3rd Edition

Ventures 3

STUDENT'S BOOK

Gretchen Bitterlin ▪ Dennis Johnson ▪ Donna Price ▪ Sylvia Ramirez
K. Lynn Savage (Series Editor)

CAMBRIDGE UNIVERSITY PRESS

CAMBRIDGE
UNIVERSITY PRESS

University Printing House, Cambridge CB2 8BS, United Kingdom

One Liberty Plaza, 20th Floor, New York, NY 10006, USA

477 Williamstown Road, Port Melbourne, VIC 3207, Australia

314–321, 3rd Floor, Plot 3, Splendor Forum, Jasola District Centre, New Delhi – 110025, India

79 Anson Road, #06–04/06, Singapore 079906

Cambridge University Press is part of the University of Cambridge.

It furthers the University's mission by disseminating knowledge in the pursuit of education, learning and research at the highest international levels of excellence.

www.cambridge.org
Information on this title: www.cambridge.org/9781108449571

First published 2008
Second edition 2014

20 19 18 17 16 15 14 13 12 11 10

Printed in Dubai by Oriental Press

A catalogue record for this publication is available from the British Library

ISBN 978-1-108-45056-0 Workbook
ISBN 978-1-108-44942-7 Online Workbook
ISBN 978-1-108-63615-5 Teacher's Edition
ISBN 978-1-108-44922-9 Class Audio CDs
ISBN 978-1-108-45035-5 Presentation Plus

Additional resources for this publication at www.cambridge.org/ventures

AUTHORS' ACKNOWLEDGMENTS

The authors would like to acknowledge and thank focus-group participants and reviewers for their insightful comments, as well as Cambridge University Press editorial, marketing, and production staffs, whose thorough research and attention to detail have resulted in a quality product.

The publishers would also like to extend their particular thanks to the following reviewers and consultants for their valuable insights and suggestions:

Barry Bakin, Instructional Technology, Los Angeles Unified School District, Los Angeles, CA;

Jim Brice, San Diego Community College District Continuing Education, San Diego, CA;

Diana Contreras, West Valley Occupational Center, Los Angeles, CA;

Druci J. Diaz, Hillsborough Country Public Schools, Tampa, FL;

Linda Foster, Instructor, Hillsborough County Schools Adult Education Department, Tampa, FL;

Margaret Geiger, M.Ed., Dallas, TX;

Ana L. Herrera, San Jacinto Adult Learning Center, El Paso, TX;

Cindi Hartmen, ESL Instructor, San Diego Continuing Education, San Diego, CA;

Patrick Jennings, Tomlinson Adult Learning Center, St. Petersburg, FL;

Lori Hess-Tolbert, Frisco, TX;

AnnMarie Kokash-Wood, Tomlinson Adult Learning Center, St. Petersburg, FL;

Linda P. Kozin, San Diego Continuing Ed, San Diego Community College District, San Diego, CA;

Caron Lieber, Palomar College, San Marcos, CA;

Reyna P. Lopez, Southwest College, Los Angeles, CA;

Rosemary Lubarov, Palo Alto Adult School, Palo Alto, CA;

Lori K. Markel, Plant City Adult and Community School, Plant City, FL;

Mary Spanarke, Center for Applied Linguistics / Washington English Center, Washington, DC;

Rosalie Tauscher, Fort Worth ISD Adult Ed, Fort Worth, TX;

Timothy Wahl, Abram Friedman Occupation Center, Los Angeles, CA;

Delia Watley, Irving ISD Adult Education and Literacy, Irving, TX;

Andrea V. White, Tarrant County College, Arlington, TX;

Sandra Wilson, Fort Worth Adult Education, Fort Worth, TX

SCOPE AND SEQUENCE

UNIT TITLE TOPIC	FUNCTIONS	LISTENING AND SPEAKING	VOCABULARY	GRAMMAR FOCUS
Welcome pages 2–5	■ Discussing goals ■ Filling out a goal form ■ Discussing past and future events	■ Listening and asking about goals ■ Asking about daily routines ■ Listening about events in the past and future	■ Review of time phrases	Verb tense review: ■ present and present continuous ■ past and future
Unit 1 Personal information pages 6–17 Topic: **Personality traits**	■ Describing and comparing likes and interests ■ Describing and discussing personality types	■ Asking about and comparing preferences ■ Describing personality types	■ Personal interests ■ Personality types ■ Adjectives that describe people	■ Verbs + gerunds ■ Comparisons with *more than, less than, as much as* ■ *must* for logical conclusions
Unit 2 At school pages 18–29 Topic: **Study skills**	■ Discussing study problems and learning strategies ■ Offering advice ■ Inquiring about people's experiences	■ Asking about study problems and learning strategies ■ Asking about someone's recent past	■ Study problems ■ Learning strategies	■ Present perfect with *how long, for, since* ■ Present perfect questions with *ever*; short answers ■ Simple past and present perfect
Review: Units 1 and 2 pages 30–31		■ Understanding a conversation		
Unit 3 Friends and family pages 32–43 Topic: **Neighbors**	■ Offering help ■ Agreeing and disagreeing ■ Giving reasons ■ Making a complaint	■ Asking about and describing problems ■ Giving reasons ■ Discussing borrowing and lending	■ *borrow* vs. *lend* ■ Two-word verbs	■ *because of* phrases and *because* clauses ■ *too* and *enough* ■ *be able to*
Unit 4 Health pages 44–55 Topic: **Healthy habits**	■ Discussing healthy foods and exercise ■ Describing events in the recent past ■ Describing past habits	■ Asking about staying healthy ■ Asking about past and present health habits	■ Healthy habits and routines ■ Medicinal plants	■ Present perfect with *recently* and *lately* ■ *used to* ■ Reported commands
Review: Units 3 and 4 pages 56–57		■ Understanding a conversation		
Unit 5 Around town pages 58–69 Topic: **Community resources and events**	■ Discussing future plans ■ Describing actions based on expectations ■ Describing community events	■ Asking about people's plans ■ Asking about people's expectations ■ Talking about community events	■ Entertainment ■ Positive and negative adjectives	■ Verbs + infinitives ■ Present perfect with *already* and *yet* ■ Verbs + infinitives and verbs + gerunds

READING	WRITING	LIFE SKILLS	PRONUNCIATION
■ Reading a paragraph about goals	■ Writing your goal and steps to reach it	■ Talking about your goal and steps to reach it	■ Pronouncing key vocabulary
■ Reading an article about personality and jobs ■ Predicting content from titles and pictures	■ Writing a descriptive paragraph with a topic sentence and supporting sentences ■ Using adjectives	■ Understanding a bar graph ■ Scanning a website for information	■ Pronouncing key vocabulary
■ Reading an article about strategies for learning English ■ Using context to identify parts of speech ■ Locating examples that support statements	■ Writing a paragraph with examples to support ideas ■ Using examples to support your ideas	■ Reading and understanding tips for taking tests ■ Talking about strategies for learning English	■ Pronouncing key vocabulary
			■ Stressing content words
■ Reading a newsletter about a neighborhood watch ■ Identifying the main idea, facts, and examples	■ Writing a complaint email ■ Supporting the main idea with examples	■ Reading and understanding an ad for volunteers ■ Writing a complaint email	■ Pronouncing key vocabulary
■ Reading an article about beneficial plants ■ Identifying the topic from the introduction and conclusion ■ Identifying parts of word families	■ Writing a descriptive paragraph ■ Writing a topic sentence ■ Completing a chart	■ Completing a medical history form ■ Talking about how to stay healthy	■ Pronouncing key vocabulary
			■ Voiced and voiceless *th* sounds
■ Reading a review of a concert ■ Using context to distinguish between positive and negative words	■ Writing an email ■ Completing a graphic organizer	■ Reading and understanding announcements about community events ■ Talking about community events	■ Pronouncing key vocabulary

UNIT TITLE TOPIC	FUNCTIONS	LISTENING AND SPEAKING	VOCABULARY	GRAMMAR FOCUS
Unit 6 **Time** pages 70–81 Topic: **Time management**	■ Prioritizing ■ Discussing how to manage time ■ Giving advice ■ Describing habits	■ Prioritizing tasks ■ Asking about habits and daily activities ■ Contrasting qualities and habits of good and weak time managers	■ Time-management words ■ Prefixes meaning *not* ■ Idioms with time	■ Adverb clauses with *when* ■ Adverb clauses with *before* and *after* ■ *when, before,* and *after* to order activities in a sequence
Review: Units 5 and 6 pages 82–83		■ Understanding a conversation		
Unit 7 **Shopping** pages 84–95 Topic: **Saving and spending**	■ Making suggestions ■ Asking for and giving advice ■ Discussing financial concerns ■ Comparing banking services	■ Asking and answering questions about buying on credit ■ Making suggestions and giving advice	■ Banking and finances ■ Compound nouns	■ *could* and *should* ■ Gerunds after prepositions ■ Collocations with *get* and *take*
Unit 8 **Work** pages 96–107 Topic: **Finding a job**	■ Discussing work-related goals ■ Discussing ways to find a job ■ Identifying procedures involved with a job interview	■ Talking about a job interview ■ Asking about ongoing activities	■ Employment ■ Separable phrasal verbs	■ Present perfect continuous ■ Separable phrasal verbs ■ Present continuous and present perfect continuous
Review: Units 7 and 8 pages 108–109		■ Understanding a conversation		
Unit 9 **Daily living** pages 110–121 Topic: **Community action**	■ Describing past activities ■ Describing past events	■ Describing a crime ■ Describing past actions ■ Asking about an emergency ■ Discussing safety items	■ Crimes ■ Emergency situations ■ Time phrases	■ Past continuous ■ Past continuous and simple past with *when* and *while* ■ Three uses of the present continuous
Unit 10 **Free time** pages 122–133 Topic: **Vacation plans**	■ Describing future possibility ■ Describing a sequence of events in the future	■ Describing vacation plans ■ Asking about future possibility ■ Describing the sequence of future events	■ Travel and vacation	■ Future real conditionals ■ Future time clauses with *before* and *after* ■ Three uses of the present perfect
Review: Units 9 and 10 pages 134–135		■ Understanding a news report		

READING	WRITING	LIFE SKILLS	PRONUNCIATION
▪ Reading an article about cultural time rules ▪ Recognizing dashes that introduce examples ▪ Identifying words with prefixes meaning *not*	▪ Writing a descriptive paragraph about a good or weak time manager ▪ Using a signal before the conclusion	▪ Reading and understanding a pie chart ▪ Talking about how to manage time	▪ Pronouncing key vocabulary
			▪ Initial *st* sound
▪ Reading an article about credit card debt ▪ Identifying problems and solutions discussed in a text	▪ Giving advice about saving money ▪ Using *first*, *second*, *third*, and *finally* to organize ideas	▪ Reading and understanding a brochure comparing checking accounts ▪ Talking about credit, credit cards, and debt	▪ Pronouncing key vocabulary
▪ Reading a blog about a job search ▪ Scanning for specific information ▪ Using a dictionary to select the best definition for a context	▪ Writing a formal thank-you email ▪ Understanding what to include in a thank-you email	▪ Reading and understanding a chart comparing job growth ▪ Preparing for a job interview ▪ Reading and understanding a blog	▪ Pronouncing key vocabulary
			▪ Linking sounds
▪ Reading an article about an emergency ▪ Recognizing time phrases ▪ Guessing meaning from context	▪ Writing about an emergency ▪ Using *Who*, *What*, *When*, *Where*, *Why*, and *How*	▪ Reading and understanding a chart comparing safety in various U.S. states ▪ Talking about emergency situations	▪ Pronouncing key vocabulary
▪ Reading an article about Alcatraz ▪ Using clues to guess the meaning of words	▪ Writing about a tourist attraction ▪ Using complex sentences to add variety	▪ Reading and understanding hotel brochures ▪ Talking about travel arrangements	▪ Pronouncing key vocabulary
			▪ Unstressed vowel sound

TO THE TEACHER

What is *Ventures*?

Ventures is a six-level, four-skills, standards-based, integrated-skills series that empowers students to achieve their academic and career goals.

- Aligned to the new NRS descriptors while covering key English Language Proficiency, College and Career Readiness Standards, and WIOA requirements.
- A wealth of resources provide instructors with the tools for any teaching situation, making *Ventures* the most complete program.
- Promotes 21st century learning complemented by a suite of technology tools.

How Does the Third Edition Meet Today's Adult Education Needs?

- The third edition is aligned to the NRS' interpretive, productive, and interactive outcomes at each level.
- To help students develop the skills they need to succeed in college and the workplace, *Ventures* 3rd Edition offers a dedicated College and Career Readiness Section (CCRS) with 10 worksheets at each level, from Level 1 to Transitions (pages 136–155).
- Audio tracks and grammar presentations linked to QR codes can be accessed using smartphones (see page x), promoting mobile learning.
- Problem-solving activities added to each unit cover critical thinking and soft skills key to workplace readiness.
- More rigorous grammar practice has been added to Lessons B and C, and more evidence-based reading practice has been added to Lesson D.

What are the *Ventures* components?

Student's Book

Each of the core **Student's Books** contains ten topic-focused units, with five review units. The main units feature six skill-focused lessons.

- **Self-contained lessons** are perfectly paced for one-hour classes. For classes longer than 1 hour, additional resources are available via the Workbook and Online Teacher's Resources.
- **Review units** recycle and reinforce the listening, vocabulary, and grammar skills developed in the two prior units and include a pronunciation activity.

Teacher's Edition

The interleaved **Teacher's Edition** includes easy-to-follow lesson plans for every unit.

- Teaching tips address common problem areas for students and additional suggestions for expansion activities and building community.
- Additional practice material across all *Ventures* components is clearly organized in the *More Ventures* chart at the end of each lesson.
- Multiple opportunities for assessment such as unit, mid-term, and final tests are available in the Teacher's Edition. Customizable tests and test audio are also available online (www.cambridge.org/ventures/resources/).

Online Teacher's Resources www.cambridge.org/ventures/resources/

Ventures Online Teacher's Resources offer hundreds of additional worksheets and classroom materials including:

- *A placement test* that helps accurately identify the appropriate level of *Ventures* for each student.
- *Career and Educational Pathways Worksheets* help students meet their post-exit employment goals.
- *Collaborative Worksheets* for each lesson develop cooperative learning and community building within the classroom.
- *Writing Worksheets* that help literacy-level students recognize shapes and write letters and numbers, while alphabet and number cards promote partner and group work.
- *Picture dictionary cards and Worksheets* that reinforce vocabulary learned in Levels Basic, 1, and 2.
- *Multilevel Worksheets* that are designed for use in multilevel classrooms and in leveled classes where the proficiency level of students differs.
- *Self-assessments* give students an opportunity to reflect on their learning. They support learner persistence and help determine whether students are ready for the unit test.

Workbook

The **Workbook** provides two pages of activities for each lesson in the Student's Book.

- If used in class, the Workbook can extend classroom instructional time by 30 minutes per lesson.
- The exercises are designed so learners can complete them in class or independently. Students can check their answers with the answer key in the back of the Workbook. Workbook exercises can be assigned in class, for homework, or as student support when a class is missed.
- Grammar charts at the back of the Workbook allow students to use the Workbook for self-study.

Online Workbooks

The self-grading **Online Workbooks** offer programs the flexibility of introducing blended learning.

- In addition to the same high-quality practice opportunities in the print workbooks, the online workbooks provide students instant feedback.
- Teachers and programs can track student progress and time on task.

Presentation Plus
www.esource.cambridge.org

Presentation Plus allows teachers to digitally project the contents of the Student's Books in front of the class for a livelier, interactive classroom. It is a complete solution for teachers because it includes the Class audio, answer keys, and the Ventures Arcade. Contact your Cambridge ESL Specialist (www.cambridge.org/cambridgeenglish/contact) to find out how to access it.

Ventures Arcade
www.cambridge.org/venturesarcade/

The Arcade is a free website where students can find additional practice for the listening, vocabulary, and grammar found in the Student's Books. There is also a Citizenship section that includes questions on civics, history, government, and the N-400 application.

Unit organization

LESSON A Listening focuses students on the unit topic. The initial exercise, ***Before you listen***, creates student interest with visuals that help the teacher assess what learners already know and serves as a prompt for the unit's key vocabulary. Next is ***Listen***, which is based on conversations. Students relate vocabulary to meaning and relate the spoken and written forms of new theme-related vocabulary. ***After you listen*** concludes the lesson by practicing language related to the theme in a communicative activity, either orally with a partner or individually in a writing activity.

LESSONS B AND C focus on grammar. The lessons move from a ***Grammar focus*** that presents the grammar point in chart form; to ***Practice*** exercises that check comprehension of the grammar point and provide guided practice; and, finally, to ***Communicate*** exercises that guide learners as they generate original answers and conversations. These lessons often include a *Culture note*, which provides information directly related to the conversation practice (such as the use of titles with last names) or a *Useful language* note, which introduces useful expressions.

LESSON D Reading develops reading skills and expands vocabulary. The lesson opens with a ***Before you read*** exercise, designed to activate prior knowledge and encourage learners to make predictions. A *Reading tip*, which focuses on a specific reading skill, accompanies the ***Read*** exercise. The reading section of the lesson concludes with ***After you read*** exercises that check comprehension. In Levels Basic, 1, and 2, the vocabulary expansion portion of the lesson is a ***Picture dictionary***. It includes a *word bank*, pictures to identify, and a conversation for practicing the new words. The words expand vocabulary related to the unit topic. In Books 3 and 4, the vocabulary expansion portion of the lesson uses new vocabulary from the reading to build skills such as recognizing word families, selecting definitions based on the context of the reading, and using clues in the reading to guess meaning.

LESSON E Writing provides practice with process writing within the context of the unit. ***Before you write*** exercises provide warm-up activities to activate the language needed for the writing assignment, followed by one or more exercises that provide a model for students to follow when they write. A *Writing tip* presents information about punctuation or paragraph organization directly related to the writing assignment. The ***Write*** exercise sets goals for the student writing. In the ***After you write*** exercise, students share with a partner.

LESSON F Another view brings the unit together with opportunities to review lesson content. ***Life-skills reading*** develops the scanning and skimming skills used with documents such as forms, charts, schedules, announcements, and ads. Multiple-choice questions (modeled on CASAS[1] and BEST[2]) develop test-taking skills. **Solve the problem** focuses on critical thinking, soft-skills, and workplace development. In Levels 1–4, ***Grammar connections*** contrasts grammar points and includes guided practice and communicative activities.

1 The Comprehensive Adult Student Assessment System. For more information, see www.casas.org.

2 The Basic English Skills Test. For more information, see www.cal.org/BEST.

The Most Complete Course for Student Success

- Helps students develop the skills needed to be college and career ready and function successfully in their community
- Covers key NRS and WIOA requirements
- Aligned with the English Language Proficiency (ELP) and College and Career Readiness (CCR) standards

Photo Stories

- Introduces the unit topic and creates an opportunity for classroom discussion.
- Activates students' prior knowledge and previews the unit vocabulary.

Unit Goals

Introduces the competencies students will learn.

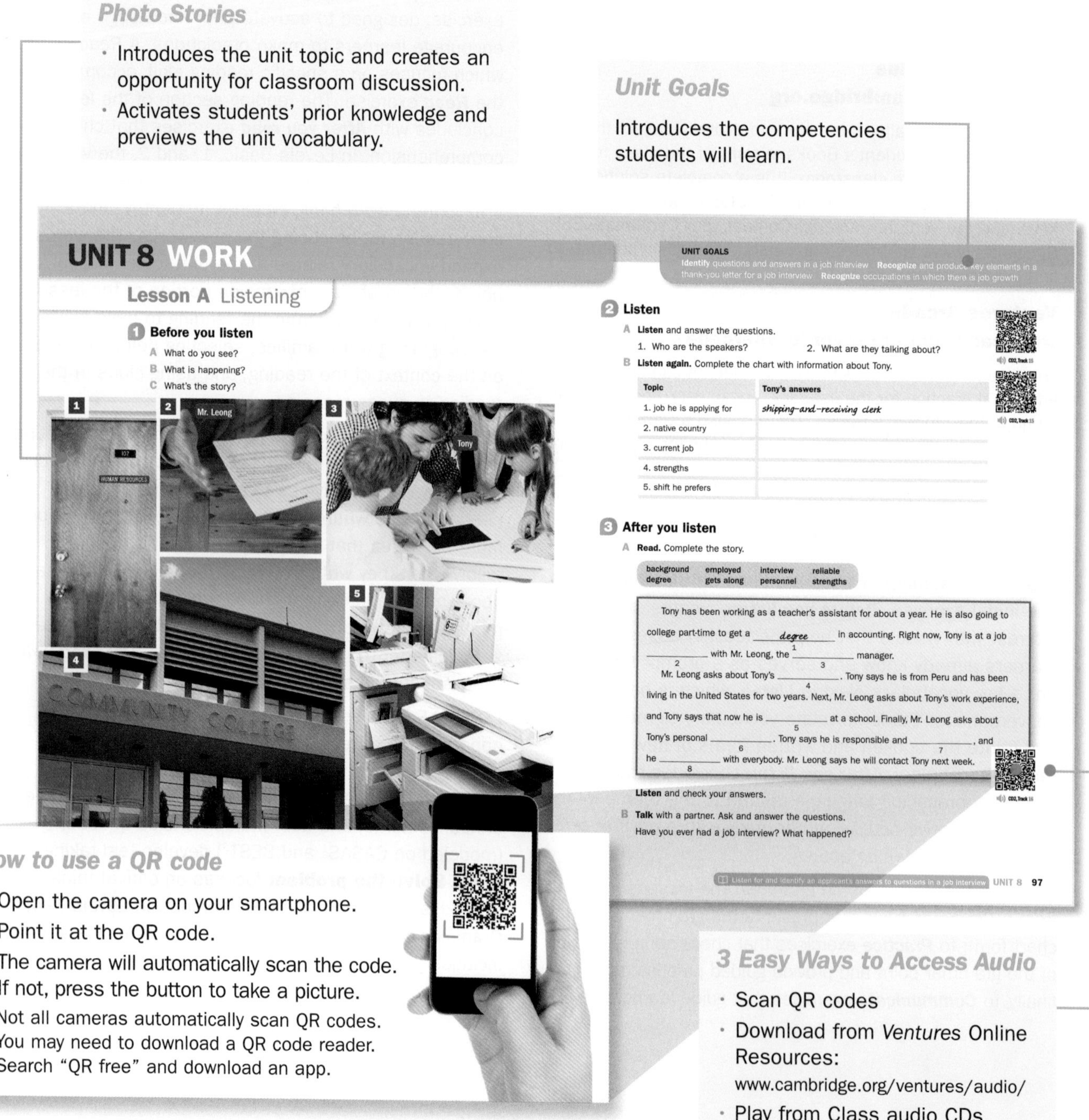

UNIT 8 WORK

Lesson A Listening

1 Before you listen

A What do you see?
B What is happening?
C What's the story?

UNIT GOALS
Identify questions and answers in a job interview **Recognize** and produce key elements in a thank-you letter for a job interview **Recognize** occupations in which there is job growth

2 Listen

A **Listen** and answer the questions.
1. Who are the speakers? 2. What are they talking about?

B **Listen again.** Complete the chart with information about Tony.

Topic	Tony's answers
1. job he is applying for	*shipping-and-receiving clerk*
2. native country	
3. current job	
4. strengths	
5. shift he prefers	

3 After you listen

A **Read.** Complete the story.

background degree employed gets along interview personnel reliable strengths

Tony has been working as a teacher's assistant for about a year. He is also going to college part-time to get a *degree* (1) in accounting. Right now, Tony is at a job ______ (2) with Mr. Leong, the ______ (3) manager. Mr. Leong asks about Tony's ______ (4). Tony says he is from Peru and has been living in the United States for two years. Next, Mr. Leong asks about Tony's work experience, and Tony says that now he is ______ (5) at a school. Finally, Mr. Leong asks about Tony's personal ______ (6). Tony says he is responsible and ______ (7), and he ______ (8) with everybody. Mr. Leong says he will contact Tony next week.

Listen and check your answers.

B **Talk** with a partner. Ask and answer the questions.
Have you ever had a job interview? What happened?

Listen for and identify an applicant's answers to questions in a job interview UNIT 8 97

How to use a QR code

- Open the camera on your smartphone.
- Point it at the QR code.
- The camera will automatically scan the code. If not, press the button to take a picture.

* Not all cameras automatically scan QR codes. You may need to download a QR code reader. Search "QR free" and download an app.

3 Easy Ways to Access Audio

- Scan QR codes
- Download from *Ventures* Online Resources: www.cambridge.org/ventures/audio/
- Play from Class audio CDs

Every unit has two grammar lessons taught using the same format.

Grammar Chart

- Presents and practices the grammar point.
- Extra grammar charts online can be used for reference and give additional support.

Grammar Presentation

Animated presentations to watch on mobile devices using QR codes allow for self-directed learning and develop digital literacy.

UNIT 8

Lesson B Present perfect continuous

1 Grammar focus: questions and statements with *for* and *since*

Use the present perfect continuous to talk about actions that started in the past, continue to now, and will probably continue in the future.

QUESTIONS	SHORT ANSWERS	
Have you been living here for a long time?	Yes, I have.	No, I haven't.
Has Tony been working here for a long time?	Yes, he has.	No, he hasn't.
Have they been working here for a long time?	Yes, they have.	No, they haven't.

How long have you been looking for a job?
How long has Tony been working as a teacher's assistant?
How long have they been working at the school?

Since October.
For about a year.

STATEMENTS

I've been waiting **for** a long time.
Lida has been waiting **since** 2:00.
We've been waiting **all** morning.

USEFUL LANGUAGE
Use *since* with specific times. *Since 2011.*
Use *for* with periods of time. *For two months.*

Additional Grammar Activities

Ensures students have the chance to practice more grammar to meet the rigor of CCRS.

2 Practice

A **Write.** Complete the sentences. Use the present perfect continuous with *for* or *since*.

1. A How long *has* Talia *been practicing* (practice) for her driving test?
   B *For* about three months.
2. A ________ you ________ (work) here for a long time?
   B No, I ________. I started six days ago.
3. A How long ________ Yin ________ (look) for a job?
   B ________ last year.
4. A ________ Mr. Rivera ________ (interview) people all day?
   B Yes, he ________.
5. A How long ________ you ________ (wait) to get an interview?
   B ________ March.
6. A How long ________ they ________ (go) to night school?
   B ________ one year.

Listen and check your answers. Then practice with a partner.

98 UNIT 8

B **Talk** with a partner. Ask and answer questions. Use *for* or *since*.

A How long has Sandra been talking on the phone?
B For 20 minutes.

Sandra — 1. talk / ________ 20 minutes
Ron — 2. wait / ________ 8:00
Latifa — 3. study / ________ morning
Jerry — 4. practice keyboarding / ________ 10:30
Felix and Pablo — 5. paint the house / ________ two days
Sharon — 6. work in the restaurant / ________ 2011
Brad — 7. look for a job / ________ several weeks
Elena — 8. attend this school / ________ last semester

Write a sentence about each picture.
Sandra has been talking on the phone for 20 minutes.

3 Communicate

A **Talk** with your classmates. Find a person who does each activity. Ask how long the person has been doing it. Complete the chart.

A Do you drive?
B Yes, I do.
A How long have you been driving?
B For about six years. / Since 2012.

Activity	Name	How long?
drive	*Josefina*	*for six years / since 2012*
cook for yourself		
attend this school		
work in this country		
speak English		
use a computer		

B **Share** information about your classmates.

Use present perfect continuous with for and since UNIT 8 99

Natural Progression

Moves from controlled to communicative activities for students to ask and answer questions about familiar text, topics, and experiences.

Real-life Practice

Engages students and provides meaningful application of the grammar.

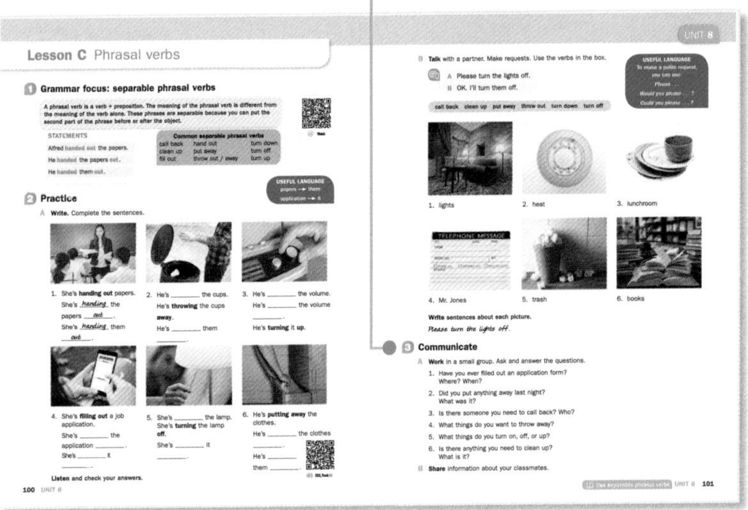

Lesson C Phrasal verbs

1 Grammar focus: separable phrasal verbs

2 Practice

A Write. Complete the sentences.

Listen and check your answers.

100 UNIT 8

B Talk with a partner. Make requests. Use the verbs in the box.

A Please turn the lights off.
B OK. I'll turn them off.

call back clean up put away throw out turn down turn off

1. lights 2. heat 3. lunchroom 4. Mr. Jones 5. trash 6. books

Write sentences about each picture.
Please turn the lights off.

3 Communicate

A Work in a small group. Ask and answer the questions.

1. Have you ever filled out an application form? Where? When?
2. Did you put anything away last night? What was it?
3. Is there someone you need to call back? Who?
4. What things do you want to throw away?
5. What things do you turn on, off, or up?
6. Is there anything you need to clean up? What is it?

B Share information about your classmates.

UNIT 8 101

Reading

- Uses a 3-step reading approach to highlight the skills and strategies students need to succeed.
- Combines reading with writing and listening practice for an integrated approach to ensure better comprehension.
- Brings text complexity into the classroom to help students read independently and proficiently.

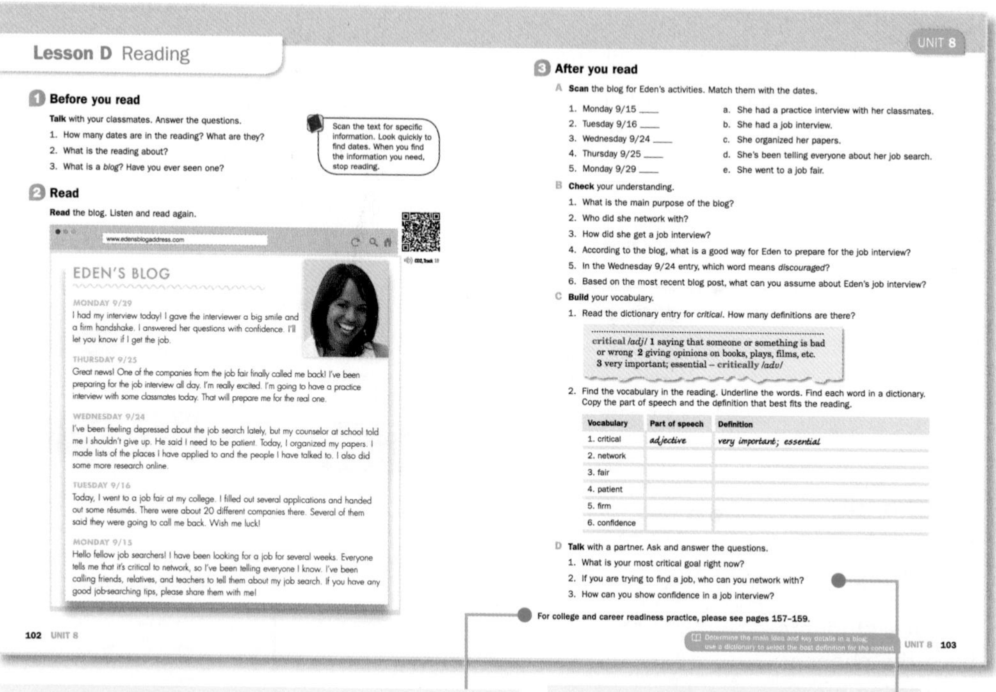

UNIT 8

Lesson D Reading

1 Before you read

Talk with your classmates. Answer the questions.

1. How many dates are in the reading? What are they?
2. What is the reading about?
3. What is a *blog*? Have you ever seen one?

Scan the text for specific information. Look quickly to find dates. When you find the information you need, stop reading.

2 Read

Read the blog. Listen and read again.

www.edensblogaddress.com

EDEN'S BLOG

MONDAY 9/29
I had my interview today! I gave the interviewer a big smile and a firm handshake. I answered her questions with confidence. I'll let you know if I get the job.

THURSDAY 9/25
Great news! One of the companies from the job fair finally called me back! I've been preparing for the job interview all day. I'm really excited. I'm going to have a practice interview with some classmates today. That will prepare me for the real one.

WEDNESDAY 9/24
I've been feeling depressed about the job search lately, but my counselor at school told me I shouldn't give up. He said I need to be patient. Today, I organized my papers. I made lists of the places I have applied to and the people I have talked to. I also did some more research online.

TUESDAY 9/16
Today, I went to a job fair at my college. I filled out several applications and handed out some résumés. There were about 20 different companies there. Several of them said they were going to call me back. Wish me luck!

MONDAY 9/15
Hello fellow job searchers! I have been looking for a job for several weeks. Everyone tells me that it's critical to network, so I've been telling everyone I know. I've been calling friends, relatives, and teachers to tell them about my job search. If you have any good job-searching tips, please share them with me!

3 After you read

A **Scan** the blog for Eden's activities. Match them with the dates.

1. Monday 9/15 ____ a. She had a practice interview with her classmates.
2. Tuesday 9/16 ____ b. She had a job interview.
3. Wednesday 9/24 ____ c. She organized her papers.
4. Thursday 9/25 ____ d. She's been telling everyone about her job search.
5. Monday 9/29 ____ e. She went to a job fair.

B **Check** your understanding.

1. What is the main purpose of the blog?
2. Who did she network with?
3. How did she get a job interview?
4. According to the blog, what is a good way for Eden to prepare for the job interview?
5. In the Wednesday 9/24 entry, which word means *discouraged*?
6. Based on the most recent blog post, what can you assume about Eden's job interview?

C **Build** your vocabulary.

1. Read the dictionary entry for *critical*. How many definitions are there?

critical /adj/ 1 saying that someone or something is bad or wrong 2 giving opinions on books, plays, films, etc. 3 very important; essential – critically /adv/

2. Find the vocabulary in the reading. Underline the words. Find each word in a dictionary. Copy the part of speech and the definition that best fits the reading.

Vocabulary	Part of speech	Definition
1. critical	adjective	very important; essential
2. network		
3. fair		
4. patient		
5. firm		
6. confidence		

D **Talk** with a partner. Ask and answer the questions.

1. What is your most critical goal right now?
2. If you are trying to find a job, who can you network with?
3. How can you show confidence in a job interview?

For college and career readiness practice, please see pages 157–159.

102 UNIT 8 | UNIT 8 103

College & Career Readiness Section

Builds critical-thinking skills and uses informative texts to help master the more complex CCR standards.

Speaking Practice

Helps students internalize the vocabulary and relate it to their lives.

Writing

- Helps students develop a robust process-writing approach.
- Supports students to meet the challenges of work and the classroom through academic and purposeful writing practice.

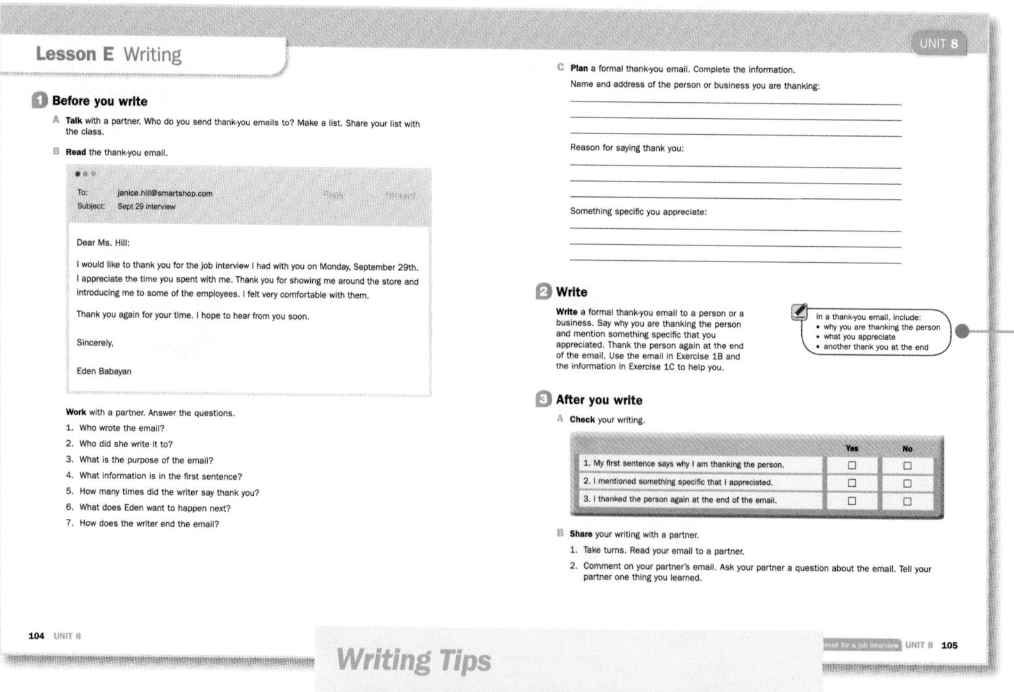

UNIT 8

Lesson E Writing

1 Before you write

A **Talk** with a partner. Who do you send thank-you emails to? Make a list. Share your list with the class.

B **Read** the thank-you email.

To: janice.hill@smartshop.com
Subject: Sept 29 interview

Dear Ms. Hill:

I would like to thank you for the job interview I had with you on Monday, September 29th. I appreciate the time you spent with me. Thank you for showing me around the store and introducing me to some of the employees. I felt very comfortable with them.

Thank you again for your time. I hope to hear from you soon.

Sincerely,

Eden Babayan

Work with a partner. Answer the questions.

1. Who wrote the email?
2. Who did she write it to?
3. What is the purpose of the email?
4. What information is in the first sentence?
5. How many times did the writer say thank you?
6. What does Eden want to happen next?
7. How does the writer end the email?

C **Plan** a formal thank-you email. Complete the information.

Name and address of the person or business you are thanking:

Reason for saying thank you:

Something specific you appreciate:

2 Write

Write a formal thank-you email to a person or a business. Say why you are thanking the person and mention something specific that you appreciated. Thank the person again at the end of the email. Use the email in Exercise 1B and the information in Exercise 1C to help you.

In a thank-you email, include:
- why you are thanking the person
- what you appreciate
- another thank you at the end

3 After you write

A **Check** your writing.

	Yes	No
1. My first sentence says why I am thanking the person.	☐	☐
2. I mentioned something specific that I appreciated.	☐	☐
3. I thanked the person again at the end of the email.	☐	☐

B **Share** your writing with a partner.

1. Take turns. Read your email to a partner.
2. Comment on your partner's email. Ask your partner a question about the email. Tell your partner one thing you learned.

104 UNIT 8 | UNIT 8 105

Writing Tips

Gives students confidence in writing with easy-to-follow writing tips and strategies.

Document Literacy

Builds real-life skills through explicit practice using authentic document types.

Grammar connections

Contrasts two grammar forms in a communicative way to help with grammar accuracy.

Test-taking Skills

Prepares students for standarized tests like the CASAS by familiarizing them with bubble answer format.

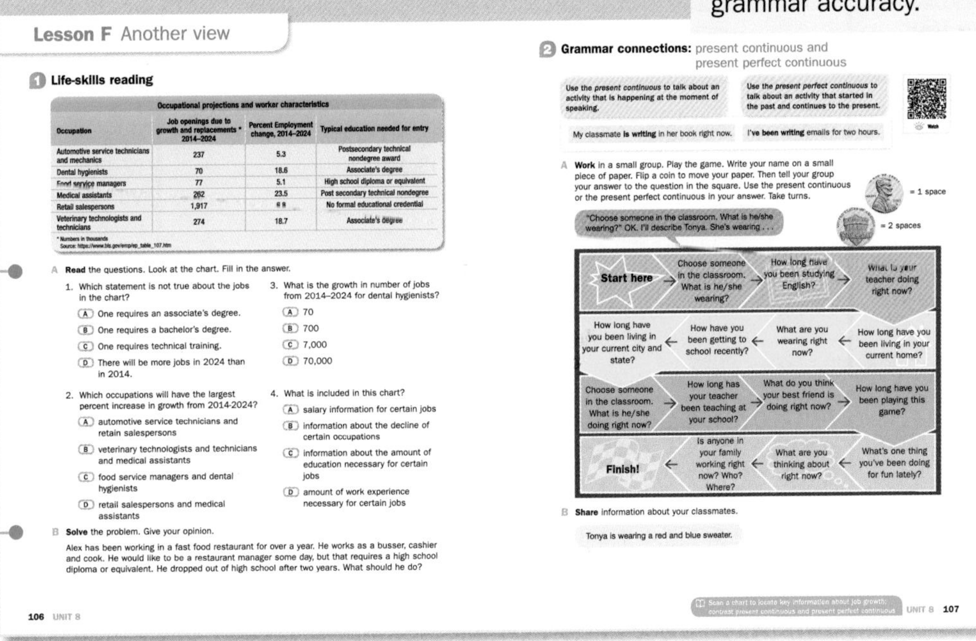

Lesson F Another view

1 Life-skills reading

Occupational projections and worker characteristics

Occupation	Job openings due to growth and replacements * 2014–2024	Percent Employment change, 2014–2024	Typical education needed for entry
Automotive service technicians and mechanics	237	5.3	Postsecondary technical nondegree award
Dental hygienists	70	18.6	Associate's degree
Food service managers	77	5.1	High school diploma or equivalent
Medical assistants	262	23.5	Post secondary technical nondegree
Retail salespersons	1,917	6.8	No formal educational credential
Veterinary technologists and technicians	274	18.7	Associate's degree

* Numbers in thousands
Source: https://www.bls.gov/emp/ep_table_107.htm

A **Read** the questions. Look at the chart. Fill in the answer.

1. Which statement is not true about the jobs in the chart?
   - (A) One requires an associate's degree.
   - (B) One requires a bachelor's degree.
   - (C) One requires technical training.
   - (D) There will be more jobs in 2024 than in 2014.
2. Which occupations will have the largest percent increase in growth from 2014-2024?
   - (A) automotive service technicians and retain salespersons
   - (B) veterinary technologists and technicians and medical assistants
   - (C) food service managers and dental hygienists
   - (D) retail salespersons and medical assistants
3. What is the growth in number of jobs from 2014–2024 for dental hygienists?
   - (A) 70
   - (B) 700
   - (C) 7,000
   - (D) 70,000
4. What is included in this chart?
   - (A) salary information for certain jobs
   - (B) information about the decline of certain occupations
   - (C) information about the amount of education necessary for certain jobs
   - (D) amount of work experience necessary for certain jobs

B **Solve** the problem. Give your opinion.

Alex has been working in a fast food restaurant for over a year. He works as a busser, cashier and cook. He would like to be a restaurant manager some day, but that requires a high school diploma or equivalent. He dropped out of high school after two years. What should he do?

106 UNIT 8

2 Grammar connections: present continuous and present perfect continuous

Use the *present continuous* to talk about an activity that is happening at the moment of speaking.	Use the *present perfect continuous* to talk about an activity that started in the past and continues to the present.
My classmate **is writing** in her book right now.	I**'ve been writing** emails for two hours.

A **Work** in a small group. Play the game. Write your name on a small piece of paper. Flip a coin to move your paper. Then tell your group your answer to the question in the square. Use the present continuous or the present perfect continuous in your answer. Take turns.

= 1 space
= 2 spaces

"Choose someone in the classroom. What is he/she wearing?" OK. I'll describe Tonya. She's wearing . . .

B **Share** information about your classmates.

Tonya is wearing a red and blue sweater.

Scan a chart to locate key information about job growth; contrast present continuous and present perfect continuous UNIT 8 107

Problem-solving Activity

Covers critical thinking and soft skills – crucial for workplace readiness – and helps students meet WIOA requirements.

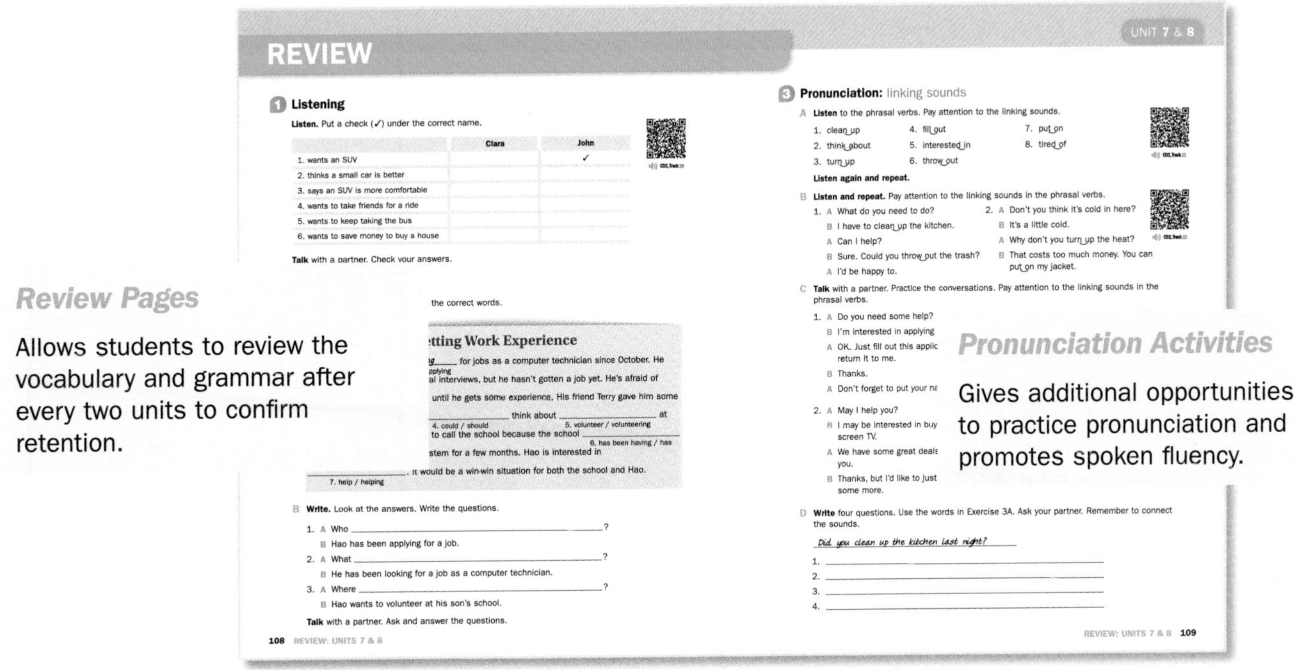

REVIEW

UNIT 7 & 8

1 Listening

Listen. Put a check (✓) under the correct name.

	Clara	John
1. wants an SUV		✓
2. thinks a small car is better		
3. says an SUV is more comfortable		
4. wants to take friends for a ride		
5. wants to keep taking the bus		
6. wants to save money to buy a house		

Talk with a partner. Check your answers.

Review Pages

Allows students to review the vocabulary and grammar after every two units to confirm retention.

the correct words.

...tting Work Experience

...g ______ for jobs as a computer technician since October. He ...al interviews, but he hasn't gotten a job yet. He's afraid of ... until he gets some experience. His friend Terry gave him some ______ think about ______ at (4. could / should) (5. volunteer / volunteering) to call the school because the school ______ (6. has been having / has) ...stem for a few months. Hao is interested in ______ (7. help / helping). It would be a win-win situation for both the school and Hao.

B **Write.** Look at the answers. Write the questions.

1. A Who ______?
   B Hao has been applying for a job.
2. A What ______?
   B He has been looking for a job as a computer technician.
3. A Where ______?
   B Hao wants to volunteer at his son's school.

Talk with a partner. Ask and answer the questions.

108 REVIEW: UNITS 7 & 8

3 Pronunciation: linking sounds

A **Listen** to the phrasal verbs. Pay attention to the linking sounds.

1. clean_up	4. fill_out	7. put_on
2. think_about	5. interested_in	8. tired_of
3. turn_up	6. throw_out	

Listen again and repeat.

B **Listen and repeat.** Pay attention to the linking sounds in the phrasal verbs.

1. A What do you need to do?
   B I have to clean_up the kitchen.
   A Can I help?
   B Sure. Could you throw_out the trash?
   A I'd be happy to.
2. A Don't you think it's cold in here?
   B It's a little cold.
   A Why don't you turn_up the heat?
   B That costs too much money. You can put_on my jacket.

C **Talk** with a partner. Practice the conversations. Pay attention to the linking sounds in the phrasal verbs.

1. A Do you need some help?
   B I'm interested in applying ...
   A OK. Just fill out this applic... return it to me.
   B Thanks.
   A Don't forget to put your na...
2. A May I help you?
   B I may be interested in buy... screen TV.
   A We have some great deals ... you.
   B Thanks, but I'd like to just ... some more.

Pronunciation Activities

Gives additional opportunities to practice pronunciation and promotes spoken fluency.

D **Write** four questions. Use the words in Exercise 3A. Ask your partner. Remember to connect the sounds.

Did you clean up the kitchen last night?

1. ______
2. ______
3. ______
4. ______

REVIEW: UNITS 7 & 8 109

CORRELATIONS

UNIT	CASAS Competencies	Florida Adult ESOL Low Beginning	LAUSD ESL Beginning Low Competencies
Welcome Unit Pages 2–5			
Unit 1 Personal information Pages 6–17	0.1.2, 0.1.4, 0.1.5, 0.1.6, 0.2.1, 0.2.4, 4.1.7, 4.6.1, 4.8.1, 4.8.2, 6.0.1, 7.1.1, 7.1.4, 7.2.1, 7.2.3, 7.2.4, 7.4.1, 7.5.1	4.01.02, 4.01.03, 4.03.07, 4.03.10, 4.03.11, 4.03.13, 4.03.15	I. 1 II. 3 IV. 29 VIII. 48, 50, 51, 52
Unit 2 At school Pages 18–31	0.1.2, 0.1.4, 0.1.5, 0.2.1, 0.2.4, 2.3.1, 2.3.2, 4.1.2, 4.6.1, 4.8.1, 4.8.2, 6.0.1, 7.1.1, 7.1.2, 7.1.3, 7.1.4, 7.2.1, 7.2.2, 7.2.4, 7.2.6, 7.3.1, 7.3.2, 7.3.4, 7.4.1, 7.4.2, 7.5.1, 7.5.6	4.01.02, 4.01.04, 4.03.07, 4.03.10, 4.03.11, 4.03.13	II. 3, 6 VIII. 50, 51, 52 IX. 64
Unit 3 Friends and family Pages 32–43	0.1.2, 0.1.3, 0.1.4, 0.1.5, 0.2.1, 0.2.3, 0.2.4, 1.4.1, 1.4.7, 1.7.4, 2.3.1, 2.3.2, 3.4.2, 4.8.1, 4.8.2, 4.8.4, 5.3.7, 5.6.1, 5.6.2, 6.0.1, 7.1.4, 7.2.1, 7.4.2, 7.5.1, 8.2.6, 8.3.2	4.01.02, 4.01.3, 4.03.01, 4.03.07, 4.03.10, 4.03.11, 4.03.15, 4.04.05, 4.05.02, 4.07.01	I. 1 II. 3, 41, 5a, 6, 9 IV. 23 VIII. 50, 51, 52
Unit 4 Health Pages 44–57	0.1.2, 0.1.3, 0.1.5, 0.1.7, 0.2.4, 2.3.2, 3.1.1, 3.2.1, 3.3.3, 3.4.2, 3.5.2, 3.5.4, 3.5.5, 3.5.8, 3.5.9, 4.8.1, 6.0.1, 7.1.4, 7.2.1, 7.3.2, 7.4.1, 7.4.2, 7.5.1, 8.1.1, 8.2.1	4.01.02, 4.03.07, 4.03.10, 4.03.11, 4.05.01, 4.05.02	I. 2 II. 3 VI. 36, 38, 41 VIII. 50, 51, 52
Unit 5 Around town Pages 58–69	0.1.2, 0.1.4, 0.1.5, 0.2.1, 0.2.4, 2.3.1, 2.3.2, 2.6.1, 2.6.2, 2.6.3, 2.7.6, 4.8.1, 6.0.1, 7.1.1, 7.1.2, 7.1.4, 7.2.1, 7.4.2, 7.4.3, 7.5.1	4.01.02, 4.01.03, 4.01.04, 4.01.08, 4.02.08, 4.03.07, 4.03.10, 4.03.11, 4.03.13, 4.03.15	II. 3 VIII. 50, 51, 52

For more details and correlations to other state standards, go to: www.cambridge.org/ventures/correlations

NRS Educational Functioning Level Descriptors	English Language Proficiency and College and Career Readiness Standards
Interpretive ■ Determine the main idea and key details in a conversation about weekend activities. ■ Determine the main idea and key details in a reading about personality and jobs. ■ Use context clues to determine the meaning of vocabulary related to personality types. **Productive** ■ Deliver a short oral presentation about a classmate's likes and dislikes. ■ Compose a paragraph about the right job for a specific personality type. ■ Report on an Internet research project about personality types. **Interactive** ■ Participate in conversations about likes and dislikes. ■ Discuss with a partner each other's writing about someone whose job is right for their personality type.	ELP Standards 1–10 Reading Anchors 1, 2, 4, 5, 7, 8, 9, 10 Speaking & Listening Anchors 1, 2, 3, 4, 6
Interpretive ■ Determine the main topic and key details in conversation about study problems and solutions. ■ Determine the main topic and key details in a written text about setting goals to practice English. ■ Use context clues to determine the meaning of vocabulary about study skills. **Productive** ■ Compose a paragraph about strategies for learning English. ■ Deliver a short oral presentation about a classmate's study problems. ■ Report on a short research project about your goals for studying English. **Interactive** ■ Participate in conversations about studying problems. ■ Discuss with a partner each other's writing about strategies for learning English.	ELP Standards 1–10 Reading Anchors 1, 2, 4, 5, 6, 7, 9, 10 Speaking & Listening Anchors 1, 2, 3, 4, 6
Interpretive ■ Determine the main topic and key details in a conversation about borrowing and lending. ■ Determine the main topic and key details in a written text about neighborhood watch. ■ Use a dictionary entry to determine the meaning of vocabulary of two-word *verbs*. **Productive** ■ Compose a paragraph about neighbors. ■ Deliver a short oral presentation about a classmate's reason for coming to this country. ■ Report on an Internet research project about volunteering. **Interactive** ■ Participate in conversations about why you came to this country. ■ Discuss with a partner each other's writing about neighbors.	ELP Standards 1–10 Reading Anchors 1, 2, 4, 5, 7, 8, 9, 10 Speaking & Listening Anchors 1, 2, 3, 4, 6
Interpretive ■ Determine the main topic and key details in a conversation about staying healthy. ■ Determine the main topic and key details in a written text about plants that help you stay healthy. ■ Use a dictionary entry to determine the meaning of vocabulary about health. **Productive** ■ Compose a paragraph about beneficial plants. ■ Deliver a short oral presentation about a classmate's health habits. ■ Report on a short research project about staying healthy. **Interactive** ■ Participate in conversations about health habits. ■ Discuss with a partner each other's writing about beneficial plants.	ELP Standards 1–10 Reading Anchors 1, 2, 4, 5, 7, 8, 9, 10 Speaking & Listening Anchors 1, 2, 3, 4, 6
Interpretive ■ Determine the main topic and key details in a conversation about weekend entertainment. ■ Determine the main topic and key details in a written text about an outdoor concert. ■ Use context clues to determine the meaning of vocabulary about weekend entertainment. **Productive** ■ Compose a paragraph about a concert, movie or performance you have seen. ■ Deliver a short oral presentation about a classmate's activities. ■ Report on an Internet research project about weekend activities in your city. **Interactive** ■ Participate in conversations about activities you have done. ■ Discuss with a partner each other's writing about a concert, movie, or performance you have seen.	ELP Standards 1–10 Reading Anchors 1, 2, 4, 5, 7, 8, 9, 10 Speaking & Listening Anchors 1, 2, 3, 4, 6

UNIT	CASAS Competencies	Florida Adult ESOL Low Beginning	LAUSD ESL Beginning Low Competencies
Unit 6 **Time** Pages 70–81	0.1.2, 0.1.4, 0.1.5, 0.2.1, 0.2.4, 1.1.3, 2.3.1, 2.7.2, 2.7.3, 4.1.7, 4.4.1, 4.4.3, 4.4.5, 4.8.1, 6.0.1, 6.7.4, 7.1.1, 7.1.2, 7.1.4, 7.2.1, 7.2.3, 7.2.4, 7.3.2, 7.4.1, 7.4.2, 7.4.8, 7.5.1	4.01.02, 4.01.5, 4.03.06, 4.03.07, 4.03.10, 4.03.11	II. 3 IV. 22 VIII. 50, 51, 52
Unit 7 **Shopping** Pages 84–95	0.1.2, 0.1.3, 0.1.5, 0.1.6, 0.2.1, 1.1.6, 1.2.1, 1.2.2, 1.2.5, 1.3.1, 1.4.1, 1.8.2, 4.8.1, 6.0.1, 6.5.1, 7.1.1, 7.1.4, 7.2.1, 7.2.3, 7.2.6, 7.3.1, 7.3.2, 7.4.2, 7.5.1, 7.5.5	4.01.02, 4.03.07, 4.03.10, 4.03.11, 4.04.01, 4.04.02, 4.04.03, 4.04.04, 4.04.07, 4.04.08, 4.04.09	II. 3, 5a IV. 23, 25c, 25d VIII. 49, 50, 51, 52
Unit 8 **Work** Pages 96–107	0.0.1, 0.1.2, 0.1.3, 0.1.5, 0.2.1, 2.3.1, 2.3.2, 2.4.1, 4.1.2, 4.1.5, 4.1.6, 4.1.7, 4.1.8, 4.4.3, 4.5.1, 4.6.1, 4.6.2, 4.8.1, 4.8.2, 6.0.1, 7.1.1, 7.1.4, 7.2.1, 7.4.1, 7.4.2, 7.4.4, 7.5.1, 7.5.2, 7.5.6	4.01.02, 4.02.02, 4.02.06, 4.03.02, 4.03.04, 4.03.07, 4.03.10, 4.03.11, 4.03.13, 4.03.15	I. 1 II. 3, 4a, 5a VII. 44a VIII. 50, 51, 52
Unit 9 **Daily living** Pages 110–121	0.1.2, 0.1.4, 0.1.5, 0.2.1, 0.2.4, 1.4.1, 2.3.1, 2.5.1, 2.7.3, 3.4.2, 4.8.1, 5.3.7, 5.6.1, 5.6.2, 6.0.1, 7.1.1, 7.2.1, 7.4.2, 7.5.1, 8.3.2	4.01.02, 4.02.05, 4.03.07, 4.03.10, 4.03.11, 4.06.04, 4.07.01	II. 3 IV. 23 VIII. 50, 51, 52
Unit 10 **Free time** Pages 122–133	0.1.2, 0.1.4, 0.1.5, 0.2.1, 0.2.4, 1.2.2, 1.2.5, 2.1.8, 2.3.1, 2.3.2, 2.3.3, 2.7.1, 4.8.1, 6.0.1, 6.5.1, 7.1.1, 7.2.1, 7.2.2, 7.2.3, 7.2.6, 7.4.1, 7.4.2, 7.5.1	4.01.02, 4.01.03, 4.03.07, 4.03.10, 4.03.11, 4.03.15, 4.04.03	II. 3 VIII. 50, 51, 52

For more details and correlations to other state standards, go to: www.cambridge.org/ventures/correlations

NRS Educational Functioning Level Descriptors	English Language Proficiency and College and Career Readiness Standards
Interpretive ■ Determine the main topic and key details in a conversation about time management. ■ Determine the main topic and key details in a written text about unspoken rules about time. ■ Use prefixes to determine the meaning of vocabulary about time. **Productive** ■ Compose a paragraph about being a strong or weak time manager. ■ Deliver a short oral presentation about a classmate's daily activities. ■ Report on a short research project about managing study time. **Interactive** ■ Participate in conversations about daily activities. ■ Discuss with a partner each other's writing about strong and weak time managers.	ELP Standards 1–10 Reading Anchors 1, 2, 4, 5, 7, 8, 9, 10 Speaking & Listening Anchors 1, 2, 3, 4, 6
Interpretive ■ Determine the main topic and key details in a conversation about buying things on credit. ■ Determine the main topic and key details in a written text about problems with a credit card. ■ Use context clues to determine the meaning of vocabulary about credit. **Productive** ■ Compose a paragraph about suggestions for saving money. ■ Deliver a short oral presentation about a classmate's credit cards and budgeting. ■ Report on a short research project using an advertisement for something you want to buy. **Interactive** ■ Participate in conversations about credit cards and budgeting. ■ Discuss with a partner each other's writing about ways to save money.	ELP Standards 1–10 Reading Anchors 1, 2, 4, 5, 7, 8, 9, 10 Speaking & Listening Anchors 1, 2, 3, 4, 6
Interpretive ■ Determine the main topic and key details in a conversation about a job interview. ■ Determine the main topic and key details in a written text about the process of finding a job. ■ Use context clues to determine the meaning of vocabulary about finding a job. **Productive** ■ Compose a thank-you letter. ■ Deliver a short oral presentation about a classmate's goals. ■ Report on an Internet research project about interview questions. **Interactive** ■ Participate in conversations about goals. ■ Discuss with a partner each other's thank-you letters.	ELP Standards 1–10 Reading Anchors 1, 2, 4, 5, 7, 8, 9, 10 Speaking & Listening Anchors 1, 2, 3, 4, 6
Interpretive ■ Determine the main topic and key details in a conversation about a crime. ■ Determine the main topic and key details in a written text about community action. ■ Use context clues to determine the meaning of vocabulary about community action. **Productive** ■ Compose a paragraph about an emergency that happened to you or someone you know. ■ Deliver a short oral presentation about a situation that happened to a classmate. ■ Report on a short research project about things you need for your house or apartment. **Interactive** ■ Participate in conversations about a situation that happened to you. ■ Discuss with a partner each other's writing about an emergency that happened.	ELP Standards 1–10 Reading Anchors 1, 2, 4, 5, 7, 8, 9, 10 Speaking & Listening Anchors 1, 2, 3, 4, 6
Interpretive ■ Determine the main topic and key details in a conversation about planning a trip. ■ Determine the main topic and key details in a written text about Alcatraz in San Francisco. ■ Use context clues to determine the meaning of vocabulary about Alcatraz in San Francisco. **Productive** ■ Compose a paragraph about a tourist attraction in your city. ■ Deliver a short oral presentation about a classmate's weekend trip plans. ■ Report on an Internet research project about a local hotel you would like to visit. **Interactive** ■ Participate in conversations about planning a weekend trip. ■ Discuss with a partner each other's writing about a local tourist attraction.	ELP Standards 1–10 Reading Anchors 1, 2, 4, 5, 7, 8, 9, 10 Speaking & Listening Anchors 1, 2, 3, 4, 6

MEET THE **VENTURES** AUTHOR TEAM

(Top row) Dennis Johnson, K. Lynn Savage; (bottom row) Gretchen Bitterlin, Donna Price, and Sylvia G. Ramirez. Together, the *Ventures* author team has more than 200 years teaching ESL as well as other roles that support adult immigrants and refugees, from teacher's aide to dean.

Gretchen Bitterlin has taught Citizenship, ESL, and family literacy through the San Diego Community College District and served as coordinator of the non-credit Continuing Education ESL program. She was an item writer for CASAS tests and chaired the task force that developed the TESOL Adult Education Program Standards. She is recipient of The President's Distinguished Leadership Award from her district and co-author of *English for Adult Competency*. Gretchen holds an MA in TESOL from the University of Arizona.

Dennis Johnson had his first language-teaching experience as a Peace Corps volunteer in South Korea. Following that teaching experience, he became an in-country ESL trainer. After returning to the United States, he began teaching credit and non-credit ESL at City College of San Francisco. As ESL site coordinator, he has provided guidance to faculty in selecting textbooks. He is the author of *Get Up and Go* and co-author of *The Immigrant Experience*. Dennis is the demonstration teacher on the *Ventures Professional Development DVD*. Dennis holds an MA in music from Stanford University.

Donna Price began her ESL career teaching EFL in Madagascar. She is currently associate professor of ESL and vocational ESL / technology resource instructor for the Continuing Education Program, San Diego Community College District. She has served as an author and a trainer for CALPRO, the California Adult Literacy Professional Development Project, co-authoring training modules on contextualizing and integrating workforce skills into the ESL classroom. She is a recipient of the TESOL Newbury House Award for Excellence in Teaching, and she is author of *Skills for Success*. Donna holds an MA in linguistics from San Diego State University.

Sylvia G. Ramirez is a Professor Emeritus at MiraCosta College, a teacher educator, writer, consultant, and a recipient of the California Hayward award for excellence in education, honoring her teaching and professional activities. She is an online instructor for the TESOL Core Certificate. Her MA is in education / counseling from Point Loma University, and she has certificates in ESOL and in online teaching.

K. Lynn Savage first taught English in Japan. She began teaching ESL at City College of San Francisco in 1974, where she has taught all levels of non-credit ESL and has served as Vocational ESL Resource Teacher. She has trained teachers for adult education programs around the country as well as abroad. She chaired the committee that developed *ESL Model Standards for Adult Education Programs* (California, 1992) and is the author, co-author, and editor of many ESL materials including *Crossroads Café*, *Teacher Training through Video*, *Parenting for Academic Success*, *Building Life Skills*, *Picture Stories*, *May I Help You?*, and *English That Works*. Lynn holds an MA in TESOL from Teachers College, Columbia University.

TO THE STUDENT

Welcome to ***Ventures***! The dictionary says that "venture" means a risky or daring journey. Its meaning is similar to the word "adventure." Learning English is certainly a journey and an adventure. We hope that this book helps you in your journey of learning English to fulfill your goals. We believe that this book will prepare you for academic and career courses and give you the English skills you need to get a job or promotion, go to college, or communicate better in your community. The audio, grammar presentations, workbooks, and free Internet practice on the Arcade will help you improve your English outside class. Setting your personal goals will also help. Take a few minutes and write your goals below.

Good luck in your studies!

The Author Team
Gretchen Bitterlin
Dennis Johnson
Donna Price
Sylvia Ramirez
K. Lynn Savage

My goals for studying English

1. My first goal for studying English:	Date: ______
2. My second goal for studying English:	Date: ______
3. My third goal for studying English:	Date: ______

WELCOME

1 Meet your classmates

A Look at the pictures. What do you see?

B What are the people doing?

2 Goals

A **Listen.** Silvia is talking about her goals with a classmate. Write the three steps that Silvia needs to take to reach her goals.

Main goal: She ___wants to open___ (1. want / open) her own beauty salon someday.

Steps to take to reach the goal:

First, she ______________ (2. need / go) to beauty school for two years. Second, she ______________ (3. need / take) an exam to get her license. Third, she ______________ (4. need / work) in a salon to get experience. She ______________ (5. hope / become) a business owner in five years because she ______________ (6. not want / work) for anyone else.

Listen again. Check your answers.

B **Work** with a partner. Talk about Vinh and Sofiya.

Name	Wants to . . .	Needs to . . .
Vinh	open a restaurant	1. learn to cook 2. take business classes 3. work in a restaurant
Sofiya	get a GED	1. improve her English 2. go to night school 3. take the GED test

Vinh wants to open a restaurant. First, he needs to learn how to cook.
Second, he needs to . . .

C **Talk** with a partner. Complete the chart. Ask and answer questions about goals.

I want to . . .	I need to . . .		
	1.	2.	3.

A What do you want to do?
B I want to . . .

A What steps do you need to take?
B First, I need to . . .

Share information with your classmates.

3 Verb tense review (present and present continuous)

A **Listen** to each sentence. Check (✓) the correct column.

CD1, Track 3

Present	Present continuous	Present	Present continuous
1. ✓		6.	
2.		7.	
3.		8.	
4.		9.	
5.		10.	

Listen again. Check your answers.

B **Listen again.** Circle the time phrases you hear. Then write them in the correct column.

CD1, Track 3

at the moment **every month** **never** **next year** **right now** **this week**

Present	Present continuous
Right now	

C **Read.** Complete the story. Use the present or present continuous.

Oksana Petrova ___*is*___ (1. be) from Russia. She ________ (2. live) in Philadelphia right now. She ________ (3. work) at an elementary school. She ________ (4. have) a job as a teacher's assistant. She ________ (5. work) at the school right now. She ________ (6. help) the students with math at the moment.

Oksana ________ (7. want) to become a teacher in the U.S. She ________ (8. study) English every evening. She ________ (9. plan) to take classes at the community college next year. She ________ (10. save) her money right now, because college classes are very expensive.

Listen and check your answers.

CD1, Track 4

D **Talk** with a partner. Ask and answer questions.

Every day	Every week	Right now	At the moment
What do you do every day?	What do you do every week?	What are you doing right now?	What are you studying at the moment?
Do you go to school every day?	Do you do homework every week?	Are you working right now?	Are you living in an apartment at the moment?

4 Verb tense review (past and future)

A **Listen** to each sentence. Check (✓) the correct column.

CD1, Track 5

Past	Future	Past	Future
1. ✓		6.	
2.		7.	
3.		8.	
4.		9.	
5.		10.	

B **Listen again.** Circle the time phrases you hear. Then write them in the correct column.

CD1, Track 5

in 2005 | last night | last year | next month | next summer | next year | soon

Past	Future
in 2005	

C **Write.** Complete the sentences. Use the past or future.

1. **A** When ___*did*___ you ___*move*___ (move) to this city?

   B I ____________ (move) here in 2011.

2. **A** How long ____________ you ____________ (stay) here?

   B Maybe I ____________ ____________ (stay) here for one more year.

3. **A** Where ____________ you ____________ (live) before you moved here?

   B I ____________ (live) in Taiwan.

4. **A** How long ____________ you ____________ (study) English?

   B I ____________ ____________ (study) English for two more years.

CD1, Track 6

Listen and check your answers.

D **Talk** with your classmates. Ask and answer the questions.

1. When did you move to this city?
2. How long will you stay here?
3. Where did you live before you moved here?
4. How long will you study English?

UNIT 1 PERSONAL INFORMATION

Lesson A Listening

1 Before you listen

A What do you see?

B What is happening?

C What's the story?

2 Listen

CD1, Track 7

A Listen and answer the questions.

1. Who are the speakers?
2. What are they talking about?

CD1, Track 7

B Listen again. Put a check (✓) under the correct name.

	Fernando	Danny
1. is tired this morning	✓	
2. likes staying home		
3. worked on his car		
4. is outgoing		
5. went out with his girlfriend		
6. wants a girlfriend		

3 After you listen

A Read. Complete the story.

alone	dislikes	going out	party animal
dance club	enjoys	outgoing	shy

Fernando and Danny are talking about their weekend. Fernando is a very friendly and *outgoing* (1) person. He ______ (2) dancing. Last night, he went to a ______ (3) and stayed until late. Danny thinks Fernando is a ______ (4).

Danny is different from Fernando. He is ______ (5) and quiet. He ______ (6) dancing. Danny was home ______ (7) the whole weekend. He likes staying at home more than ______ (8). He wants a girlfriend who likes staying home, too.

Listen and check your answers.

CD1, Track 8

B Talk with a partner. Ask and answer the questions.

1. What are some things you enjoy doing on the weekend?
2. Are you outgoing or shy? Give some examples.

Lesson B Verbs + gerunds

1 Grammar focus: questions and statements

A gerund is the base form of a verb + *ing*. Gerunds often follow verbs that talk about preferences. Use a gerund like a noun: *I love dancing*.

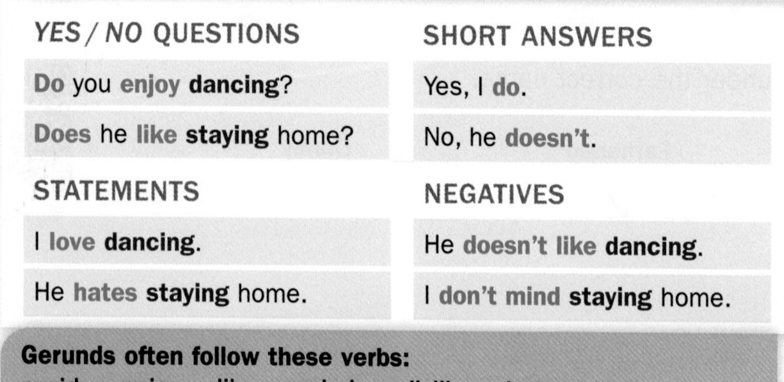

YES / NO QUESTIONS	SHORT ANSWERS
Do you **enjoy dancing**?	Yes, I **do**.
Does he **like staying** home?	No, he **doesn't**.
STATEMENTS	**NEGATIVES**
I **love dancing**.	He **doesn't like dancing**.
He **hates staying** home.	I **don't mind staying** home.

Gerunds often follow these verbs:
avoid enjoy like mind dislike hate love prefer

USEFUL LANGUAGE
Do you mind? = *Does it bother you?*
I don't mind. = *It doesn't bother me.*
* Don't say ~~*I mind*~~.

2 Practice

A **Write.** Complete the sentences. Use gerunds.

clean	do	go	pay	shop	use
close	eat	listen	play	take	wait

1. Does Katrina like ___shopping___ for clothes online?
2. My brother enjoys ________________ soccer.
3. Mrs. Tanaka doesn't mind ________________ the house.
4. Do you prefer ________________ at home or in restaurants?
5. I love ________________ to the birds in the morning.
6. Do you enjoy ________________ social media?
7. Most people don't enjoy ________________ bills every month.
8. Winston dislikes ________________ English homework.
9. I hate ________________ for the bus.
10. Do you prefer ________________ to bed early or late?
11. Danny avoids ________________ dance lessons.
12. Would you mind ________________ that window?

USEFUL LANGUAGE
"Social media" includes all the internet applications we use to share information, such as Facebook, Instagram, and Twitter.

Listen and check your answers.

B **Talk** with a partner. Ask and answer questions about the pictures. Use gerunds.

A Do Liz and Fred love working in the garden?
B Yes, they do. They love working in the garden.

A Does Karl enjoy taking out the garbage?
B No, he doesn't. He doesn't enjoy taking out the garbage.

Liz and Fred

1. love / work in the garden

Karl

2. enjoy / take out the garbage

Ramon

3. like / go to the beach

Kim

4. dislike / stand in line

Nasim

5. mind / work out

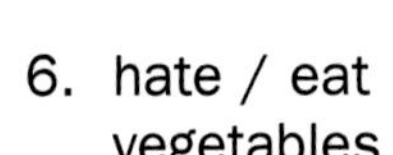
Marissa and Ethan

6. hate / eat vegetables

Joe

7. enjoy / play video games

the students

8. like / take / tests

Write a sentence about each picture.

Liz and Fred love working in the garden.

3 Communicate

A **Work** in a small group. Ask and answer questions about the activities.

A Tam, do you like being alone?
B I don't mind it. What about you?

USEFUL LANGUAGE
Say *What about you?* OR *How about you?* to ask the same question someone asked you.

- be alone
- dance
- learn languages
- walk in the rain
- use social media
- play sports
- read magazines
- cook
- talk on the phone
- exercise
- clean the house
- buy things online

B **Share** information about your classmates.

Lesson C Comparisons

1 Grammar focus: *more than, less than, as much as*

We can use *more than* or *less than* to compare two things that we like in different amounts. We can use *as much as* to talk about two things that we like the same amount.

STATEMENTS

I enjoy walking **more than** driving.	They enjoy singing **as much as** dancing.
She likes cooking **less than** eating.	

Watch

2 Practice

A **Write.** Complete the sentences. Use *more than*, *less than*, or *as much as*.

1. Sally enjoys cooking *more than* washing dishes.

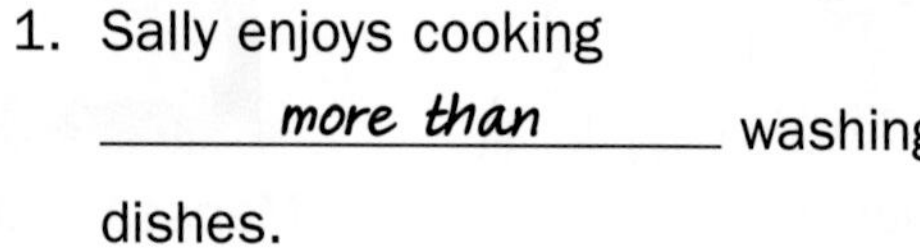

2. Sally likes washing dishes ____________ cooking.

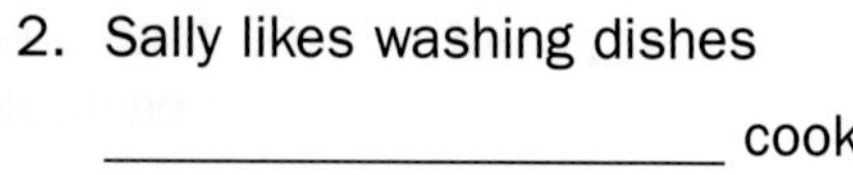

3. Alfredo loves listening to music ____________ playing an instrument.
4. Alfredo enjoys playing an instrument ____________ listening to music.

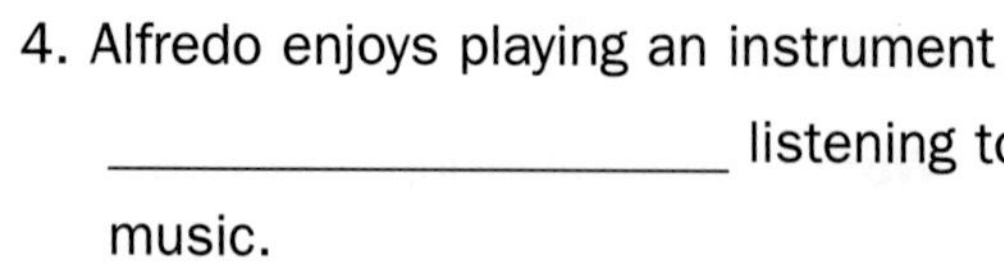

5. Pam likes working ____________ going to school.
6. Pam enjoys going to school ____________ working.
7. Marta enjoys painting ____________ jogging.

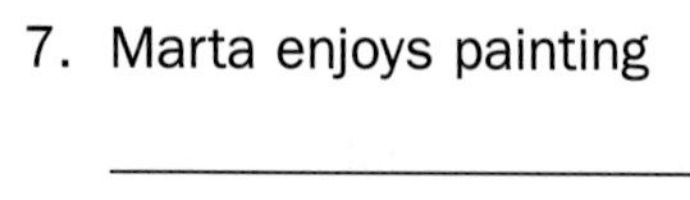

8. Marta likes jogging ____________ painting.

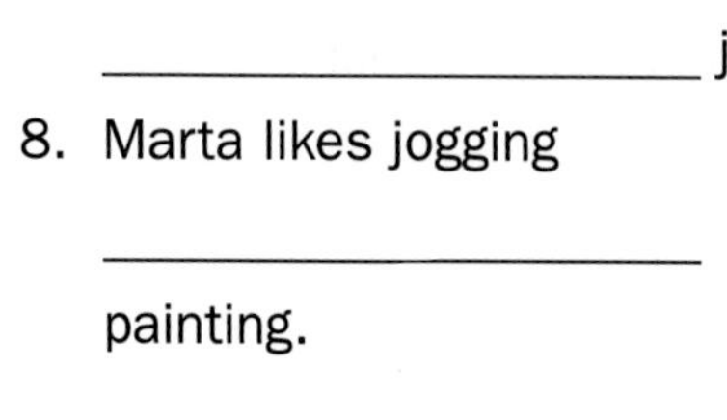

Listen and check your answers.

CD1, Track 10

B **Work** with a partner. Talk about the bar graph. Use *more than*, *less than*, and *as much as*.

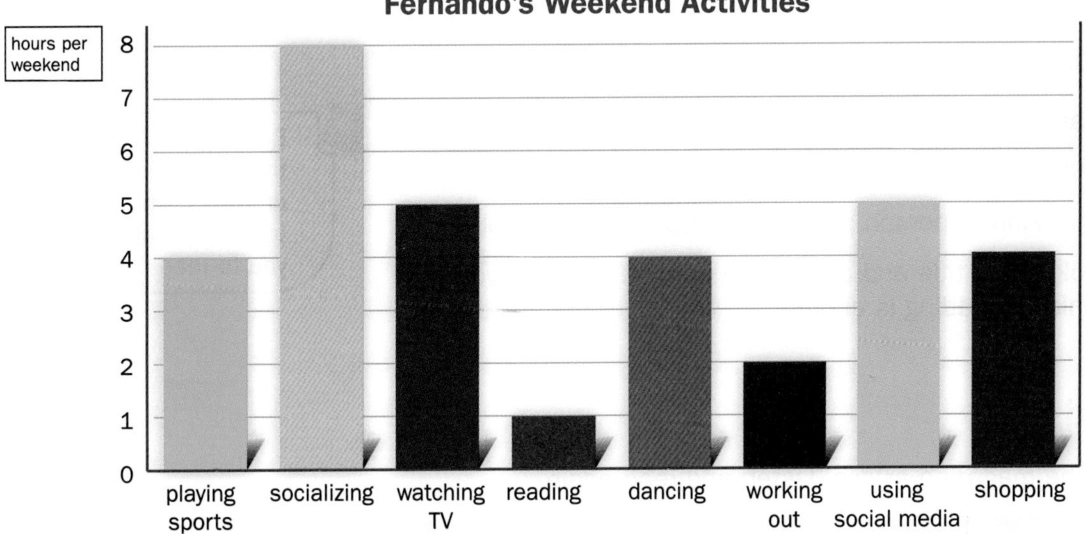

A Fernando likes socializing more than reading.

B That's right.

USEFUL LANGUAGE
socializing = spending time with friends or family

1. socializing / reading
2. playing sports / dancing
3. socializing / working out
4. watching TV / socializing
5. reading / playing sports
6. working out / reading
7. using social media / watching TV
8. reading / shopping

Write sentences about Fernando's weekend activities.

Fernando enjoys socializing more than reading.

3 Communicate

A **Work** in a small group. Ask and answer questions about the activities in Exercise 2B.

Which do you like more, playing sports or socializing?

I like socializing more than playing sports.

B **Share** information about your classmates.

Amelia likes socializing more than playing sports.

Lesson D Reading

1 Before you read

Look at the reading tip. Answer the questions.

1. What jobs do the people in the pictures have?
2. What kind of person probably enjoys doing each job?
3. Look at the title and pictures to predict. What do you think the reading is about?

Before you read, look at the title and the pictures. Predict, or guess, what you are going to read about. This will help you to read faster.

2 Read

Read the magazine article. Listen and read again.

CD1, Track 11

Your *Personality* and Your Job

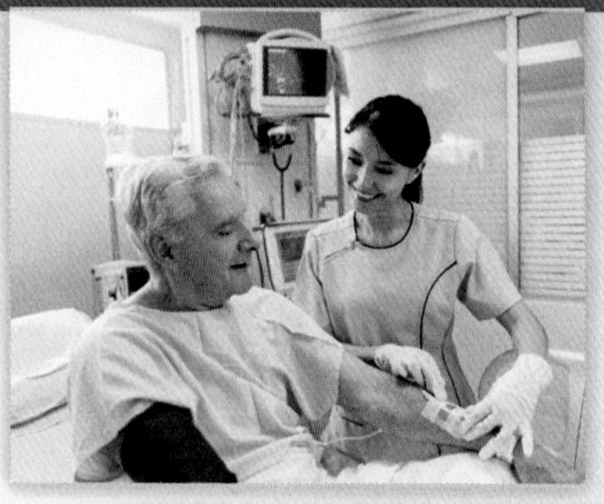

What is the perfect job for you? It depends a lot on your personality. People think, act, and feel in different ways, and there are interesting jobs for every kind of person. Three common personality types are outgoing, intellectual, and creative.

Outgoing people enjoy meeting others and helping them. They are good talkers. They are friendly, and they get along well with other people. They often become nurses, counselors, teachers, or social workers.

Intellectual people like thinking about problems and finding answers to hard questions. They often enjoy reading and playing games like chess. Many intellectual people like working alone more than working in a group. They may become scientists, computer programmers, or writers.

Creative people enjoy making things. They like to imagine things that are new and different. Many of them become artists such as painters, dancers, or musicians. Architects, designers, and photographers are other examples of creative jobs.

Before you choose a career, think about your personality type. If you want to be happy in your work, choose the right job for your personality.

3 After you read

A **Check** your understanding.

1. According to the article, why is it important to know your personality type?
2. What three personality types does this article discuss?
3. What do intellectual people like doing? What jobs are good for them?
4. What do creative people enjoy doing? What jobs are good for them?
5. According to the article, would an outgoing person enjoy being a scientist? Why or why not?
6. Does the author believe that one personality type is better than others? Cite evidence from the article to support your answer.

B **Build** your vocabulary.

1. Find these words in the reading, and underline them.

artists **creative** **intellectual** **outgoing** **personality** **type**

2. Find these phrases in the reading, and circle them.

enjoy meeting others
like to imagine things that are new and different
like thinking about problems
think, act, and feel in different ways
painters, dancers, or musicians
every kind of person

3. Look at the phrases in Exercise B2. They are clues to help you guess the meaning of these words. Write the phrases under the words.

1. personality ______________________
2. type ______________________
3. outgoing ______________________
4. intellectual ______________________
5. creative ______________________
6. artists ______________________

4. Match the words and the definitions.

1. personality ____
2. type ____
3. outgoing ____
4. intellectual ____
5. creative ____
6. artist ____

a. a kind of person or thing
b. good at making things that are new and different
c. enjoys thinking and finding answers
d. a person who paints, dances, writes, or draws
e. the natural way a person thinks, feels, and acts
f. friendly

C **Talk** with a partner. Ask and answer the questions.

1. What personality type are you? Why do you think so?
2. What is a good job for you?

For college and career readiness practice, please see pages 136–138.

Determine the central idea and details in an article; interpret words and phrases as they are used in a text

Lesson E Writing

1 Before you write

USEFUL LANGUAGE
Adjectives are words that describe people, places, and things.

A **Work** in a small group. Think of adjectives that describe someone at work. Write them on the lines.

artistic	hard-working	honest	____________	____________
creative	highly-trained	patient	____________	____________
friendly	helpful	reliable	____________	____________

B **Talk** with a partner. Look at the pictures. Answer the questions.

1. What are these people doing? What are their jobs?
2. What are some adjectives that can describe these people?

a.

b.

c.

d.

e.

f.

C **Read** the paragraph.

Marcos
September 9

The Right Job

My sister, Leona, has the right job for her personality. She's a nurse. She works in a big hospital in the Philippines. Leona is a very outgoing person. She's very friendly with all her patients, and she enjoys talking to everybody in the hospital. She is warm and helpful. I think a nurse is a good job for her because it fits her personality.

Work with a partner. Answer the questions.

1. What does the first sentence say about Leona?
2. What is Leona's job?
3. Where does she work?
4. Leona is an outgoing person. Which sentences explain this?
5. Which adjectives describe Leona?
6. Is a nurse a good job for Leona? Why?

2 Write

Write a paragraph about the right job for someone you know. Describe the person and what he/she likes or enjoys. Use a topic sentence and supporting sentences. Use Exercises 1B and 1C to help you.

A good paragraph is organized. Use a clear topic sentence and supporting sentences.

3 After you write

A **Check** your writing.

	Yes	No
1. I included a job and a personality type.	☐	☐
2. I described the person and what he/she likes or enjoys.	☐	☐
3. I used a topic sentence and supporting sentences.	☐	☐

B **Share** your writing with a partner.

1. Take turns. Read your paragraph to a partner.
2. Comment on your partner's paragraph. Ask your partner a question about the paragraph. Tell your partner one thing you learned.

Lesson F Another view

USEFUL LANGUAGE
DM = divorced male
N/S = nonsmoker
SF = single female
SM = single male

1 Life-skills reading

Fun-loving DM (46, 5'11", salt-and-pepper hair, N/S) enjoys taking motorcycle trips, camping outdoors, and spending time at the ocean. Seeking outgoing SF (40–50) for bike trips and fun.

Warm, kind, intelligent SM (27, 5'8") enjoys playing guitar, cooking, taking pictures. Seeking gentle SF (25–30) for musical evenings at home.

Caring SF (30, 5'5") loves playing tennis. Seeking good-looking, honest, active SM (28–35) with a good heart to share life together.

A **Read** the questions. Look at the online dating site. Fill in the answer.

1. How tall is the man on the motorcycle?
   - (A) under 5 feet
   - (B) 5 feet 2 inches
   - (C) 5 feet 11 inches
   - (D) over 6 feet
2. What word describes the younger man?
   - (A) friendly
   - (B) fun-loving
   - (C) gentle
   - (D) kind
3. What does the woman enjoy doing?
   - (A) playing guitar
   - (B) playing tennis
   - (C) taking motorcycle trips
   - (D) none of the above
4. Which ad seeks a single person?
   - (A) the first ad
   - (B) the second ad
   - (C) the third ad
   - (D) all of the above

B **Solve** the problem. Give your opinion.

You post your personal profile on an internet dating site. Someone responds to your profile and asks for your home address because the person wants to meet you. What should you do?

2 Grammar connections: *must* for logical conclusions

Use *must* and the base form of a verb to make conclusions based on the facts you know.

Julia works until 11:00 p.m. every night.	→ She must have a difficult job.
	→ She must not eat dinner at home.

A **Work** in a small group. Choose a situation and make conclusions. Take turns.

A David's phone bill is usually over $200 a month.
B He must talk on the phone a lot.
C He must send a lot of texts, too.
D He must not have a free Internet phone service.

1. David's phone bill is usually over $200 a month.
2. Susan gets up at 10:30 a.m. every morning.
3. Brenda buys a new car every year.
4. Sally spends a lot of time at the library.
5. Carlos goes to the gym five times a week.
6. George and Linda never cook at home.
7. Ivan doesn't have a computer.
8. Shawn and Olivia go to dance clubs a lot.

B **Talk** with a partner. Say something interesting about yourself. Your partner makes conclusions about you.

A I went to 20 concerts last year.
B You **must love** music.
A Yes, I do. I love it!

Scan an online dating site to locate key information; use *must* for logical conclusions

UNIT 2 AT SCHOOL

Lesson A Listening

1 Before you listen

A What do you see?

B What is happening?

C What's the story?

2 Listen

CD1, Track 12

A **Listen** and answer the questions.

1. Who are the speakers?
2. What are they talking about?

B **Listen again.** Put a check (✓) next to Alex's study problems. Then write Bella's advice.

CD1, Track 12

Study problems	Bella's advice
1. ☑ too many things to do	*make a to-do list; do important things first*
2. ☐ always late for school	
3. ☐ can't concentrate	
4. ☐ can't pronounce English words	
5. ☐ can't remember vocabulary	

3 After you listen

A **Read.** Complete the story.

active **boring** **discouraged** **list** **vocabulary**
advice **concentrate** **index cards** **paper**

Alex has been at the library for a long time, and he is *discouraged* (1). He has many things to do. He needs to study for a test and write a ______ (2). He needs to finish reading a book, but he can't ______ (3). He says the book is ______ (4).

Alex's friend Bella gives him some study ______ (5). First, she tells Alex to make a ______ (6) of all the things he needs to do. Next, she says he has to be a more ______ (7) reader. Finally, she tells him to write ______ (8) words on ______ (9) and study them when he has free time. With Bella's help, Alex plans to study smarter, not harder.

Listen and check your answers.

CD1, Track 13

B **Talk** with a partner. Ask and answer the questions.

1. What study problems do you have?
2. What can you do to study better?

Lesson B Present perfect

1 Grammar focus: *how long, for, since*

Use *how long* + present perfect to ask about something that started in the past and continues to the present. To answer *how long* questions, use *for* with a period of time (five months) and *since* with a specific point in time (Monday).

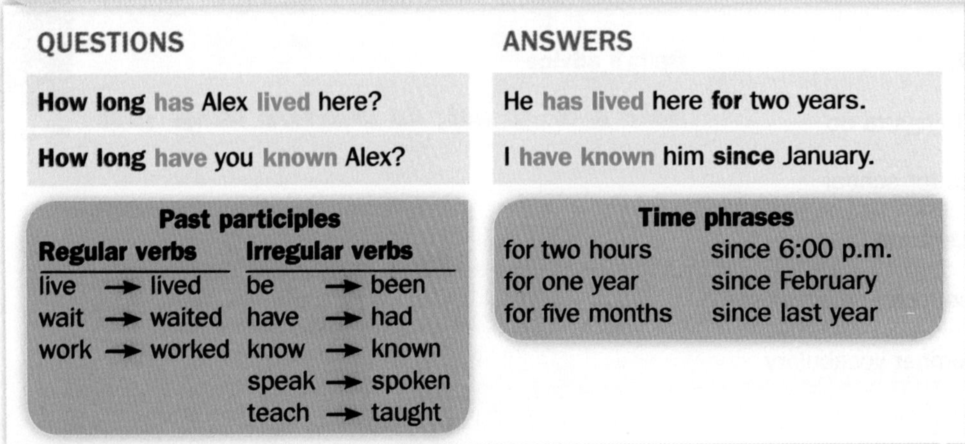

QUESTIONS	ANSWERS
How long has Alex lived here?	He has lived here **for** two years.
How long have you known Alex?	I have known him **since** January.

Past participles

Regular verbs		Irregular verbs	
live	lived	be	been
wait	waited	have	had
work	worked	know	known
		speak	spoken
		teach	taught

Time phrases

for two hours	since 6:00 p.m.
for one year	since February
for five months	since last year

2 Practice

A Write. Complete the sentences. Use the present perfect in the question. Use *for* or *since* in the answer.

1. A How long ___has___ Manya ___been___ in the computer lab? (be)
   B ___Since___ six o'clock.
2. A How long __________ Avi __________ Bella? (know)
   B __________ four months.
3. A How long __________ Kayla __________ at the library? (work)
   B __________ September.
4. A How long __________ Mrs. Bateson __________ at the adult school? (teach)
   B __________ 20 years.
5. A How long __________ you __________ in Canada? (live)
   B __________ one year.
6. A How long __________ Omar __________ two jobs? (have)
   B __________ last year.
7. A How long __________ Pete __________ for the bus? (wait)
   B __________ one hour.

Listen and check your answers. Then practice with a partner.

CD1, Track 14

B **Talk** with a partner. Ask and answer questions about Alex. Use *since*.

A How long has Alex been in the United States?

B Since January 2016.

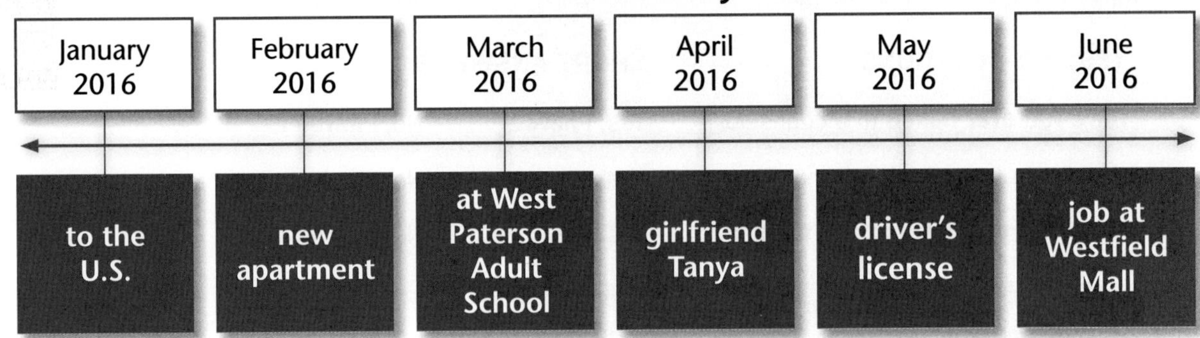

1. be in the U.S.
2. live in his new apartment
3. study at West Paterson Adult School
4. know his girlfriend Tanya
5. have a driver's license
6. work at Westfield Mall

Write today's date. Then write sentences about Alex. Use *for*.

Today is July 23, 2018.

Alex has been in the U.S. for two years and six months.

3 Communicate

A **Work** in a small group. Ask and answer questions with *how long*.

A How long have you studied English?

B For three years.

A That's interesting. How long have you lived in this country?

B Since 2003.

A Wow!

1. study / English
2. live / in this country
3. be / at this school
4. work / in this country
5. have / your job
6. know / our teacher
7. be / married
8. lived / in your present home

USEFUL LANGUAGE
To express interest or surprise, you can say:
That's interesting.
Really?
Wow!

B **Share** information about your classmates.

Lesson C Present perfect

1 Grammar focus: questions with *ever*; short answers

Use *ever* with the present perfect to ask *Yes / No* questions about things that happened at any time in the past.

YES / NO QUESTIONS	SHORT ANSWERS	
Have you **ever** **talked** to a counselor?	Yes, I **have**.	No, I **haven't**.
Has Sonia **ever** **studied** French?	Yes, she **has**.	No, she **hasn't**.
Have they **ever** **tried** to ask for help?	Yes, they **have**.	No, they **haven't**.

Past participles

Regular verbs	Irregular verbs	
ask → asked	do → done	make → made
talk → talked	forget → forgotten	read → read
try → tried	get → gotten	take → taken
	lose → lost	write → written

2 Practice

A **Write.** Complete the sentences. Use ever.

1. **A** Has Laura ever talked to her school counselor? (Laura / talk)
   B No, she hasn't.
2. **A** ______ your teacher's name? (you / forget)
   B Yes, I ______.
3. **A** ______ a book in English? (Joseph / read)
   B No, he ______. But he wants to.
4. **A** ______ late to school? (Mary and Paula / be)
   B No, they ______.
5. **A** ______ to speak English with your neighbors? (you / try)
   B Yes, I ______.
6. **A** ______ the wrong bus to school? (Tomas / take)
   B No, he ______.

Listen and check your answers. Then practice with a partner.

B **Talk** with a partner. Ask and answer questions about study habits.

A Have you ever made a to-do list?

B No, never.

A Have you ever asked questions in class?

B Yes, I have.

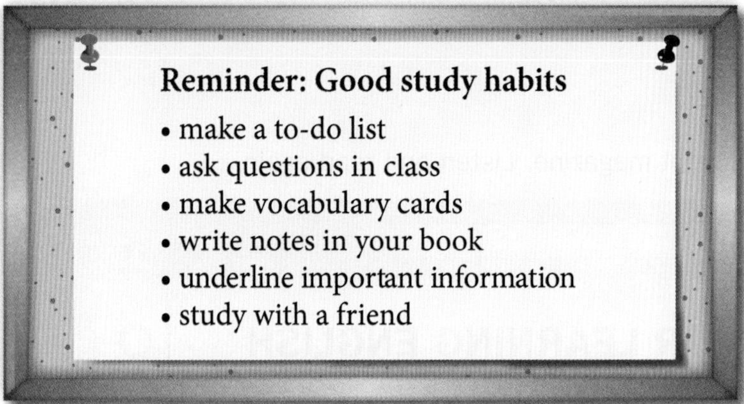

Write sentences about your partner.

Omar has never made a to-do list. He has asked questions in class.

USEFUL LANGUAGE
has never = hasn't ever

3 Communicate

A **Work** in a small group. Ask and answer questions about study problems. Complete the chart.

A Have you ever had trouble concentrating?

B Yes, I have.

Study problems	Name: ____________	Name: ____________
have trouble concentrating	*Yes*	
forget to study for a test		
lose your textbook		
do the wrong homework		
be late to school		
(your idea)		

B **Share** information about your classmates. Give advice.

Ana has had trouble concentrating.

She should do her homework in a quiet place.

Lesson D Reading

1 Before you read

Look at the title and strategies. Answer the questions.

1. Read the title. What do you think the word *strategies* means?
2. How many strategies are there? What are they?

2 Read

Read the article from an online student magazine. Listen and read again.

CD1, Track 16

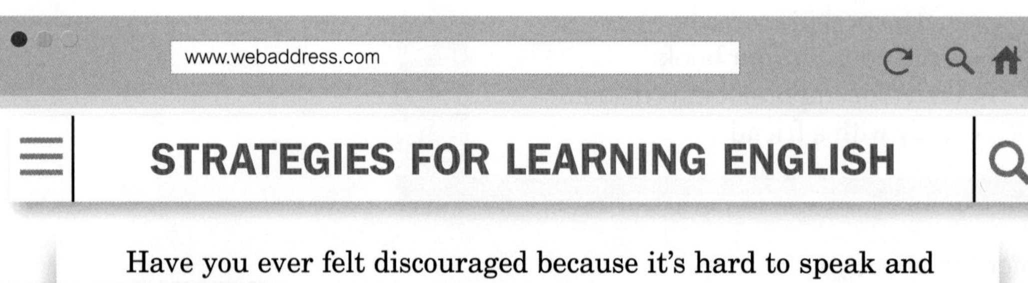

STRATEGIES FOR LEARNING ENGLISH

Have you ever felt discouraged because it's hard to speak and understand English? Don't give up! Here are three strategies to help you learn faster and remember more.

STRATEGY #1 SET GOALS.

Have you ever set goals for learning English? When you set goals, you decide what you want to learn. After you determine your purpose for learning, you can make a plan to help you reach your goals. Maybe your goal is to learn more vocabulary. There are many ways to do this. For example, you can read in English for 15 minutes every day. You can also learn one new word every day.

STRATEGY #2 LOOK FOR OPPORTUNITIES TO PRACTICE ENGLISH.

Talk to everyone. Speak with people in the store, at work, and in the park. Don't worry about making mistakes. And don't forget to ask questions. For example, if your teacher uses a word you don't understand, ask a question like "What does that word mean?"

STRATEGY #3 GUESS.

Don't try to translate every word. When you read, concentrate on clues such as pictures or other words in the sentence to help you understand. You can also make guesses when you are talking to people. For example, look at their faces and hand gestures – the way they move their hands – to help you guess the meaning.

Set goals, look for opportunities to practice, and guess. Do these things every day, and you will learn more English!

In a reading, *for example* means *details will follow*.

3 After you read

A Check your understanding.

1. What is the article about?
2. What is an example of setting goals?
3. What is an example of looking for opportunities to practice English?
4. You ask someone in line at a supermarket, "What time is it?" What strategy are you using?
5. If you read a story without using a dictionary, what clues help you guess?
6. Which strategy do you think will help you learn English faster? Use evidence from the article to support your answer.

B Build your vocabulary.

1. Look at the chart. Find the vocabulary words in the article. Underline them.
2. Use the context to decide the part of speech of each word – *noun* or *verb*. Write it in the chart.
3. Circle the best definition to match the part of speech.

Vocabulary	Part of speech	Definition
1. set	*verb*	a. a group of related things, such as dishes (b.) to choose or decide on something, such as a goal
2. plan		a. something you have decided to do b. to decide about something you want to do
3. practice		a. an activity you do to improve your ability b. to do something regularly to improve your ability
4. guess		a. an answer that you think is right, but you're not sure b. to give an answer that you think is right
5. clues		a. information you use to guess or solve problems b. to give someone useful information
6. pictures		a. paintings, drawings, or photographs b. to paint, draw, or photograph something
7. gestures		a. hand movements that have a special meaning b. to tell something by moving your hands

C Talk with a partner. Ask and answer the questions.

1. Have you ever set goals for learning English? What were they?
2. How do you practice something new? Give an example.
3. When you speak, what gestures do you use?

For college and career readiness practice, please see pages 139–141.

Determine the central idea and details of an article and make inferences; use context to determine part of speech and meaning

Lesson E Writing

1 Before you write

A **Work** in a small group. Complete the chart with examples of strategies for learning English. Use the reading on page 24 and your own ideas.

Strategy	Examples from reading	Your examples
Set goals.	*Read for 15 minutes in English every day.*	*Write in English every day for five minutes.*
Practice English.		
Guess.		

B **Read** the paragraph.

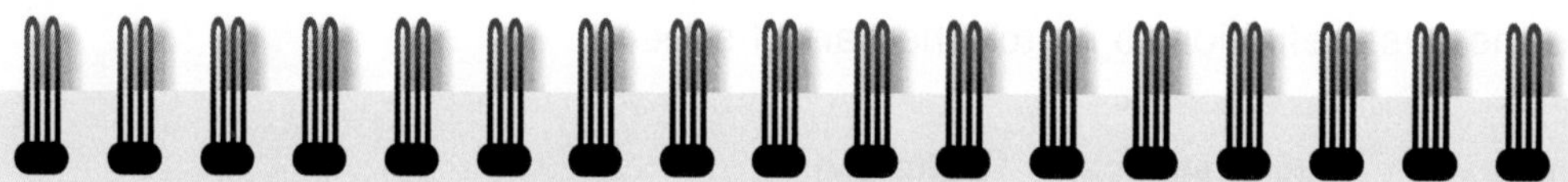

My Strategies for Learning English

There are two strategies I'm going to use to help me learn English. My first strategy is to learn more English vocabulary. There are many ways I will do this. For example, I'm going to learn one new English word every day. I'm also going to write my new words in a notebook. Another strategy I will use is looking for places to practice my English. For example, I'm going to talk to more English speakers at the store and at work. I can't wait to try these new strategies because I want to speak, read, and write English better.

Use examples to support your ideas.

Work with a partner. Answer the questions.

1. What is the writer's first strategy?
2. What examples does the writer give of the first strategy?
3. What is the writer's second strategy?
4. What example does the writer give of the second strategy?
5. The writer says, "I can't wait to try these new strategies." What does that mean?
6. Do you think these strategies could help you?

C **Write** a plan for a paragraph about strategies for learning English. Answer the questions.

1. What is one strategy you want to try?	
2. What is one example of this strategy?	
3. What is another strategy you want to try?	
4. What is one example of this strategy?	
5. Why do you want to try these strategies?	

2 Write

Write a paragraph about strategies for learning English. Include a topic sentence that focuses on strategies. Write about two strategies and give one or two examples for each one. Use Exercises 1B and 1C to help you.

3 After you write

A **Check** your writing.

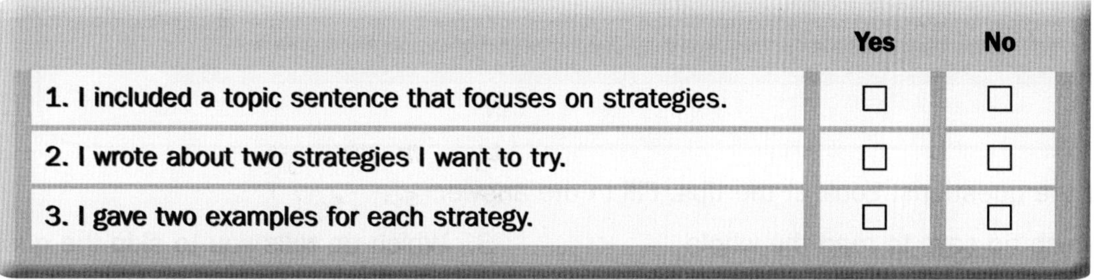

	Yes	No
1. I included a topic sentence that focuses on strategies.	☐	☐
2. I wrote about two strategies I want to try.	☐	☐
3. I gave two examples for each strategy.	☐	☐

B **Share** your writing with a partner.

1. Take turns. Read your paragraph to a partner.
2. Comment on your partner's paragraph. Ask your partner a question about the paragraph. Tell your partner one thing you learned.

Lesson F Another view

1 Life-skills reading

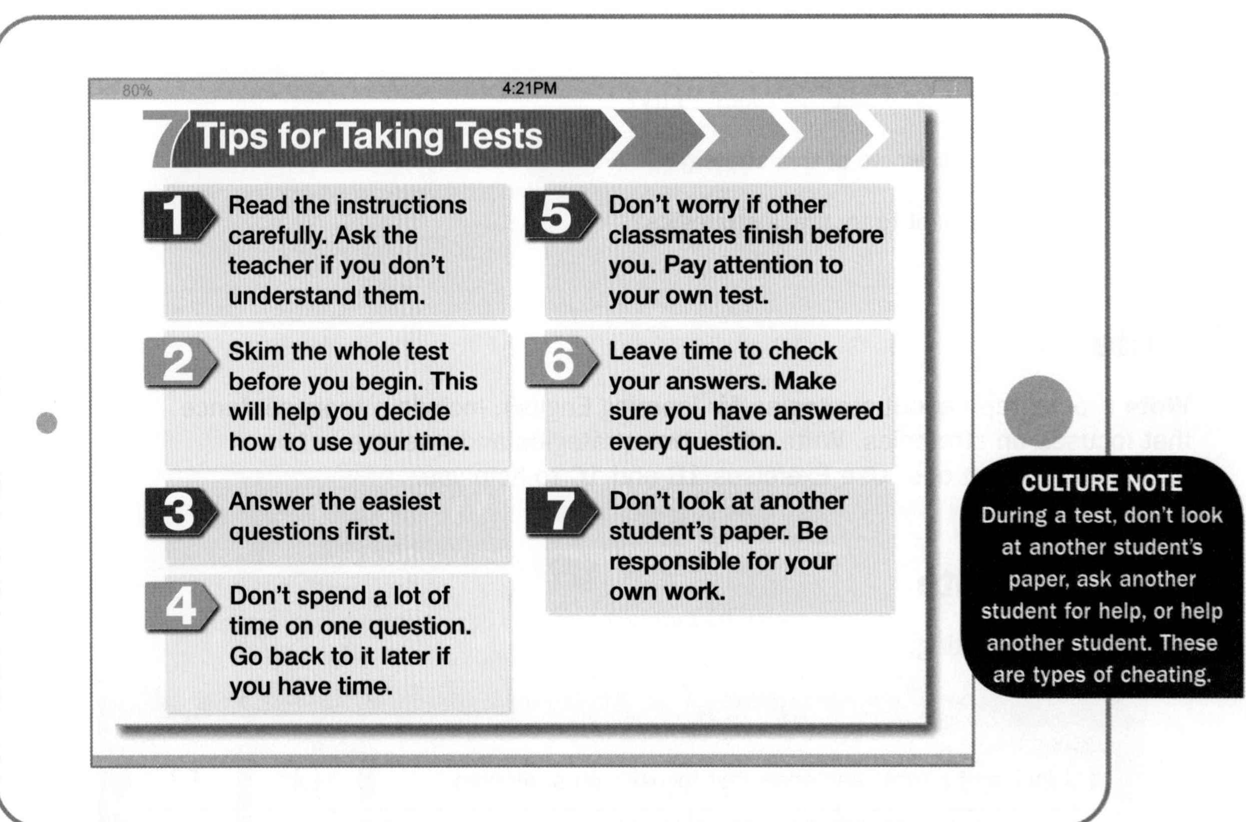

CULTURE NOTE
During a test, don't look at another student's paper, ask another student for help, or help another student. These are types of cheating.

A **Read** the questions. Look at the tips. Fill in the answer.

1. Which tip says to read the whole test quickly before you answer any questions?
   - (A) Tip 1
   - (B) Tip 2
   - (C) Tip 6
   - (D) Tip 7
2. Which tip tells you to answer the questions you know first?
   - (A) Tip 1
   - (B) Tip 2
   - (C) Tip 3
   - (D) Tip 4
3. Which tip tells you to skip the questions you don't know and go back to them later?
   - (A) Tip 3
   - (B) Tip 4
   - (C) Tip 5
   - (D) Tip 6
4. What word means *read quickly for the main idea*?
   - (A) responsible
   - (B) spend
   - (C) skim
   - (D) decide

B **Solve** the problem. Give your opinion.

Luz is taking a test in class. She discovers that she has marked the wrong answer, and she needs to change her answer. Her pencil doesn't have an eraser. She looks over to her friend Maria's desk. Maria has an extra eraser on her desk. What should Luz do?

2 Grammar connections: simple past and present perfect

Use the *simple past* for an activity that happened at a specific time in the past. Use the *present perfect* for an activity that began in the past and continues to the present.

Rita **studied** Arabic in 2012.	Rita **has studied** Arabic since 2012.

A **Talk** with a partner. You need an English tutor. Look at the chart and compare the two tutors. Use the simple past and present perfect to talk about the tutors' experience. With your partner, choose the tutor you think is best.

A Rita would be a good tutor. She studied Spanish for four years, and she took French classes. She has also studied Arabic since 2012.

B Maybe, but she hasn't had any tutoring experience. Dao has tutored English since 2015. He also . . .

Rita Lawrence

1966 – 1976	live in Phoenix, AZ
1976 – 1980	study Spanish in college
1980	graduate from college with B average, degree in education
1980 – 1986	teach English in Mexico
1987	get married to English teacher
1988 – 2012	stay home with children
2009 – 2012	study French at night school
2012 – now	teach at an elementary school
2012 – now	study Arabic online
2015 – now	volunteer at a hospital translating Spanish to English

Dao Lin

1990- 2004	live in Shanghai, China
2004	move to Chicago, IL
2004 – 2008	learn English in high school
2008 – 2012	study English and computer science in college
2012	graduate from college with A average, degree in computer science
2012	travel around U.S. for four months
2012 – 2014	work for travel agency
2014 – now	work as a computer technician
2015 – now	tutor English at a high school
2016 – now	live with aunt and uncle, who only speak Chinese

B **Share** your decision with the class.

We chose Rita because . . .

We chose Dao because . . .

Scan an article about test taking tips to locate key details; compare simple past and present perfect

REVIEW

1 Listening

Listen. Put a check (✓) under the correct name.

CD1, Track 17

	Vladimir	Marisol
1. asks the teacher questions		✓
2. asks another student questions		
3. writes vocabulary on index cards		
4. talks to co-workers		
5. is shy		
6. is outgoing		

Talk with a partner. Check your answers.

2 Grammar

A **Write.** Complete the story. Use the correct words.

Homework Problems

Jameela ___has had___ (1. has / has had) a lot of problems with her son, Faisal, __________ (2. for / since) the past two months. He doesn't enjoy __________ (3. studying / study) science. He __________ (4. get / has gotten) bad grades on his tests. The teacher said that Faisal __________ (5. doesn't do / hasn't done) his homework __________ (6. for / since) December. Faisal said he hates __________ (7. do / doing) his science homework because he doesn't understand it. Jameela __________ (8. works / has worked) overtime at her job __________ (9. for / since) the past two months, so she __________ (10. hasn't been / won't be) able to help him. What should Jameela and her son do?

B **Write.** Look at the answers. Write the questions.

1. A How long ___has Jameela had problems with her son___?
   B Jameela has had problems with her son for the past two months.
2. A __________ ever __________?
   B Yes, he has. Faisal has gotten bad grades on his tests for the past two months.
3. A How long __________?
   B Jameela has worked overtime for the past two months.

Talk with a partner. Ask and answer the questions.

3 Pronunciation: stressing content words

A **Listen** to the stressed content words in each sentence. Content words include main verbs, nouns, adverbs, adjectives, and question words.

CD1, Track 18

1. She loves playing cards with friends.
2. He hates working in the garden.
3. Do you like being alone?
4. She enjoys cooking less than eating.
5. I like living in the city.
6. How long has Shen studied English?
7. He's been here for six months.
8. Have you ever studied Korean?
9. I've never studied Chinese.
10. He graduated from college in 2013.

Listen again and repeat. Stress the content words.

B **Listen and repeat.** Then underline the content words.

CD1, Track 19

1. What is the perfect job for you?
2. The perfect job depends on your personality.
3. Have you ever felt discouraged?
4. Have you ever set goals for learning English?
5. What does that word mean?
6. Intellectual people often enjoy working alone.
7. She has volunteered at a hospital for two years.
8. He got married in 2010.
9. How long have you lived in your present house?
10. She spends a lot of time studying at the library.

Read your sentences to a partner. Compare your answers.

C **Read** the paragraph. Underline the content words.

My sister has the right job for her personality. She's a nurse. She works in a big hospital in the Philippines. She is a very outgoing person. She's very friendly with all her patients, and she enjoys talking to people in the hospital. She is warm and helpful. I think a nurse is a good job for her because it fits her personality.

Talk with a partner. Compare your answers. Read the paragraph to your partner. Stress the content words.

UNIT 3 FRIENDS AND FAMILY

Lesson A Listening

1 Before you listen

A What do you see?

B What is happening?

C What's the story?

2 Listen

CD1, Track 20

A **Listen** and answer the questions.

1. Who are the speakers?
2. What are they talking about?

B **Listen again.** Put a check (✓) next to Ana's problems.

CD1, Track 20

1. ☑ been busy	4. ☐ car alarm broken
2. ☐ children sick	5. ☐ smoke alarm needs battery
3. ☐ ceiling is too high	6. ☐ neighbors are noisy

3 After you listen

A **Read.** Complete the story.

alarm	**battery**	**come over**	**favor**	**noisy**
appreciates	**borrow**	**complain**	**noise**	**owe**

Ana and Maria are neighbors. Ana calls Maria because she needs a ___favor___ (1). The smoke ________ (2) in Ana's kitchen is beeping. She needs to change the ________ (3), but the ceiling in her kitchen is too high. Ana asks to ________ (4) Maria's ladder.

Maria says her husband, Daniel, will ________ (5) with a ladder and help Ana. Ana says, "I ________ (6) you one." This means she ________ (7) Maria and Daniel's help, and she will do a favor for them in the future.

Next, Maria tells Ana about their ________ (8) neighbors. The neighbors had a party on Saturday night. Because of the ________ (9), Maria and Daniel couldn't sleep. Ana tells Maria that she should ________ (10) to the apartment manager.

Listen and check your answers.

CD1, Track 21

B **Talk** with a partner. Ask and answer the questions.

1. Have you ever borrowed something from a neighbor? What did you borrow?
2. Have you ever lent something to a neighbor? What did you lend?

USEFUL LANGUAGE
When you *borrow* something *from* someone, you receive it. When you *lend* something *to* someone, you give it for a short time.

Lesson B Clauses and phrases with *because*

1 Grammar focus: *because* clauses and *because of* phrases

Use a *because* clause or *because of* phrase to give an explanation for something. Use *because* in a clause with a subject and verb. Use *because of* before a noun to make a phrase.

BECAUSE + CLAUSE	*BECAUSE OF* + NOUN PHRASE
Ana can't reach the smoke alarm **because** the ceiling is too high.	Ana can't reach the smoke alarm **because of** the high ceiling.
Because the ceiling is too high, Ana can't reach the smoke alarm.	**Because of** the high ceiling, Ana can't reach the smoke alarm.

USEFUL LANGUAGE
When you read aloud, pause when you see a comma. *Because of the high ceiling,* (pause) *Ana can't reach the smoke alarm.*

2 Practice

A Write. Complete the sentences. Use *because* or *because of*.

A Nice Surprise

Lei wanted to bake a cake ___because___(1) it was her neighbor Margy's birthday. Lei needed to go to the store ________(2) she didn't have any flour. However, her car had a flat tire. She probably got the flat tire ________(3) her tires were very old. ________(4) this problem, she couldn't drive to the store. She couldn't walk to the store ________(5) the distance. It was more than a mile away. Lei had a clever idea. She went to Margy and asked to borrow a cup of flour. Margy was happy to help ________(6) she had a lot of flour and ________(7) she was a good neighbor. Two hours later, Lei returned to Margy's house with a beautiful cake. When Margy opened the door, Lei shouted, "Happy birthday!" Margy was very surprised and happy. ________(8) the nice surprise, Margy had a wonderful birthday!

Listen and check your answers.

B **Talk** with a partner. Ask and answer *why* questions about the problems.

A Why couldn't you sleep last night?
B Because of my noisy neighbors.

A Why couldn't you make the cake?
B Because I didn't have any eggs.

Problem	Reason
1. You couldn't sleep last night.	noisy neighbors
2. You couldn't make a cake.	didn't have any eggs
3. The neighbors couldn't lock the door.	lock was broken
4. You couldn't change the alarm battery.	didn't have a ladder
5. The children couldn't play outside.	the rain
6. You couldn't come to school.	car had a flat tire
7. You couldn't buy the house.	high price
8. You couldn't go to the party.	had to work
9. You couldn't go hiking.	the bad weather
10. You couldn't call me.	was busy

Write a sentence about each problem.

I couldn't sleep last night because of my noisy neighbors.

3 Communicate

A **Work** in a small group. Ask and answer questions. Complete the chart.

A Why did you come to this country, Shakir?
B Because of my children. They live here.
A Why do you live in your neighborhood?
B Because it's close to my job.

Name	Why did you come to this country?	Why do you live in your neighborhood?
Shakir	*children live here*	*close to job*

B **Share** information about your classmates.

Lesson C Adverbs of degree

1 Grammar focus: *too* and *enough*

Use *too* + adjective to talk about more than the right amount. The meaning is negative. Use *adjective* + *enough* to talk about the right amount of something. *Use not* + adjective + *enough* to talk about less than the right amount. The meaning is negative.

too + ADJECTIVE	ADJECTIVE + *enough*
The ceiling is **too high**.	The ladder is **tall enough**.
It's **too high** to reach.	It's **tall enough** to reach the ceiling.

not + ADJECTIVE + *enough*
The woman is **not tall enough**.
She is **not tall enough** to reach the ceiling.

Adjectives

big	expensive	far
close	experienced	high

Use the shorter sentence when the listener knows what you are talking about. Example: *The ladder is tall enough.*

2 Practice

A Write. Complete the sentences. Use *too* or *enough*.

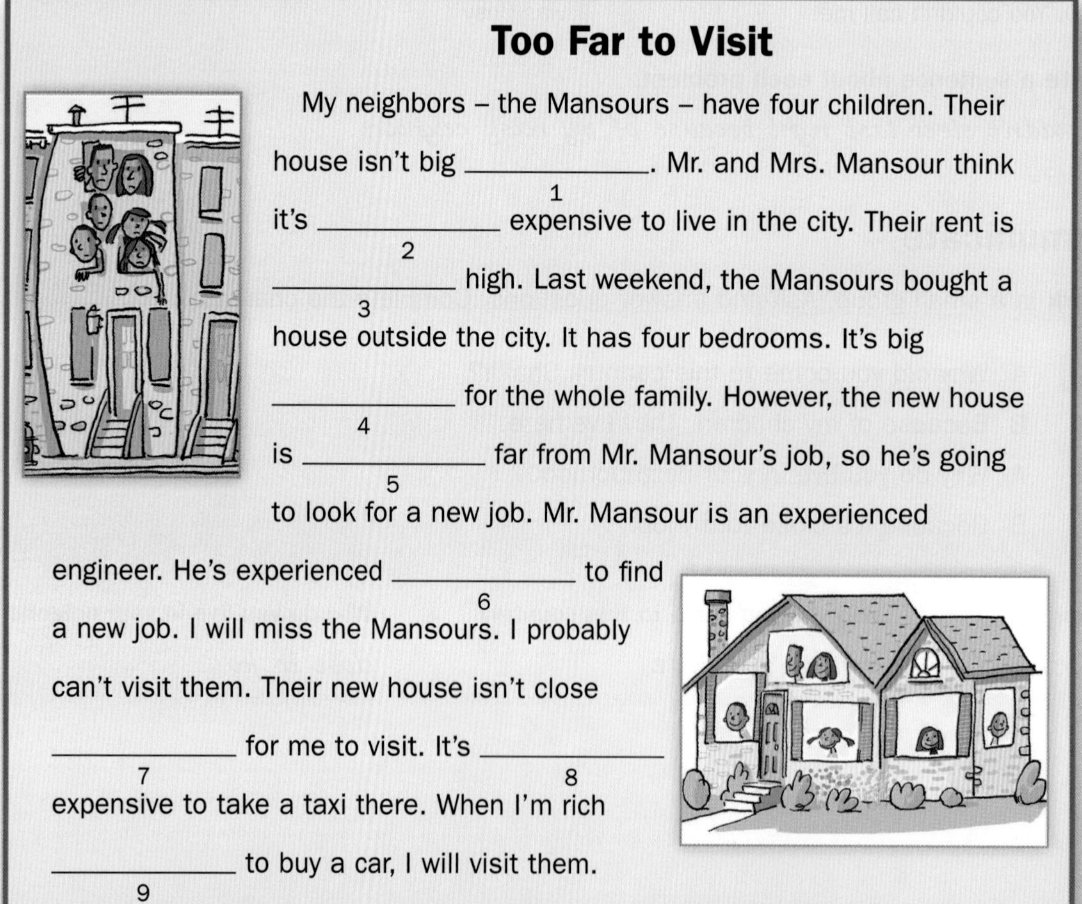

Too Far to Visit

My neighbors – the Mansours – have four children. Their house isn't big ______1______. Mr. and Mrs. Mansour think it's ______2______ expensive to live in the city. Their rent is ______3______ high. Last weekend, the Mansours bought a house outside the city. It has four bedrooms. It's big ______4______ for the whole family. However, the new house is ______5______ far from Mr. Mansour's job, so he's going to look for a new job. Mr. Mansour is an experienced engineer. He's experienced ______6______ to find a new job. I will miss the Mansours. I probably can't visit them. Their new house isn't close ______7______ for me to visit. It's ______8______ expensive to take a taxi there. When I'm rich ______9______ to buy a car, I will visit them.

Listen and check your answers.

B **Work** with a partner. Talk about the pictures. Use ***too***, ***enough***, and ***not . . . enough***.

A Can they swim today?
B I don't think so. It's too cold to swim today.
A Yeah, you're right. It really isn't warm enough.

A Can she swim today?
B Yes, it's hot enough to swim.

1. cold / swim / warm

2. hot / swim

3. young / drive / old

4. old / drive

5. weak / lift the TV / strong

6. strong / lift the TV

7. short / reach the books / tall

8. tall / reach the books.

Write sentences about each picture.

It's too cold to swim.

It isn't warm enough to swim.

3 Communicate

Work in a small group. Talk about what you are *too young*, *too old*, *young enough*, or *old enough* to do. Give your opinions.

USEFUL LANGUAGE
I agree. = My opinion is the same as yours.
I disagree. / *I don't agree.* = My opinion is different from yours.

I'm too young to get married.

I agree. Young people should wait to get married.

Lesson D Reading

1 Before you read

Look at the title and the picture. Answer the questions.

1. Have you ever heard of Neighborhood Watch? What is it?
2. Is there a Neighborhood Watch in your area?

The first sentence of a paragraph usually tells the main idea. The other sentences give details. Facts and examples are types of details.

2 Read

Read the article from a neighborhood newsletter. Listen and read again.

CD1, Track 24

Neighborhood Watch Success Story

by Latisha Holmes, President, Rolling Hills Neighborhood Watch

People often ask me about the role of Neighborhood Watch. My answer is *Because of Neighborhood Watch, our neighborhood is safer and nicer.* Members of Neighborhood Watch help each other and look after the neighborhood. For example, we look after our neighbors' houses when they aren't home. We help elderly neighbors with yard work. Once a month, we get together to paint over graffiti.

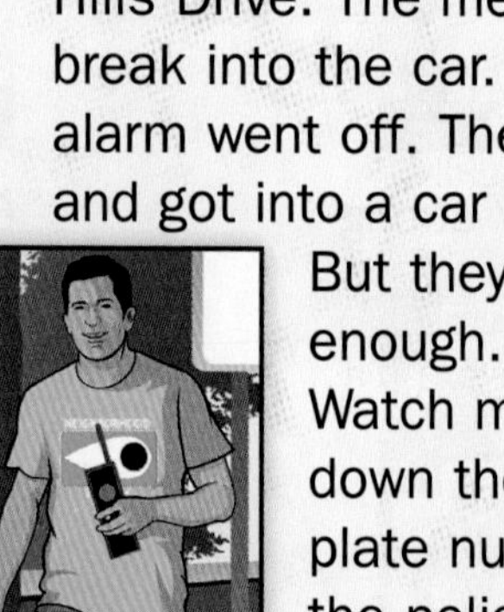

Last Wednesday, the Neighborhood Watch team had another success story. Around 8:30 p.m., members of our Neighborhood Watch were out on a walk. Near the Corner Café, they noticed two men next to George Garcia's car. George lives on Rolling Hills Drive. The men were trying to break into the car. Suddenly, the car alarm went off. The men ran away and got into a car down the street. But they weren't quick enough. Our Neighborhood Watch members wrote down the car's license plate number and called the police. Later that night, the police arrested the two men.

I would like to congratulate our Neighborhood Watch team on their good work. Because so many people participate in Neighborhood Watch, Rolling Hills is a safer neighborhood today.

For information about Neighborhood Watch, please call 773-555-1234.

3 After you read

A **Check** your understanding.

1. What is the main idea of the first paragraph?
2. What are three examples of the role of Neighborhood Watch?
3. What did the Neighborhood Watch team see? What did they do?
4. In the 3rd paragraph, what word means the same as *tell someone they did a good job*?
5. According to the author, why is Rolling Hills a safer neighborhood today?

B **Build** your vocabulary.

1. Read the dictionary entry for the word *get*. Find the definition of *get together*.

> **get** /get/ [T] **getting,** *past* **got,** *past part* **gotten** to take (something) into your possession
> **get together** *v/adv* [I/T] to meet; to have a meeting or party

2. *Get together* is a two-word verb. Look at the article in Exercise 2. Match the two-word verbs.

get	look	break	run	get
after	into	together	into	away

3. Write each verb in Exercise B2 next to its definition.

1. to meet	*get together*
2. to enter (a car legally)	
3. to enter (a car illegally)	
4. to escape; to leave a place very fast	
5. to take care of	

4. Complete the sentences with the verbs in Exercise B3.

a. Let's *get together* for coffee tomorrow, OK?
b. Somebody tried to ____________ my neighbor's house.
c. I saw the girl next door ____________ a car and drive away.
d. My cats always ____________ when the door is open.
e. All the people on my street ____________ each other's houses.

C **Talk** with a partner. Ask and answer the questions.

1. Do you enjoy getting together with friends? What do you do?
2. Do you and your neighbors look after each other? How?

For college and career readiness practice, please see pages 142–144.

Determine the main idea and key details in a neighborhood newsletter; recognize two-word verbs and their meaning

Lesson E Writing

1 Before you write

A **Talk** with a partner. Answer the questions.

1. Have you ever complained to your landlord or apartment manager?
2. What was the problem?
3. How did you complain – in person, by telephone, or in writing?
4. What happened?

B **Read** the complaint email.

Reply Forward

From: Luis Ramos (luis.ramos@umail.com)
To: Acme Properties (info@acmeproperties.com)
Subject: Neighbors

Acme Properties
100 25th Avenue
New York, NY 10011

To Whom It May Concern:

My name is Luis Ramos. I live at 156 South Flower Street, Apartment 3. I am writing because my neighbors in Apartment 9 are too noisy. I asked them to be quiet, but they still have loud parties almost every night. Because of the noise, my children can't sleep.

Can you please tell them to be quiet? I hope you will take care of this as soon as possible.

Thank you in advance.

Sincerely,
Luis Ramos

CULTURE NOTE
When you don't know the name of the person you are writing to, use *To Whom It May Concern.*

Work with a partner. Answer the questions.

1. What is the email about?
2. Who is the email to?
3. Does the writer know the person's name?
4. Who wrote the email?
5. What is the problem?
6. What does the writer want Acme Properties to do?

C **Complete** the complaint email.

advance because because of sincerely soon very

Reply Forward

From: Alina Krasinski (akrasinksi@umail.com)
To: Flower Street Management (info@flowerstreet.com)
Subject: Leaking Sink

To Whom It May Concern:

My name is Alina Krasinski. I live at 156 South Flower Street, Apartment 6. I am writing *because* (1) the pipes under my kitchen sink are leaking. ____________ (2) the leak, my water bill will be ____________ (3) high next month. The water is also bad for the kitchen floor. Can you please come as ____________ (4) as possible to fix the leak?

Thank you in ____________ (5).

____________ (6),

Alina Krasinski

A complaint email should include:
- the problem
- examples
- a request to fix the problem

D **Talk** with your classmates. What housing problems do people complain about?

2 Write

Write a complaint email. Use *To Whom It May Concern* or the person's name. Include the problem, an example, and a request to fix the problem. Use the emails in Exercises 1B and 1C to help you.

3 After you write

A **Check** your writing.

	Yes	No
1. I used *To Whom It May Concern* or the person's name.	☐	☐
2. I included the problem and an example.	☐	☐
3. I included a request to fix the problem.	☐	☐

B **Share** your writing with a partner.

1. Take turns. Read your email to a partner.
2. Comment on your partner's email. Ask your partner a question about the email. Tell your partner one thing you learned.

Lesson F Another view

1 Life-skills reading

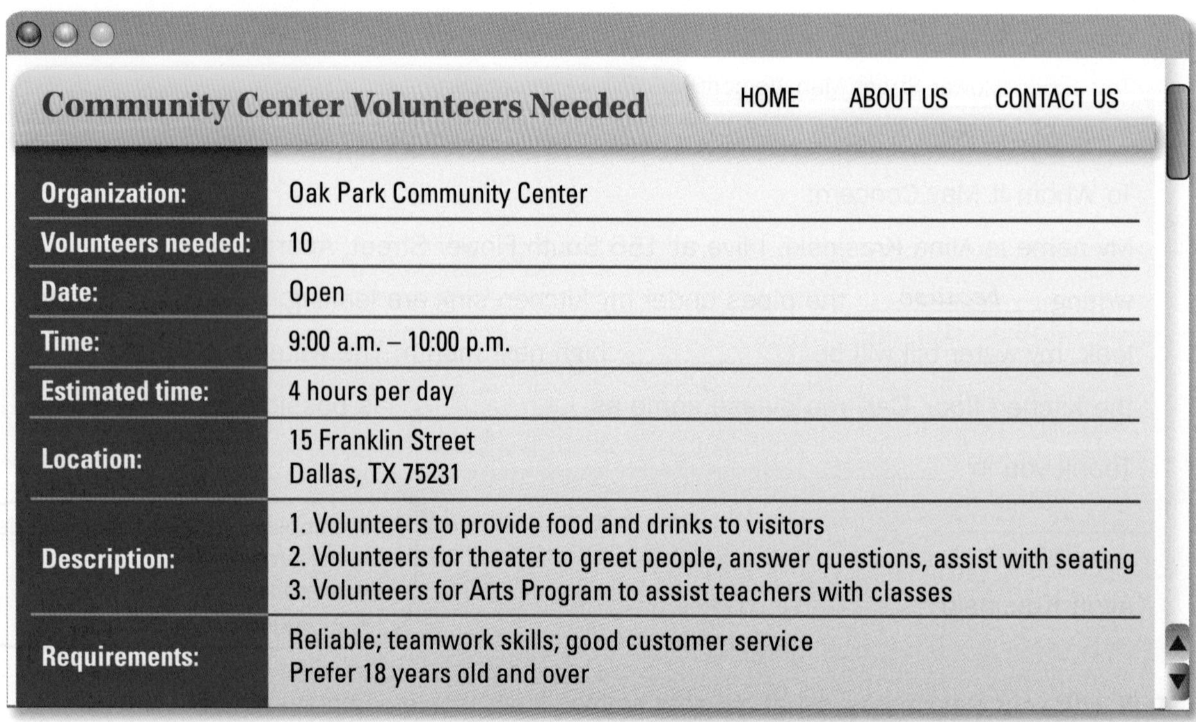

Community Center Volunteers Needed

HOME ABOUT US CONTACT US

Organization:	Oak Park Community Center
Volunteers needed:	10
Date:	Open
Time:	9:00 a.m. – 10:00 p.m.
Estimated time:	4 hours per day
Location:	15 Franklin Street Dallas, TX 75231
Description:	1. Volunteers to provide food and drinks to visitors 2. Volunteers for theater to greet people, answer questions, assist with seating 3. Volunteers for Arts Program to assist teachers with classes
Requirements:	Reliable; teamwork skills; good customer service Prefer 18 years old and over

A **Read** the questions. Look at the ad. Fill in the answer.

1. How long do volunteers need to work?
   - (A) one hour a day
   - (B) four hours a day
   - (C) eight hours a day
   - (D) nine hours a day

2. Which word under *requirements* best matches the example of *coming to work on time every day*?
   - (A) good customer service
   - (B) teamwork skills
   - (C) reliable
   - (D) none of the above

3. What can a volunteer do at this center?
   - (A) greet people
   - (B) help the art teachers
   - (C) serve food
   - (D) all of the above

4. Which statement is true?
   - (A) Volunteers must be artists.
   - (B) Volunteers must be experienced cooks.
   - (C) Volunteers must be over 21 years old.
   - (D) Volunteers must be team players.

B **Solve** the problem. Give your opinion.

Ann is volunteering at a senior center. She enjoys the opportunity to practice her English with the people, but one senior man stands too close to her and says things that embarrass her. What should she do?

2 Grammar connections: *be able to*

Use *be able to* for ability.	be able to = can
I'm able to drive.	Isabel isn't able to drive.

A **Work** in a small group. Play the game. Write your name on a small piece of paper. Flip a coin to move your paper. Then tell your group about the topic in the square. Use ***be able to*** in your answer. Take turns.

A This says, "A food you are **able to** make in less than 15 minutes." OK. I'm **able to** make cookies in less than 15 minutes.

B My space says, "Something you aren't **able to** lift." I'm not able to lift my nephew!

= 1 space

= 2 spaces

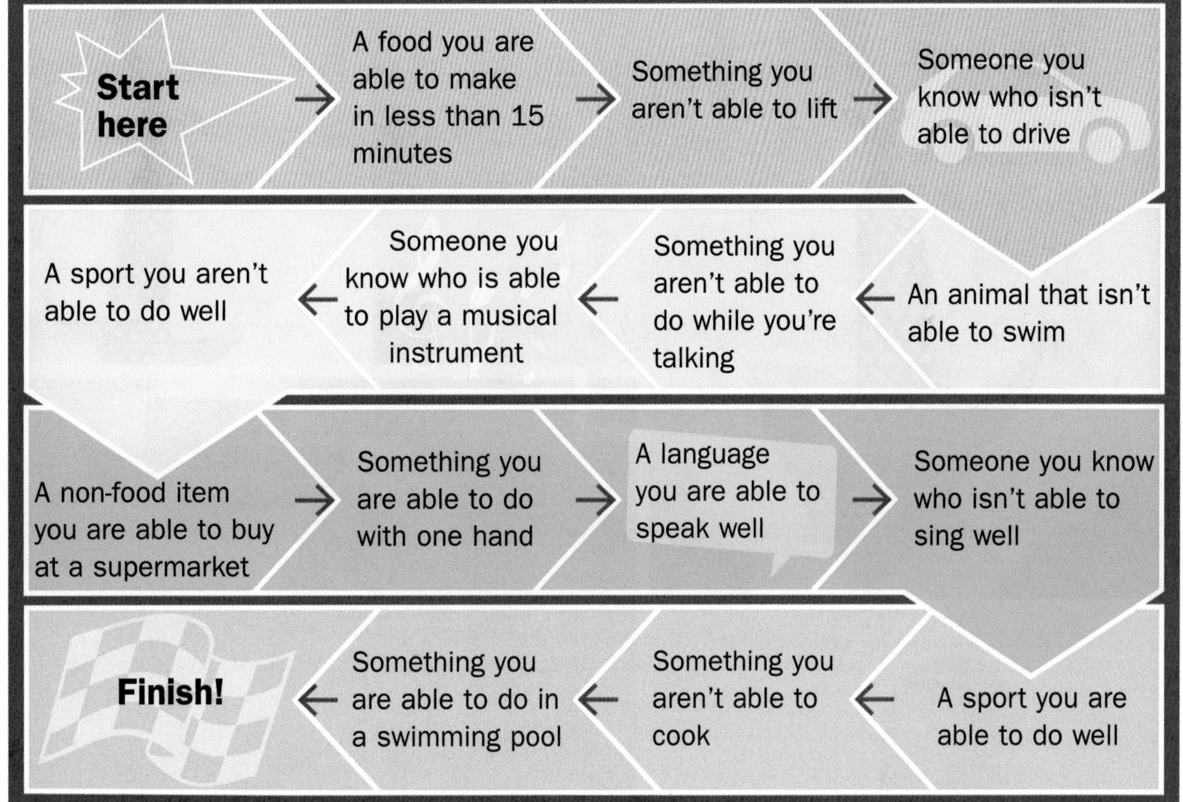

B **Share** information about your classmates.

Katia is able to make cookies in less than 15 minutes.

Carlos isn't able to lift his nephew.

Scan an ad for volunteers to locate key information; use *be able to* for ability

UNIT 4 HEALTH

Lesson A Listening

1 Before you listen

A What do you see?

B What is happening?

C What's the story?

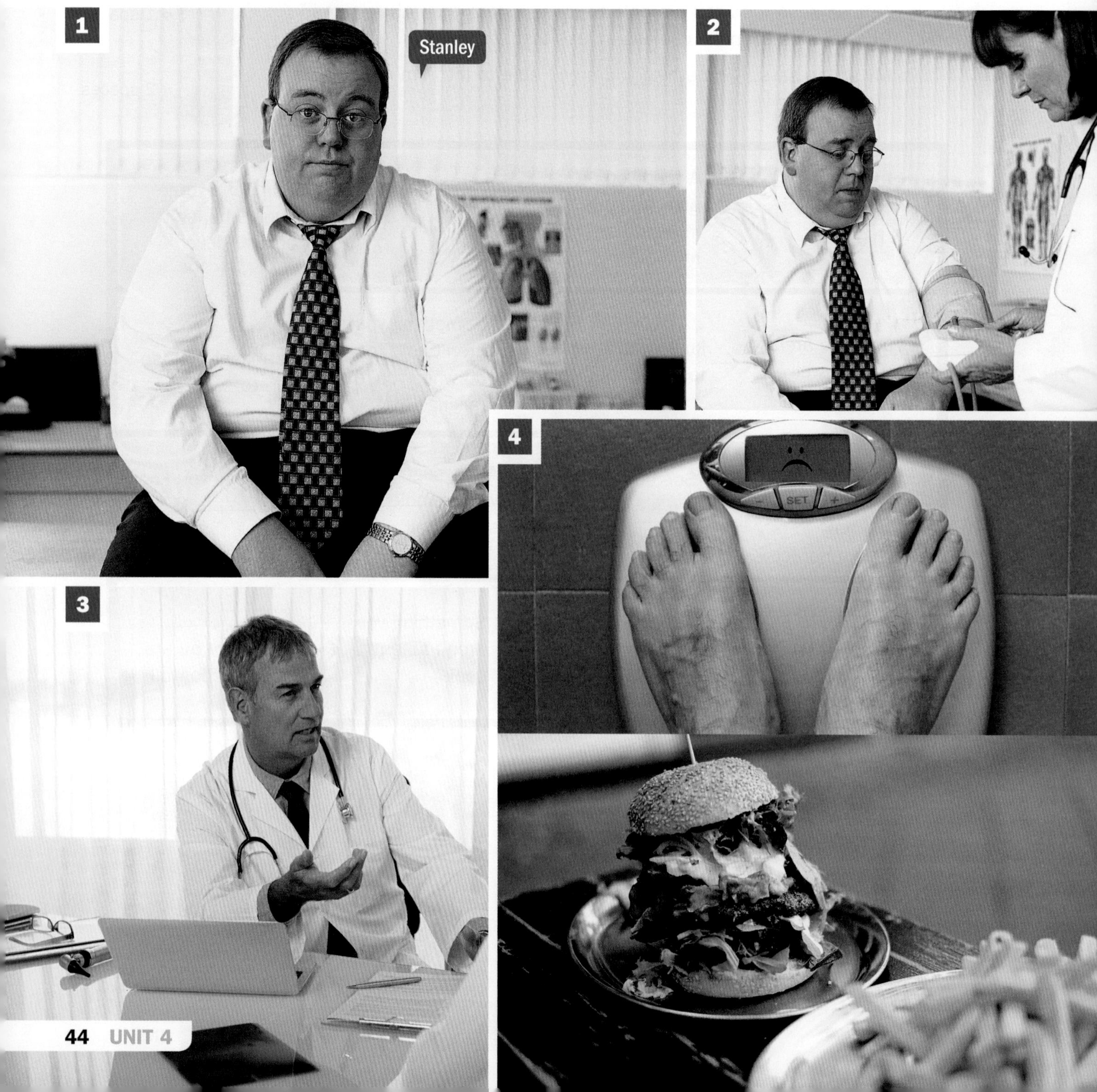

2 Listen

CD1, Track 25

A **Listen** and answer the questions.

1. Who are the speakers?
2. What are they talking about?

B **Listen again.** Put a check (✓) next to the doctor's advice.

CD1, Track 25

1. ☐ sleep more	5. ☐ eat hamburgers
2. ☑ take a walk every day	6. ☐ eat breakfast
3. ☐ ride a bicycle	7. ☐ eat fish
4. ☐ take the elevator at work	8. ☐ take medication

3 After you listen

A **Complete** the story.

advice	**exercise**	**healthy**	**pressure**	**weight**
diet	**health**	**medication**	**tired**	

Stanley is at the doctor's office. His ___*health*___ (1) has always been good, but he has been really ______ (2) lately. The doctor looks at Stanley's chart. He sees a couple of problems. One problem is Stanley's ______ (3). He has gained 20 pounds. Another problem is his blood ______ (4). The doctor tells him he needs regular ______ (5) – for example, walking or riding a bike. He also tells Stanley to change his ______ (6) – to eat more fish and vegetables. If Stanley doesn't do these things, he will need to take pills and other ______ (7). Stanley wants to be ______ (8), so he is going to try to follow the doctor's ______ (9).

Listen and check your answers.

CD1, Track 26

B **Talk** with a partner. Ask and answer the question.

What are three things you do to stay healthy?

Lesson B Present perfect

1 Grammar focus: *recently* and *lately*

Use *recently* and *lately* with the present perfect to suggest that something was done in the past, but not too long ago.

QUESTIONS	STATEMENTS
Have you gained weight **recently**?	I have gained weight **recently**.
Has Sheila gone to the gym **lately**?	Sheila hasn't gone to the gym **lately**.
Have they seen the doctor **recently**?	No, they haven't seen him **recently**.

Past participles

Regular verbs				Irregular verbs			
check	→ checked	start	→ started	eat	→ eaten	lose	→ lost
exercise	→ exercised	visit	→ visited	give	→ given	see	→ seen
gain	→ gained	weigh	→ weighed	go	→ gone	sleep	→ slept

2 Practice

A **Write.** Complete the sentences. Use the present perfect.

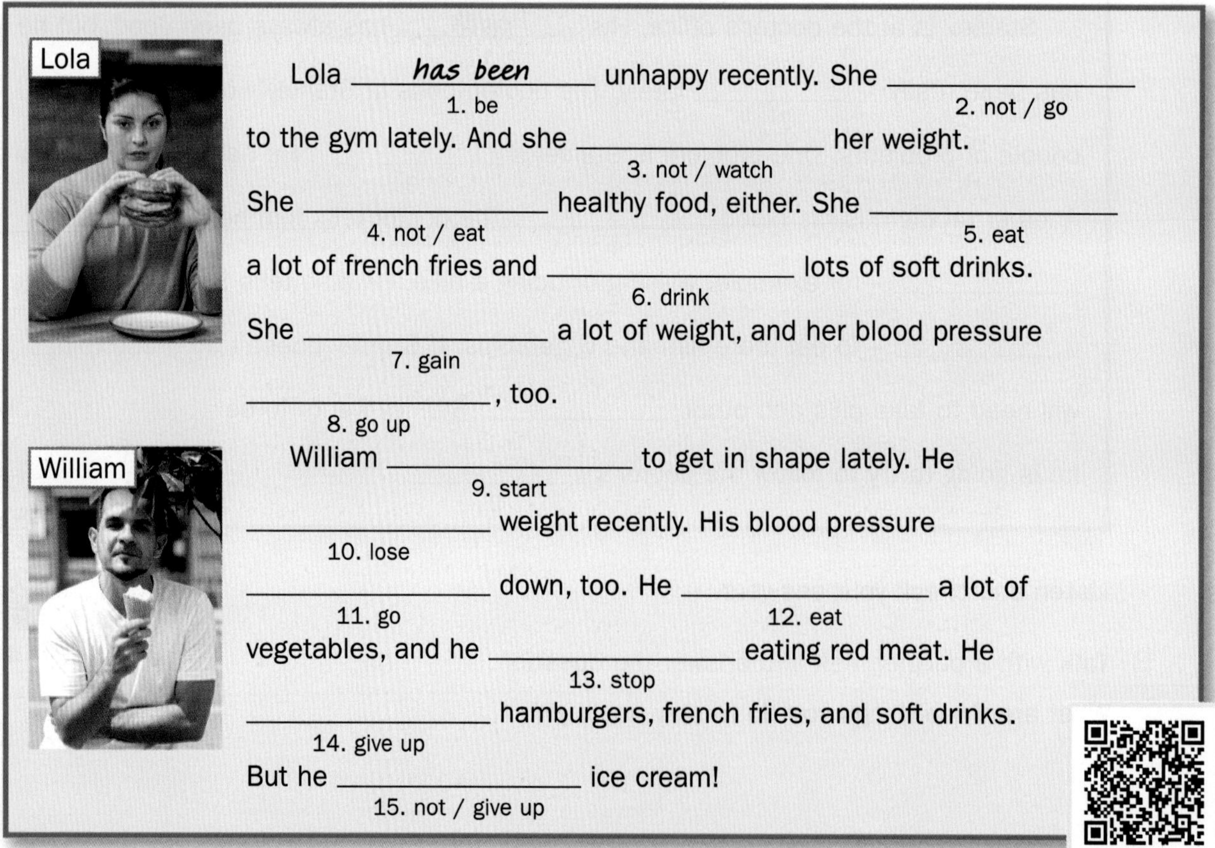

Listen and check your answers.

B **Talk** with a partner. Ask and answer questions. Use the present perfect with ***recently*** and ***lately***.

A Has Elisa lost weight recently?
B Yes, she has.

A Has Roberto given up desserts lately?
B No, he hasn't.

1. Elisa / lose weight

2. Roberto / give up desserts

3. Joy / start taking vitamins

4. Ahmet / gain weight

5. Martin and Julie / exercise a lot

6. Lee / sleep much

7. Robert and Susan / ride their biycles

8. James / take walks

Write a sentence about each picture. Use the present perfect with *recently* and *lately*.

Elisa has lost weight recently.

3 Communicate

A **Work** with a partner. Ask and answer questions. Complete the chart.

A Have you eaten a lot of fish lately?
B Yes, I have. How about you?

A Have you had a cold lately?
B No, I haven't. What about you?

Partner's name: ______________________	**Yes**	**No**
1. eat a lot of fish		
2. have a cold		
3. check your blood pressure		
4. see a doctor		
5. go to the gym		
6. visit a dentist		

B **Share** information about your partner.

Lesson C *Used to*

1 Grammar focus: statements and questions

Use *used to* to talk about a past situation or a past habit that is not true now. Use *didn't use to* to talk about a situation or habit that is true now, but wasn't true in the past.

Watch

STATEMENTS	*YES / NO* QUESTIONS	SHORT ANSWERS
I **used to** eat a lot of fatty foods.	**Did** you **use to** eat a lot of fatty foods?	Yes, I did.
She **didn't use to** go to bed late.	**Did** she **use to** go to bed late?	No, she didn't.
They **used to** exercise every day.	**Did** they **use to** exercise every day?	Yes, they did.

2 Practice

A **Write.** Complete the sentences. Use ***use to*** or ***used to***.

1. A Did he ___*use to*___ stay up all night?
   B Yes, he ____________ but he goes to bed early now.
2. A How often do you eat meat?
   B I ____________ eat meat every night, but now I usually have fish.
3. A ____________ she ____________ drive to work?
   B No, she ____________. She ____________ her bike, but now she drives.
4. A What do they usually do after work?
   B They ____________ go straight home, but now they take dance classes twice a week.
5. A Do you exercise every day?
   B I ____________ exercise every day, but now I exercise only on weekends.
6. A ____________ you ____________ eat red meat?
   B Yes, I ____________, but now I'm a vegetarian.
7. A Do you take the stairs?
   B No, I don't. I ____________, but now I take the elevator.
8. A Does he usually eat dessert?
   B Not now, but he ____________.

Listen and check your answers. Then practice with a partner.

CD1, Track 28

B **Work** with a partner. Talk about Michael as a young man and Michael today.

Michael used to play sports, but he doesn't anymore. Now he watches sports on TV.

When Michael was young	Michael now
1. play sports	watch sports on TV
2. skip breakfast	eat three meals a day
3. take vitamins	not take vitamins
4. drink coffee	drink tea
5. sleep late	get up early
6. eat fruit between meals	eat candy and chips between meals
7. work out every afternoon	take a nap every afternoon
8. walk to the store	drive to the store

Write sentences about Michael.

When Michael was young, he used to play sports. Now he watches sports on TV.

3 Communicate

A **Work** in a small group. Complete the sentences. Talk about your health habits.

1. When I was a child, I used to . . . , but now I . . .
2. In my country, I used to . . . , but now I . . .
3. When I was a teenager, I used to . . . , but now I . . .
4. When I first came to this country, I used to . . . , but now I . . .
5. When I had more time, I used to . . . , but now I . . .

B **Share** information about your classmates.

1 Before you read

Look at the reading tip. Then read the first and last paragraphs. Answer the questions.

1. Which two plants is the reading about?
2. How long have people used them?

The first paragraph of a reading is the **introduction**. It tells you the topic. The last paragraph is the conclusion. It often repeats the topic with different words.

2 Read

Read the blog post. Listen and read again.

CD1, Track 29

Two Beneficial Plants

Since the beginning of history, people in every culture have used plants to stay healthy and to prevent sickness. Garlic and chamomile are two beneficial plants.

Garlic is a plant in the onion family. The green stem and the leaves of the garlic plant grow above the ground. The root – the part under the ground – is a bulb with sections called cloves. They look like the pieces of an orange. The bulb is the part that people have traditionally used for medicine. They have used it for insect bites, cuts, earaches, and coughs. Today, some people also use it to treat high blood pressure and high cholesterol.

Chamomile is a small, pretty plant with flowers that bloom from late summer to early fall. The flowers have white petals and a yellow center. Many people use dried chamomile flowers to make tea. Some people give the tea to babies with upset stomachs. They also drink chamomile tea to feel better when they have a cold or the flu, poor digestion, or trouble falling asleep.

For thousands of years, people everywhere have grown garlic, chamomile, and other herbal medicines in their gardens. Today, you can buy them in health-food stores. You can get them in dried, powdered, or pill form.

3 After you read

A **Check** your understanding.

1. Underline the word beneficial in the first paragraph. Do you think it has a positive or a negative meaning? Circle the phrases in the first paragraph that helped you decide.
2. What is the word for the sections of the garlic bulb?
3. What have people used garlic for?
4. What does the chamomile plant look like?
5. According to the author, what do people use chamomile tea for?
6. Which plant could you use for high blood pressure?
7. What examples does the author give to support the idea that garlic and chamomile are beneficial?

B **Build** your vocabulary.

1. Read the dictionary entry for *digestion*. What part of speech is it? What does it mean? What is the antonym? What is the verb? What is the adjective?

> **digestion** /n/ the ability of the body to change food so the body can use it; antonym: **indigestion; digest** /v/ – **digestive** /adj/

2. Use a dictionary. Fill in the chart with the missing forms.

Noun	Verb	Adjective
digestion	*digest*	*digestive*
	prevent	
	treat	
herbs		

3. Complete the sentences. Write the correct form of the word from Exercise B2.
   a. You shouldn't swim right after you eat. You should wait to *digest* your food.
   b. Chamomile, basil, oregano, and thyme are examples of __________.
   c. Some people drink orange juice to __________ a cold. They don't want to get sick.
   d. A hot bath is a good __________ for sore muscles.

C **Talk** with a partner. Ask and answer the questions.

1. What do you do to prevent a sore throat? A cold? Weight gain?
2. In your opinion, what is the best treatment for a headache? A stomachache? An earache?
3. What herbs do you like to cook with? What's your favorite herb?

For college and career readiness practice, please see pages 145–147.

Identify the topic and supporting examples in an explanatory article about plants; recognize word families

Lesson E Writing

1 Before you write

A Talk with your classmates. Answer the questions and complete the chart.

Name	Use beneficial plants?	Name of plant(s)	Used for what?
Lynn	Yes	Apple cider vinegar	Weight loss
1.			
2.			
3.			

Aloe vera

B Read the paragraph.

Licorice

Licorice is a popular herb in my native country, Greece. The plant has feathery leaves and purple flowers. It tastes sweet. My mother used to use licorice to make a medicine for my grandmother's arthritis. Mother grew the licorice plant in our backyard. She used to cut the licorice roots into pieces and put them inside a warm, wet cloth. Then she put the cloth on my grandmother's shoulders and knees. The licorice helped with the pain. Today, I use licorice when I have sore muscles.

The first sentence of a paragraph is called the *topic sentence*. It names the topic and gives basic information about it.
Licorice (topic) *is a popular herb in my native country, Greece.* (basic information)

Work with a partner. Put the information from the paragraph in order.

____ how the writer's mother used the plant
_1_ where the plant grows
____ how the plant helped
____ how the plant tastes
____ how the plant looks
____ how the writer uses the plant today

C **Write** a plan for a paragraph about a beneficial plant. Answer the questions.

What's the name of the beneficial plant?	
What do people use it for?	
Where does the plant grow?	
What does the plant look like?	
Can you eat the plant? What does it taste like?	
What does the plant smell like?	
What does the plant feel like?	

2 Write

Write a paragraph about a plant that people use as medicine. Name the herb and give basic information about it in the topic sentence. Describe the plant and how people use it. Use Exercises 1B and 1C to help you.

3 After you write

A **Check** your writing.

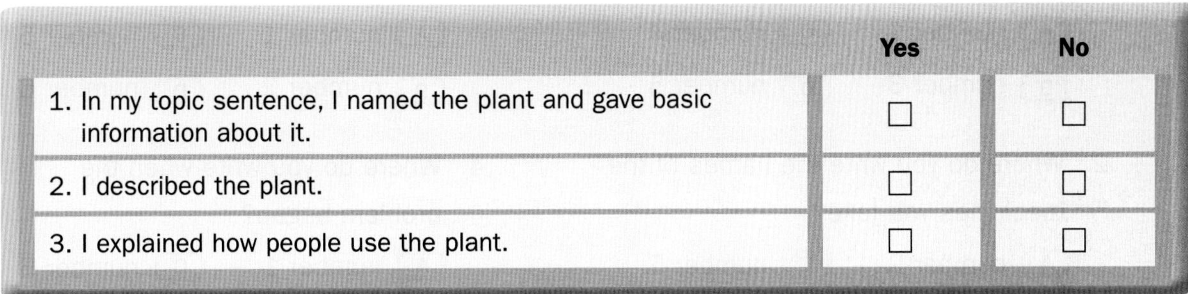

	Yes	No
1. In my topic sentence, I named the plant and gave basic information about it.	☐	☐
2. I described the plant.	☐	☐
3. I explained how people use the plant.	☐	☐

B **Share** your writing with a partner.

1. Take turns. Read your paragraph to a partner.
2. Comment on your partner's paragraph. Ask your partner a question about the paragraph. Tell your partner one thing you learned.

Lesson F Another view

1 Life-skills reading

Medical History Form

1. Chief complaint: Describe the problem and approximately when it began.

Problem	**Date problem began**

2. Have you ever had any of the following?

☐ allergies	☐ back pain	☐ frequent headaches	☐ high blood pressure
☐ arthritis	☐ chest pains	☐ heart attack	☐ high cholesterol
☐ asthma	☐ diabetes	☐ heart disease	☐ tuberculosis

3. Are you pregnant? Yes No
4. Are you currently taking medications? Yes No
5. If yes, list all medications, including vitamins and herbal supplements.

____

6. List any major illness, injury, or surgery that you have had in the past year.

____

The above information is correct to the best of my knowledge.

7. Signature: ____________ **8.** Date: ____________

A **Read** the questions. Look at the form. Fill in the answer.

1. Where do you write the reason for this doctor visit?
   Ⓐ number 1 Ⓑ number 3 Ⓒ number 4 Ⓓ number 5
2. Where do you write the names of the medicines you take?
   Ⓐ number 2 Ⓑ number 4 Ⓒ number 5 Ⓓ number 7
3. Where do you write that you had back surgery last year?
   Ⓐ number 1 Ⓑ number 2 Ⓒ number 5 Ⓓ number 6
4. Where do you write when the problem began?
   Ⓐ number 1 Ⓑ number 3 Ⓒ number 5 Ⓓ number 6

B **Solve** the problem. Give your opinion.

You are in the reception area of a doctor's office. The receptionist has given you a form. You need to fill it out before you can see the doctor. There are lots of words on the form that are new for you. You don't know what they mean. What should you do?

2 Grammar connections: reported *commands*

Use the base form of the verb to give a command (to tell someone to do something). Use *don't* + the base form of the verb to give a negative command (to tell someone not to do something). To report a command, use *tell* + indirect object + infinitive (*to* + base form of verb).

COMMANDS	REPORTED COMMANDS			
	Subject (who gave command)	**Verb**	**Indirect object** (told who)	**Infinitive** (*to* + base form of verb)
"Open wide."	The dentist	**told**	**me**	**to open** wide.
"Don't skip breakfast."	The doctor	**told**	**him**	**not to skip** breakfast.

A **Work** with a partner. Complete the chart.

1. Who gave the command?

the dentist **the doctor** **the eye doctor** **the nurse** **the receptionist**

2. Write the reported command.

Commands	**Who said it?**	**Reported Commands**
1. Step on the scale.	*the nurse*	*The nurse told me to step on the scale.*
2. Don't move during the X-ray.	*the dentist*	*The dentist told me not to move during the X-ray.*
3. Use an electric toothbrush.		
4. Get more exercise.		
5. Cover your left eye.		
6. Brush after every meal.		
7. Roll up your sleeve.		
8. Don't write below the line.		
9. Use these drops at night.		
10. Take blood pressure medication.		
11. Don't forget to take your medicine.		
12. Wear your glasses to read.		

B **Talk** with a partner.

Use a reported command from the list above. Your partner guesses who said it. Take turns.

REVIEW

1 Listening

Listen. Put a check (✓) under the correct name(s).

CD1, Track 30

	Jenny	Sara
1. used to have time to call friends	✓	
2. used to work 50 hours a week		
3. used to exercise more		
4. used to cook healthy food		
5. used to take care of herself		
6. used to take the stairs at work		

Talk with a partner. Check your answers.

2 Grammar

A **Write.** Complete the story. Use the correct words.

A Happy Ending

Last year, Frank went to his doctor *because of* (1. because / because of) his health. His doctor told him that his blood pressure was ________ (2. enough / too) high. Frank got very nervous because he didn't ________ (3. use to / used to) have health problems.

Frank ________ (4. started / has started) to get in shape lately. He ________ (5. use to / used to) take the elevator at work, but now he takes the stairs. He ________ (6. has / has had) a lot more energy lately. The hardest thing he ________ (7. has given up / gives up) recently is his favorite food – ice cream!

B **Write.** Look at the answers. Write the questions.

1. **A** ________ Frank ________ lately?
   B Yes, he has. Frank has started to get in shape.
2. **A** ________ Frank ________?
   B Yes, he did. Frank went to the doctor last year because of his health.
3. **A** ________ Frank ________?
   B Yes, he did. Frank used to take the elevator at work.

Talk with a partner. Ask and answer the questions.

3 Pronunciation: voiced and voiceless *th* sounds

A **Listen** to the *th* sounds in these phrases.

1. **th**is morning
2. sore **th**roat
3. **Th**at's too bad!
4. heal**th** problems
5. **th**e neighbors
6. on Sou**th** Street
7. **th**ey are
8. **th**is mon**th**
9. asked **th**em
10. **th**ree times
11. How are **th**ings?
12. **th**anks

CD1, Track 31

Listen again and repeat.

B **Listen and repeat.** Then underline the words with the voiced and voiceless *th* sounds.

CD1, Track 32

1. A Where's Tommy <u>this</u> morning?
   B He's sick. He has a sore throat.
   A That's too bad!
   B He often has health problems.
   A I'm sorry to hear that.

2. A The neighbors on South Street are really noisy.
   B Yes, they are.
   A This month, I've asked them three times to be quiet.
   B Let's write them a letter.
   A That's a good idea.

Talk with a partner. Compare your answers.

C **Talk** with a partner. Practice the conversations. Pay attention to the words with the *th* sounds.

1. A What can your friends do to be more healthy?
   B Well, they can exercise more this month.
   A That's a good idea.
   B And they can eat healthy meals three times a day.

2. A How are things?
   B Not great. I have three tests this week.
   A Oh, I think you'll do fine.
   B Thanks.

D **Write** four questions. Use the words in Exercise 3A. Ask your partner.

Have you eaten this morning?

1. ______________________________
2. ______________________________
3. ______________________________
4. ______________________________

UNIT 5 AROUND TOWN

Lesson A Listening

1 Before you listen

A What do you see?

B What is happening?

C What's the story?

UNIT GOALS
Describe events in the community **Identify** positive and negative words from context clues
Interpret announcements

2 Listen

CD1, Track 33

A **Listen** and answer the questions.

1. Who are the speakers?
2. What are they talking about?

CD1, Track 33

B **Listen again.** Read and match the events. You may use an event more than once.

1. It opens at 10:00. __c__
2. It starts at 10:30. ____
3. It starts at 11:00. ____
4. The family will do this first. ____
5. The family will do this if the weather is nice. ____

a. outdoor concert
b. garden tour
c. art exhibit
d. storytelling

3 After you listen

A **Read.** Complete the story.

admission **afford** **concert** **events** **exhibit** **options** **storytelling** **tour**

It is Thursday. Wen and Mei are talking about their plans for the weekend. They can't ___afford___ (1) to spend a lot of money on entertainment. They decide to check the newspaper for free community ________ (2) on Sunday. They have many ________ (3). There's an outdoor ________ (4) in the park, a walking ________ (5) of the gardens, a modern art ________ (6) at the art museum, and storytelling for children at the library. All these events have free ________ (7).

The problem is that all these things are happening on Sunday at the same time. Mei and Wen decide to take their son to the ________ (8) first. Then, if the weather is nice, they will go to the concert. Later, they might go to the art museum.

Listen and check your answers.

CD1, Track 34

B **Talk** with a partner. Ask and answer the questions.

What kind of entertainment do you enjoy on the weekend?

Lesson B Verbs + infinitives

1 Grammar focus: questions and answers

Infinitives often follow verbs that talk about future plans.

infinitive = *to* + base form of verb

QUESTIONS	ANSWERS	
Where do you plan **to go**?	I plan **to go** to the park.	
Where does he plan **to go**?	He plans **to go** to the park.	
Do you plan **to go** to the park?	Yes, I do.	No, I don't.
Does he plan **to go** to the park?	Yes, he does.	No, he doesn't.

Infinitives often follow these verbs

agree	decide	hope	need	promise	want
(can / can't) afford	expect	intend	plan	refuse	would like

2 Practice

A Write. Complete the sentences.

1. **A** How much do you *expect to pay* (expect / pay) for the concert?
   B No more than $25.
2. **A** What have you ____________ (decide / do) for your birthday?
   B I'm going to an exhibit at the art museum.
3. **A** Can you ____________ (afford / buy) a ticket for the show?
   B Not really. I need to start saving money.
4. **A** What did you ____________ (agree / do) next weekend?
   B We agreed to go to the park.
5. **A** How is Tom going to go to the park?
   B He ____________ (intend / ride) his bike.
6. **A** Have you ever ____________ (refuse / go) on a trip with your family?
   B No, I haven't.
7. **A** What did they promise their relatives?
   B They ____________ (promise / visit) this weekend.
8. **A** What is Chen going to eat at the picnic?
   B He ____________ (want / eat) ice-cream and cake.

USEFUL LANGUAGE
afford to do something = have enough money to do it

Listen and check your answers. Then practice with a partner.

B **Talk** with a partner. Ask and answer questions about Sharon's plans. Look at her calendar. Use the verbs in the box and an infinitive.

A What does Sharon plan to do on Tuesday?

B She plans to go to a concert with Linda.

expect hope intend need plan want

www.calendar.com

May

Sunday	Monday	Tuesday	Wednesday	Thursday	Friday	Saturday
		1	2	3	4	5
		8:30 a.m. Do errands. Clean the house. 12:30 p.m. Go with Linda to a concert.	5:30 p.m. Meet Joe at the gym.	9:00 a.m. See the dentist. 3:00 p.m. See the new art exhibit.	7:30 a.m. Go to work with John. 6:00 p.m. Have dinner with Andrew???	Sit on the beach all day!

Write sentences about Sharon's plans.

On Tuesday, Sharon plans to go to a concert with Linda.

3 Communicate

A **Work** in a small group. Choose one item from each column. Answer questions about your plans.

A What do you expect to do tomorrow?

B I plan to meet my friends for lunch tomorrow.

expect	(infinitive of any verb)	tomorrow
hope		next week
intend		next month
need		next year
plan		two years from now
promise		in a few weeks
want		three years from now
would like		five years from now

B **Share** information about your classmates.

Lesson C Present perfect

1 Grammar focus: *already* and *yet*

Use *already* and *yet* with the present perfect to talk about actions you expect to happen. Use *already* in questions and affirmative answers. Use *yet* in questions and negative answers.

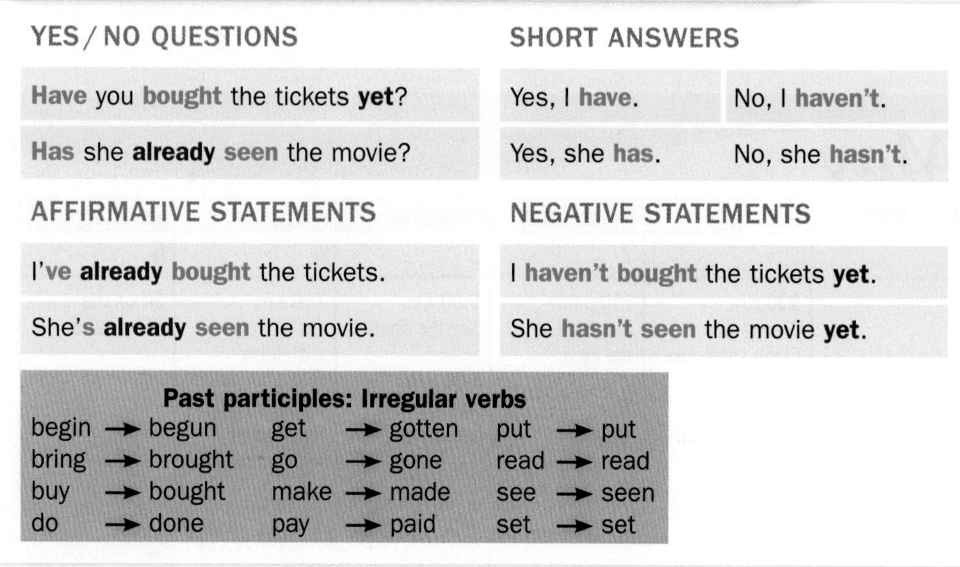

YES / NO QUESTIONS	SHORT ANSWERS	
Have you **bought** the tickets **yet**?	Yes, I **have**.	No, I **haven't**.
Has she **already seen** the movie?	Yes, she **has**.	No, she **hasn't**.

AFFIRMATIVE STATEMENTS	NEGATIVE STATEMENTS
I**'ve already bought** the tickets.	I **haven't bought** the tickets **yet**.
She**'s already seen** the movie.	She **hasn't seen** the movie **yet**.

Past participles: Irregular verbs

begin → begun	get → gotten	put → put
bring → brought	go → gone	read → read
buy → bought	make → made	see → seen
do → done	pay → paid	set → set

2 Practice

A Write. Complete the sentences. Use *already* or *yet* and the correct form of the verb.

1. It's 11:00 p.m. The salsa concert has *already* *ended*. (end)
2. It's 8:00 a.m. The science museum opens at 9:00. It hasn't ________ ________. (open)
3. It's July 5th. The Independence Day parade has ________ ________. (finish)
4. It's the beginning of August. School begins in September. School activities haven't ________ ________. (begin)
5. It's 2:00 a.m. The dance club stays open until 3:00. It hasn't ________ ________. (close)
6. It's Friday evening. The weekend has ________ ________. (start)
7. It's 7:45 p.m. The movie starts at 8:00. We haven't ________ the movie ________. (miss)
8. It's Monday. I've ________ ________ tickets for next Sunday's soccer game. (buy)
9. It's Sunday night. Have you ________ the homework ________? (do)
10. There's a new Japanese restaurant down the street. Have you ________ there ________? (eat)
11. It's 8:30 a.m. The children have ________ ________ for school. (leave)
12. There's a new art exhibit at the museum. Have you ________ it ________? (see)

Listen and check your answers.

B **Talk** with a partner. Jaime and Andrea are helping at their school's fundraiser. Ask and answer questions about them. Use *yet*.

A Has Jaime bought refreshments yet?
B Yes, he has.
A Has Andrea set up the tables yet?
B No, she hasn't.

CULTURE NOTE
A fundraiser is an event where people collect money for a school, an organization, or a cultural activity.

Things to do before the fundraiser

Jaime	*Andrea*
✓ *buy refreshments*	*set up the tables*
✓ *borrow more chairs*	✓ *organize the volunteers*
call the chair-rental store	✓ *make the food*
get name tags	*bring the music CDs*
pick up the DJ	✓ *put up the decorations*

Write sentences about Jaime and Andrea. Use *already* and *yet*.

Jaime has already bought refreshments.

Andrea hasn't set up the tables yet.

3 Communicate

A **Work** with a partner. Ask and answer questions. Complete the chart.

A Have you done your homework yet?
B Yes, I have.
A Have you already paid your bills?
B No, I haven't.

Activities	Yes	No
1. do your homework	☐	☐
2. pay your bills	☐	☐
3. go to a baseball game in this country	☐	☐
4. read the newspaper today	☐	☐
5. (your question)	☐	☐
6. (your question)	☐	☐

B **Share** information about your classmates.

Lesson D Reading

1 Before you read

Talk with your classmates. Answer the questions.

1. Do you like salsa music?
2. Have you ever gone to an outdoor concert? Where? When?

When you see a new word, try to guess if the meaning is positive or negative.
*The volume was **excessive**. I had to wear my earplugs.*
You can guess that *excessive* has a negative meaning.

2 Read

Read the concert review. Listen and read again.

CD1, Track 37

Salsa Starz at Century Park

If you missed the outdoor concert at Century Park last Saturday evening, you missed a great night of salsa music and dancing – and the admission was free!

The performers were the popular band Salsa Starz. Bandleader Ernesto Sanchez led the five-piece group and two dancers. Sanchez is a versatile musician. He sang and played maracas and guitar. The other musicians were also superb. The group's excellent playing and great energy galvanized the crowd. No one sat down during the entire show!

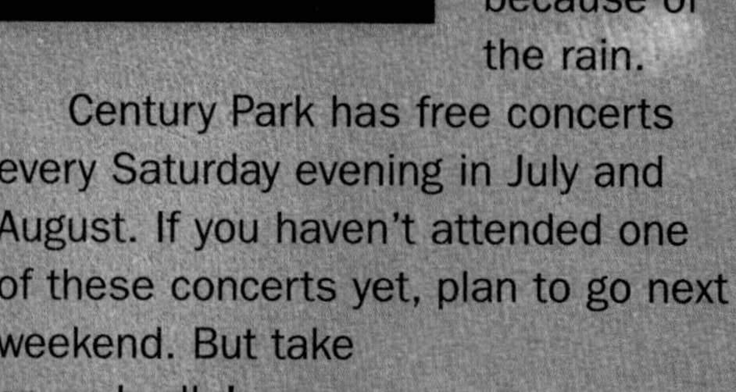

However, the evening had some problems. At first, the sound level of the music was excessive. I had to wear earplugs. Then, the level was too low. The change in sound was irritating. In addition, the stage was plain and unremarkable. I expected to see lights and lots of color at the performance. The weather was another problem. The night started out clear. By 10:00 p.m., some ominous black clouds moved in, and soon it started to rain. The band intended to play until 11:00, but the show ended early because of the rain.

Century Park has free concerts every Saturday evening in July and August. If you haven't attended one of these concerts yet, plan to go next weekend. But take an umbrella!

3 After you read

A Check your understanding.

1. Read the first and last paragraph of the concert review. What is the author's purpose for writing this review?
2. Where did Salsa Starz perform?
3. What were two positive and three negative things about the concert?
4. What phrase in the article mean the same as *also*?
5. Did the audience like the concert? How do you know?
6. How do you think the reviewer rated the overall performance? Find the words in the reading to support your opinion.

**** excellent *** very good ** OK * bad

B Build your vocabulary.

1. Find these words in the reading, and underline them. Which words are positive? Which words are negative? What clues helped you guess?

Word	Positive	Negative	Clue
1. versatile	☑	☐	*He sang and played maracas and guitar.*
2. superb	☐	☐	
3. galvanized	☐	☐	
4. excessive	☐	☐	
5. irritating	☐	☐	
6. unremarkable	☐	☐	
7. ominous	☐	☐	

2. Work with your classmates. Write four more words in the reading that have a positive or negative meaning. Write *P* next to positive words. Write *N* next to negative words.

a. ______________________ c. ______________________

b. ______________________ d. ______________________

C Talk with a partner.

1. Tell your partner about a superb restaurant.
2. Tell about a versatile artist.
3. Tell about an irritating experience.
4. Tell about an unremarkable TV program.
5. Tell about an event that was canceled because of ominous weather.

For college and career readiness practice, please see pages 148–150.

Determine the central idea of a text by locating, identifying and analyzing positive and negative details; distinguish between positive and negative words

Lesson E Writing

1 Before you write

A **Talk** with your classmates.

1. Do you use email? How often?
2. What do you use it for?

B **Read** the email.

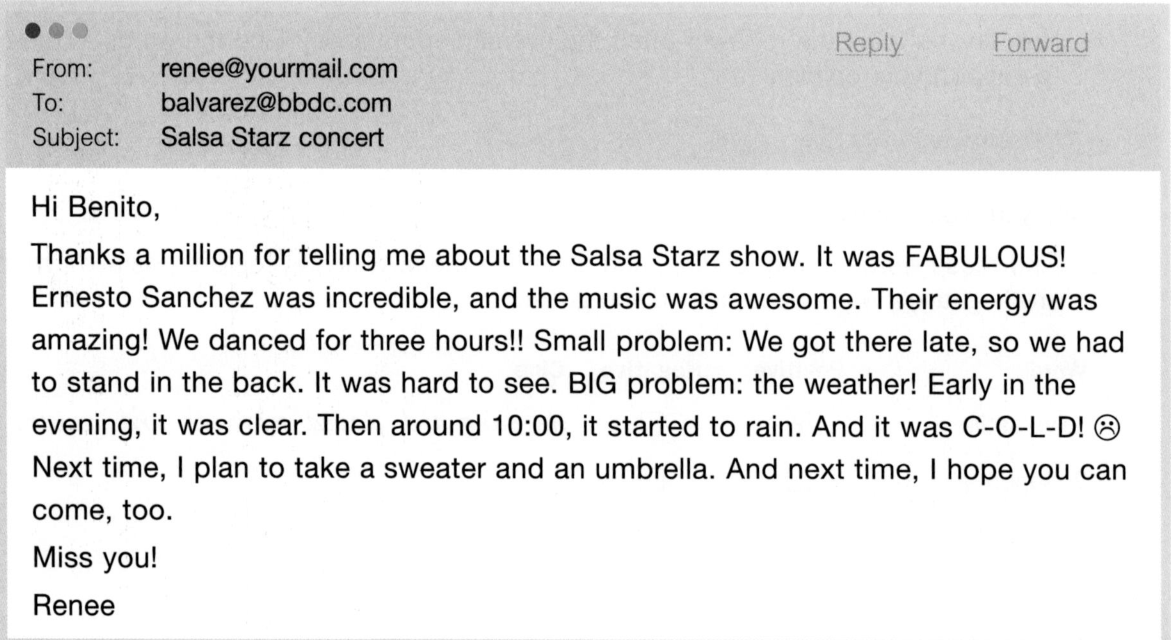

Reply Forward

From: renee@yourmail.com
To: balvarez@bbdc.com
Subject: Salsa Starz concert

Hi Benito,

Thanks a million for telling me about the Salsa Starz show. It was FABULOUS! Ernesto Sanchez was incredible, and the music was awesome. Their energy was amazing! We danced for three hours!! Small problem: We got there late, so we had to stand in the back. It was hard to see. BIG problem: the weather! Early in the evening, it was clear. Then around 10:00, it started to rain. And it was C-O-L-D! ☹ Next time, I plan to take a sweater and an umbrella. And next time, I hope you can come, too.

Miss you!

Renee

Work with a partner. Complete the diagram with positive and negative information about the concert.

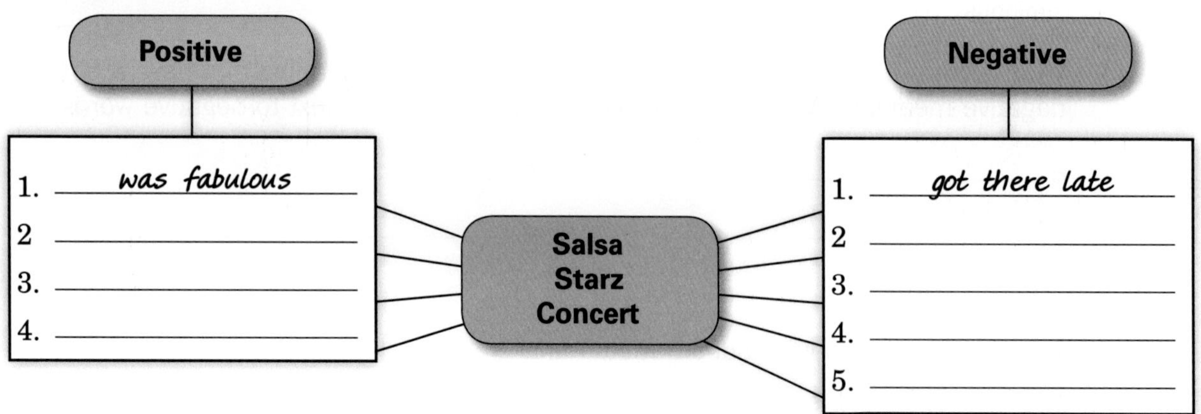

C **Write** the name of a concert, a movie, or a performance you have seen in the middle of the diagram. Complete the diagram with positive and negative information.

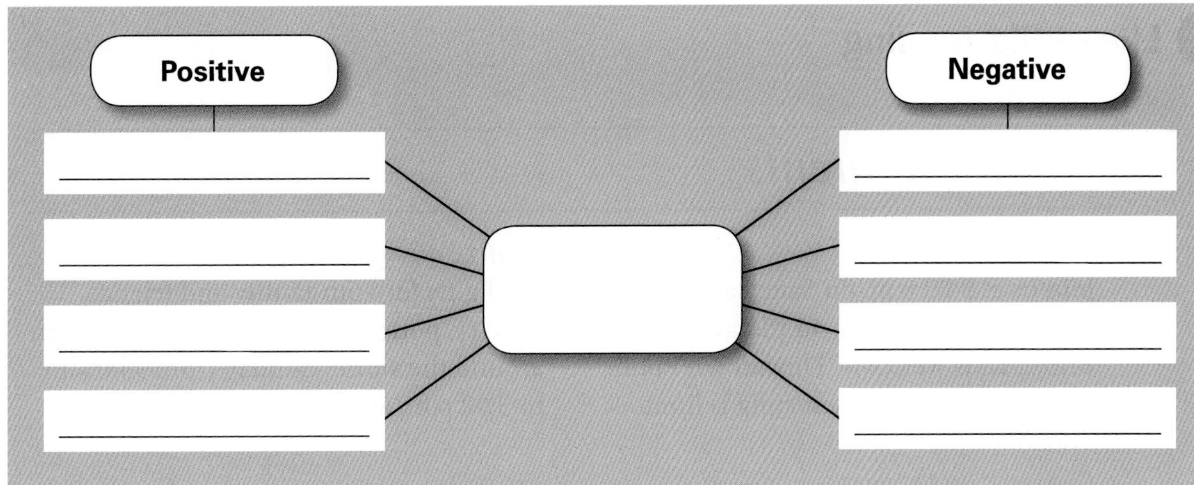

Share your information with a partner.

2 Write

Write an email about a concert, a movie, or a performance you have seen. Name the event in your first sentence. Use positive and negative words to describe the event. Use an informal writing style in the email. Use Exercises 1B and 1C to help you.

The style of a friendly email is informal.

- Some sentences are not complete.
  Miss you!
  BIG problem: the weather!
- Writers use capital letters and symbols to express their feelings.
  It was FABULOUS!
  It was C-O-L-D! ☹

3 After you write

A **Check** your writing.

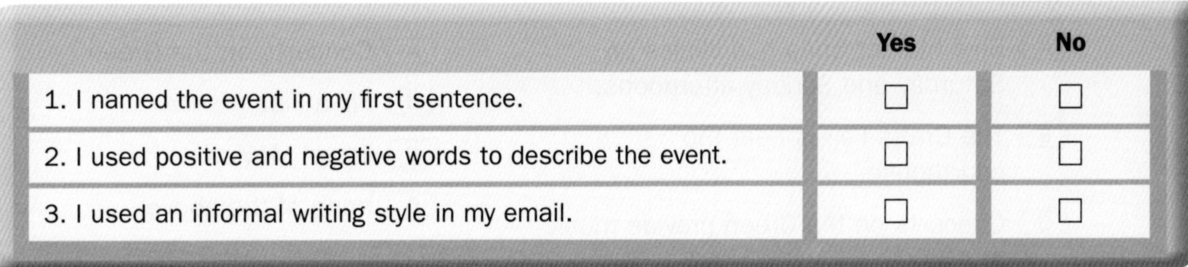

	Yes	No
1. I named the event in my first sentence.	☐	☐
2. I used positive and negative words to describe the event.	☐	☐
3. I used an informal writing style in my email.	☐	☐

B **Share** your writing with a partner.

1. Take turns. Read your email to a partner.
2. Comment on your partner's email. Ask your partner a question about the email. Tell your partner one thing you learned.

Lesson F Another view

1 Life-skills reading

Announcements

Travel Movies
Join us at 7:00 p.m. on Saturday and Sunday to see movies on India, Japan, and Brazil. Kids welcome. Downtown Public Library. Come early – seating is limited.

Concerts on the Green
Hear the Riverside Brass Band every Friday this month at noon. North end of City Park, near the courthouse.

Crafts Fair
Find gifts for your family and friends. Jewelry, pottery, paintings, and food from around the world. Sunday from 9:00 a.m. to 5:00 p.m. at Broadway and 5th Street.

Fix a Flat
Bike Master Shop offers basic bicycle maintenance clinics this Saturday at 4:30 p.m. and Sunday at 9:00 a.m. in front of the Bike Master Shop.

A **Read** the questions. Look at the announcements. Fill in the answer.

1. Which event does not happen during the day?
   - (A) Concerts on the Green
   - (B) Crafts Fair
   - (C) Fix a Flat
   - (D) Travel Movies
2. Which statement is true?
   - (A) Bike Master Shop has clinics on Saturday and Sunday afternoons.
   - (B) The Crafts Fair is near the courthouse.
   - (C) Concerts on the Green provide music at 12:00.
   - (D) Travel Movies are in the afternoon.
3. Which event would be good for bike riders?
   - (A) Crafts Fair
   - (B) Fix a Flat
   - (C) Travel Movies
   - (D) none of the above
4. Which event is at noon on Saturday?
   - (A) Concerts on the Green
   - (B) Fix a Flat
   - (C) Travel Movies
   - (D) none of the above

B **Solve** the problem. Give your opinion.

Mei and her family went to a craft fair at a park last Saturday. Mei stopped at a booth to try on some earrings. When she got home at 5:30, she realized she left her glasses on a table at the earring booth. They were expensive glasses and Mei needs them for work. What should she do?

2 Grammar connections: verbs + infinitives and verbs + gerunds

An infinite is *to* + the base form of a verb. Infinitives often follow verbs that talk about future plans. A gerund is the base form of the verb + *ing*. Gerunds often follow verbs that talk about preferences. Both infinitives and gerunds can follow some verbs.

VERBS + INFINITIVES	VERBS + GERUNDS	VERBS + INFINITIVES OR GERUNDS
decide need refuse intend plan want	avoid enjoy miss dislike finish suggest	continue like start hate prefer
We **intend to study** tonight.	Tomas **dislikes exercising.**	I **like to cook.**
We **need to go** home.	They **enjoy swimming.**	I **like cooking.**

A **Work** in a small group. Ask the questions with *to do* or *doing*. Complete the survey.

A What do you enjoy doing on the weekend, Viktor?

B I enjoy walking in the park.

A What do you intend to do after class?

B I intend to study at the library.

What do you . . .	______ **(name)**	______ **(name)**	______ **(name)**
enjoy ______ on the weekend?			
intend ______ after class?			
avoid ______ at home?			
hate ______ in the morning?			
refuse ______ on the weekend?			
plan ______ at the end of the year?			
like ______ in the summer?			
miss ______ from your childhood?			

B **Share** information about your classmates.

Viktor enjoys walking in the park. He intends to study at the library after class. He . . .

Scan an announcement about community events to locate key information; contrast verbs + infinitives and verbs + gerunds

UNIT 6 TIME

Lesson A Listening

1 Before you listen

A What do you see?

B What is happening?

C What's the story?

1

2

3

4

2 Listen

CD2, Track 2

A **Listen** and answer the questions.

1. Who are the speakers?
2. What are they talking about?

B **Listen again.** Complete Winston's to-do list. Then number the tasks in order of priority.

CD2, Track 2

Things to Do	*Priority*
• *take out the trash*	*1*
•	
•	
•	
•	

3 After you listen

A **Read.** Complete the story.

chores **deadline** **due** **impatient** **order** **prioritize** **procrastinating** **tasks** **to-do**

Winston is listening to music in his room. His mother comes in and tells him to stop *procrastinating* (1). She is very ______ (2) because he hasn't taken out the trash, and he hasn't done his homework.

Winston has too many things to do. His mother suggests making a ______ (3) list. First, she tells him to list all the tasks he needs to do. Next, she tells him to ______ (4) – to put his ______ (5) in ______ (6) of importance. His mother says he needs to do his homework and ______ (7) first. He decides to do his English and math homework first because they are ______ (8) the next day. He also has a history project, but the ______ (9) is next Tuesday. After he finishes his homework, he will practice guitar. But before he does anything else, he has to take out the trash.

CD2, Track 3

Listen and check your answers.

B **Talk** with a partner. Ask and answer the questions.

When you have a lot of things to do, how do you decide what to do first?

Lesson B Adverb clauses

1 Grammar focus: clauses with *when*

A clause is a group of words that has a subject and a verb. The word *when* often joins two clauses in which the activities occur at the same time. Use *when* + present tense verbs to talk about habits.

When I **have** a lot to do, I **make** a to-do list.
When she **feels** tired, she **takes** a break.
I **make** a to-do list **when** I **have** a lot to do.
She **takes** a break **when** she **feels** tired.

USEFUL LANGUAGE
Use a comma when the *when* clause is at the beginning of the sentence. When you are speaking or reading out loud, pause after the comma.

2 Practice

A **Write.** Combine the sentences. Use *when*. Circle the adverb clause.

Tips for Managing Your Time

1. You have many things to do. Make a to-do list.
   When *you have many things to do*, *make a to-do list*.
2. You have a deadline. Write it on your calendar.
   When ______, ______.
3. Don't let people interrupt you. You need to concentrate.
   ______ when ______.
4. You want to focus on a task. Turn off the television.
   When ______, ______.
5. You feel tired. Take a break.
   When ______, ______.
6. Give yourself a reward. You finish something difficult.
   ______ when ______.
7. Don't procrastinate. You have a deadline.
   ______ when ______.
8. You are tired. Don't do difficult tasks.
   When ______, ______.
9. Prioritize tasks. You have many things to do.
   ______ when ______.

Listen and check your answers.

CD2, Track 4

B **Talk** with a partner. Make sentences with *when*.

A When Mr. Jackson has a deadline, **he doesn't answer** the phone.

B Ms. Clark **answers every call** when she has a deadline.

expect **hope** **intend** **need** **plan** **want**

Mr. Jackson

Ms. Clark

1. doesn't answer the phone	answers every call
2. closes his office door	allows people to interrupt
3. works on one task at a time	works on several things at once
4. begins work immediately	procrastinates
5. does difficult tasks first	saves difficult tasks for last
6. doesn't check email	checks email frequently
7. makes no personal phone calls	makes many personal phone calls

Write sentences about Mr. Jackson and Ms. Clark.

Mr. Jackson doesn't answer the phone when he has a deadline.

3 Communicate

A **Work** in a small group. Interview your classmates. Complete the chart.

A What do you do when you have a deadline?

B I usually procrastinate.

C I start working right away.

What do you do when you . . .	**Name:** ________	**Name:** ________	**Name:** ________
have a deadline?			
have many things to do?			
finish a difficult task?			
have trouble concentrating?			
(your idea)			

B **Share** information about your classmates.

Lesson C Adverb clauses

1 Grammar focus: clauses with *before* and *after*

Use *before* and *after* clauses to order activities in a sequence. The *after* clause introduces the first activity. The *before* clause introduces the second activity.

After I watch the news, I eat dinner.	watch the news = first activity eat dinner = second activity
Before she eats breakfast, she reads the newspaper.	reads the newspaper = first activity eats breakfast = second activity
She reads the newspaper **before** she eats breakfast.	reads the newspaper = first activity eats breakfast = second activity
I eat dinner **after** I watch the news.	watch the news = first activity eat dinner = second activity

USEFUL LANGUAGE
Use a comma when *before* and *after* clauses are at the beginning of a sentence. When you read out loud, pause after the comma.

2 Practice

A Look at the two activities in the exercise and find them on Bonnie's Morning Schedule. Which happens first? Which happens second? Number them. Then write two sentences: one with *after* and one with *before*.

Bonnie's Morning Schedule

6:55 take a shower	7:35 bring in the newspaper
7:15 get dressed	7:40 eat breakfast
7:30 make coffee	8:00 leave for work

take a shower 1 **/ get dressed** 2

1. After Bonnie takes a shower, she gets dressed.
2. Bonnie takes a shower before she gets dressed.

get dressed / make coffee

3. Before ______, ______.
4. ______ after ______.

bring in the newspaper / eat breakfast

5. ______ before ______.
6. ______ after ______.

eat breakfast / leave for work

7. After ______, ______.
8. Before ______, ______.

make coffee / bring in the newspaper

9. After ______, ______.
10. Before ______, ______.

Listen and check your answers.

B **Talk** with a partner. Ask and answer questions about Ken, a soap opera star. Use *before* and *after*.

A What does Ken do before he eats breakfast?

B Before Ken eats breakfast, he works out.

A What does Ken do after he works out?

B Ken eats breakfast after he works out.

1. works out

2. eats breakfast

3. goes to the studio

4. memorizes his lines

5. puts on makeup

6. talks to the director

7. performs his scene

8. goes home and rests

Write sentences about Ken's day.

Ken works out before he eats breakfast.

3 Communicate

A **Work** in a small group. Ask and answer questions about daily activities. Complete the chart.

A What do you do every day, Emma?

B I study.

A What do you do before you study?

B I watch TV.

A What do you do after you study?

B I go to bed.

Name	Everyday activity	Before activity	After activity
Emma	*study*	*watch TV*	*go to bed*

B **Share** information about your classmates.

Lesson D Reading

1 Before you read

Look at the title. Answer the questions.

1. What are some rules about time in this country?
2. What are some rules about time in other countries?

2 Read

Read this article. Listen and read again.

CD2, Track 6

Rules about Time

Dashes often signal a definition, explanation, or example. The dashes in this reading signal examples.

Every culture has rules about time. These rules are usually unspoken, but everybody knows them.

In some countries such as the United States, England, and Canada, punctuality is an unspoken rule. It is important to be on time, especially in business. People usually arrive a little early for business appointments. Business meetings and personal appointments often have strict beginning and ending times. When you are late, other people might think you are rude, disorganized, or irresponsible.

These countries also have cultural rules about time in social situations. For example, when an invitation for dinner says 6:00 p.m., it is impolite to arrive more than five or ten minutes late. On the other hand, when the invitation is for a party from 6:00 to 8:00 or a reception from 3:30 to 5:30, you can arrive anytime between those hours. For public events with specific starting times – movies, concerts, sports events – you should arrive a few minutes before the event begins. In fact, some theaters do not allow people to enter if they arrive after the event has started.

Other cultures have different rules about time. In Brazil, it is not unusual for guests to arrive an hour or two after a social event begins. In the Philippines, it is not uncommon for people to miss scheduled events – a class or an appointment – to meet a friend at the airport. Many Filipinos believe that relationships with people are more important than keeping a schedule.

When you are living or working with people from different cultures, it is important to know that culture's unspoken rules about time. Without this knowledge, there can be misunderstandings.

3 After you read

A Check your understanding.

1. What are "unspoken" rules?
2. Find the word *punctuality* in the second paragraph. Underline it. What phrase in the next sentence is a clue to its meaning?
3. According to the article, punctuality is an unspoken rule in the United States, England, and Canada. What examples in business and social situations does the article give to support that statement?
4. When should you arrive for the following events in the U.S.?
   - a reception
   - a concert
   - a sporting event
   - a medical appointment
   - a business meeting
   - dinner at someone's house
   - a party
   - a movie
5. Some theaters do not allow people to enter after the event has started. In your opinion, what is the reason?
6. Manolo's Filipino family expects him to meet them when they arrive at the train station. The train arrives at the same time as his English class. What do you think he will do? Why?

B Build your vocabulary.

1. English has several prefixes that mean "not." Write words from the reading that begin with these prefixes.

   un- *unspoken* ir- ______________

   dis-______________ im- ______________

2. Work with a partner. Explain the meaning of the words you wrote.
3. Work with a partner. Write more words with the prefixes. Use a dictionary if needed. Use each word in a sentence.

un-	*dis-*	*ir-*	*im-*

C Talk with a partner. Ask and answer the questions.

1. Look at your answers for the events listed in question four. When should you arrive for those events in your native country?
2. Someone is late to a job interview. Do you believe that person is irresponsible? Why or why not?
3. You are 30 minutes late for lunch with a friend. Do you believe that is impolite? Why or why not?

For college and career readiness practice, please see pages 151–153.

Read closely to determine what the text says explicitly and to make logical inferences from it: recognize prefixes that mean *not*

Lesson E Writing

1 Before you write

A **Work** in a small group. Discuss the questions. Complete the diagrams.

1. What does a good time manager do?

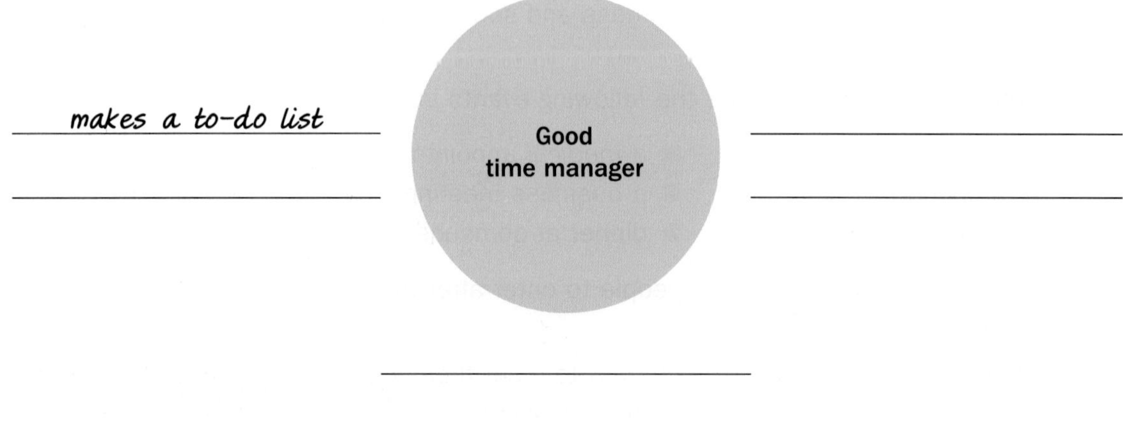

2. What does a weak time manager do?

procrastinates

Weak
time manager

B **Complete** the chart about yourself.

My Time Management Skills

How I manage time well	How I manage time poorly
1.	1.
2.	2.
3.	3.

Talk with a partner. In general are you a good time manager or a weak time manager? Tell why you think so.

C **Read** the paragraph.

How Lucinda Manages Her Time

Lucinda is not a very good time manager. For example, this is the way she does her homework. First, she sits down and takes out her books. Two minutes later, she decides to get a cup of coffee. She goes to the kitchen, makes coffee, and returns to her desk. Before she starts reading, she checks her email. Then the phone rings. It's her best friend. They talk for 20 minutes. After they hang up, it's 9:00 p.m. – time for Lucinda's favorite TV show. She watches the show from 9:00 to 10:00. Then, she studies from 10:00 until 1:30 a.m. Of course, she is tired in the morning. In summary, Lucinda is a weak time manager because she procrastinates.

Use one of the following phrases before your conclusion to introduce it:
In conclusion,
To conclude,
In summary,

Work with a partner. Answer the questions.

1. What is the topic sentence?
2. How many examples does the writer give about Lucinda?
3. Which phrase introduces the conclusion?

2 Write

Write a paragraph about yourself or someone you know who is a good or a weak time manager. Say what kind of time manager you are writing about in the topic sentence. Include examples to support your topic sentence and a phrase to introduce your conclusion. Use Exercises 1A and 1C to help you.

3 After you write

A **Check** your writing.

	Yes	No
1. My topic sentence says what kind of time manager I am writing about.	☐	☐
2. I included examples to support my topic sentence.	☐	☐
3. I used a phrase to introduce my conclusion.	☐	☐

B **Share** your writing with a partner.

1. Take turns. Read your paragraph to a partner.
2. Comment on your partner's paragraph. Ask your partner a question about the paragraph. Tell your partner one thing you learned.

Write an expository paragraph with examples of good or weak time management; use a phrase to introduce a conclusion

Lesson F Another view

1 Life-skills reading

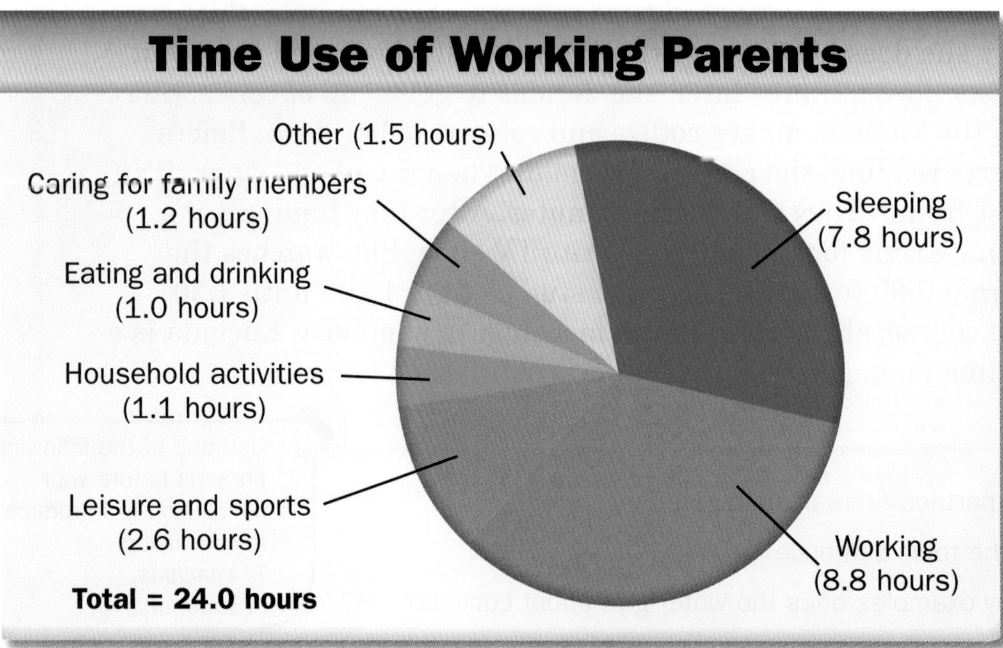

Bureau of Labor Statistics, American Time Use Survey

Time use on an average work day for employed persons ages 25 to 54 with children.

A **Read** the questions. Look at the pie chart. Fill in the answer.

1. Who is the chart about?
   - (A) employed people with children
   - (B) employed people without children
   - (C) unemployed people with children
   - (D) none of the above

2. Which activity do these people spend the least time doing?
   - (A) caring for family members
   - (B) eating and drinking
   - (C) household activities
   - (D) none of the above

3. Which activity do these people spend the most time doing?
   - (A) eating and drinking
   - (B) leisure and sports
   - (C) working
   - (D) none of the above

4. Which statement is true?
   - (A) People spend less time working than eating, drinking, and sleeping combined.
   - (B) People spend more time working than eating, drinking, and sleeping combined.
   - (C) People spend as much time working as eating, drinking, and sleeping combined.
   - (D) none of the above

B **Solve** the problem. Give your opinion.

Lisa is a single mom with two teenage girls, ages 13 and 15. Lisa works full time. Recently her boss asked her to work overtime every Monday. The pay is good, so she wants to accept, but she is already very busy. What can Lisa do differently if she wants to work overtime on Mondays?

2 Grammar Connections: *when / before / after*

Use *when*, *before* and *after* to order activities in a sequence.

Use **when** to talk about two activities that happened at the same time.
Use **after** to introduce the first activity in a sequence.
Use **before** to introduce the second activity in a sequence.

A **Work** in a small group. Play the game. Write your name on a small piece of paper. Flip a coin to move your paper. Then tell your group about the topic in the square. Use *when*, *before* or *after* in your answer. Take turns.

A This asks, "What do you do when people interrupt you?" When people interrupt me, I usually stop talking and listen, but sometimes I ask them to let me finish.

B Mine asks, "What do you do to reward yourself after you finish a difficult task?" After I finish a difficult task, I often eat ice cream or cake to reward myself.

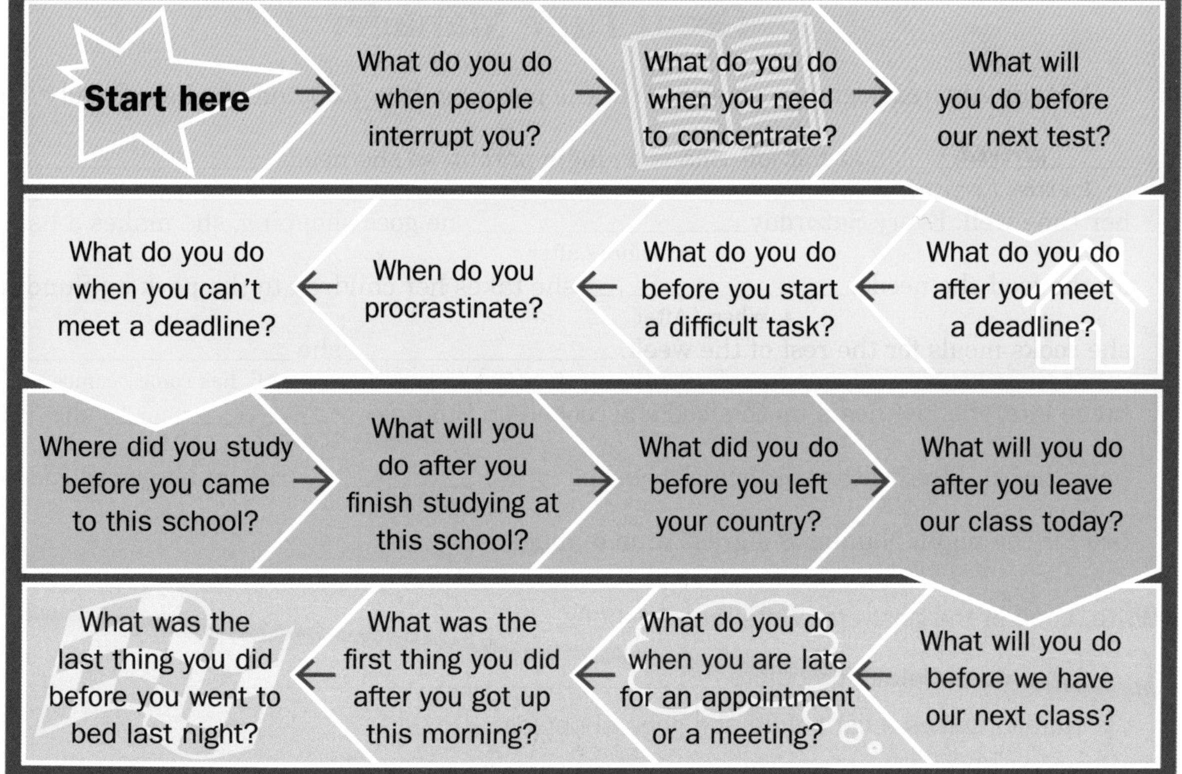

REVIEW

1 Listening

Listen. Put a check (✓) under the correct name.

	Trina	Minh
1. has decided to visit family		✓
2. is going to Las Vegas		
3. hasn't bought plane tickets yet		
4. has already made reservations		
5. won a free hotel room		

Talk with a partner. Check your answers.

2 Grammar

A **Write.** Complete the story. Use the correct words.

A Great Time Manager

Natalia Alvarez begins work at 8:00 in the morning. It is 7:50 and she has already ___*arrived*___ (1. arrive / arrived) at her job. She is a single parent, so she needs ________ (2. manage / to manage) her time well. Every Saturday ________ (3. before / after) she goes shopping, she makes a list of all the food she needs. ________ (4. When / After) she takes her children to the park on Sunday, she cooks meals for the rest of the week. ________ (5. before / when) she ________ (6. has come / comes) home late, she just heats up the food she cooked on Sunday. ________ (7. Before / After) she helps her children with their homework, she ________ (8. do / does) the laundry and goes to bed for the night. Natalia is a great time manager.

B **Write.** Look at the answers. Write the questions.

1. **A** What does Natalia do before ____________________?
   B Natalia makes a list before she goes shopping.
2. **A** What ____________________?
   B She cooks meals for the rest of the week after she goes to the park.
3. **A** When ____________________?
   B She does the laundry after she helps her children with their homework.

Talk with a partner. Ask and answer the questions.

3 Pronunciation: initial *st* sound

A **Listen** to the initial *st* sound.

CD2, Track 8

1. **St**udy English.
2. **St**art the computer.
3. Tell the **st**ory.
4. What **st**ate do you live in?
5. Go to the **st**ore.
6. **St**udents need to **st**udy.
7. Let's see the Salsa **St**arz.
8. **St**op procrastinating.

Listen again and repeat.

B **Listen and repeat.** Then underline the initial *st* sound.

1. **A** Hi, Stuart. I'm going to the store. What do you need?
   B Can you get me some stamps? It's the first of the month, and I have to pay bills.
   A Sure.
   B Thanks. I'll start writing the checks now and stop procrastinating.

2. **A** Hello, Stephanie.
   B Hi, Steve. Are you still a student here?
   A Yes. I'm studying appliance repair.
   B Really? Maybe you can fix my stove when you're finished.
   A I hope so.

CD2, Track 9

Talk with a partner. Compare your answers.

C **Talk** with a partner. Ask and answer the questions. Say the words with the initial *st* sound carefully.

1. How long have you studied at this school?
2. When you go to the store, what do you usually buy?
3. When did you move to this state?
4. When did you start working?

D **Write** five questions. Use the following words. Ask your partner the questions. Remember to pay attention to the initial *st* sound.

1. study: ____
2. store: ____
3. start: ____
4. story: ____
5. student: ____

UNIT 7 SHOPPING

Lesson A Listening

1 Before you listen

A What do you see?

B What is happening?

C What's the story?

2 Listen

CD2, Track 10

A **Listen** and answer the questions.

1. Who are the speakers?
2. What are they talking about?

B **Listen again.** Complete the chart.

CD2, Track 10

	How much / many?
1. cost of a new car	$27,500
2. cost of a car with tax and fees	
3. money in the savings account	
4. interest rate (%)	
5. months to pay	
6. cost of a used car	

3 After you listen

A **Read.** Complete the story.

afford **balance** **cash** **credit** **debt** **financing** **interest** **pay off** **suggests**

Ken and his wife, Julie, are looking at cars. Ken wants to buy a new car that costs over $27,000. Julie thinks that they can't ___afford___ (1) to spend that much money. The ____________ (2) in their savings account is less than $8,000. She's afraid of getting into ____________ (3). But Ken says they can get ____________ (4) to help pay for the new car. The ____________ (5) rate is low, and they can take five years to ____________ (6) the loan. Ken isn't worried about buying things on ____________ (7).

Julie disagrees. She ____________ (8) that they could buy a used car. She says her father never had a credit card. He always paid ____________ (9) for everything.

Listen and check your answers.

CD2, Track 11

B **Talk** with a partner. Ask and answer the questions.

1. What things do people often buy on credit?
2. Is it a good idea to buy things on credit? Why or why not?

USEFUL LANGUAGE
to buy on credit = to buy something now and pay for it later

Lesson B Modals

1 Grammar focus: *could* and *should*

Use *could* to give suggestions. Use *should* to give advice. *Should* gives stronger advice than *could*.

COULD FOR SUGGESTIONS	
You **could get** a smaller car and save money.	
He **could keep** his money in a savings account.	
***SHOULD* FOR ADVICE**	
What **should** I do?	You **should open** a savings account.

2 Practice

A **Write.** Complete the sentences. Use *could* or *should*.

1. **A** My rent is going up again. What should I do?
   B Here's my advice. You're a good tenant. I think you ___should___ talk to your landlord.
2. **A** I have to fix my credit. What should I do?
   B You ____________ talk to a debt counselor. He can help you.
3. **A** Can you suggest a nice restaurant? It's my wife's birthday.
   B You ____________ try Chao's – or how about Anita's?
4. **A** It's my niece's sixteenth birthday next week. What could I get her?
   B Why don't you get tickets to a concert? Or you ____________ buy her a CD.
5. **A** That vocational school is very expensive. I can't afford it. Can you give me any advice?
   B Well, you're a good student. I think you ____________ apply for a scholarship.
6. **A** I need a new car. Where do you suggest I look for one?
   B How about looking in the newspaper? Or you ____________ look online.
7. **A** I just got another parking ticket. It's getting harder and harder to park in this neighborhood.
   B I think you ____________ sell that car. You don't really need it.
8. **A** I'm going to be in New York City in July. Any ideas for things to do?
   B Well, you ____________ see a Broadway show, or you ____________ walk in Central Park, or you ____________ go to a museum. There are so many things to do.

USEFUL LANGUAGE
For suggestions, you can say:
Why don't you + verb . . . ?
How about + noun . . . ?
How about + verb + *ing* . . . ?

Listen and check your answers. Then practice with a partner.

CD2, Track 12

B **Talk** with a partner. Take turns. Read the problems. Make suggestions or give advice.

A My car broke down.

B You could take the bus, or you could ask someone for a ride.

1. "My car broke down."

2. "My rent is going up $150!"

3. "It's getting cold in here."

4. "I can't afford a new washing machine."

5. "These shoes look terrible."

6. "I don't have enough cash to pay for these groceries."

7. "I got a bad haircut."

8. "My neighbors are really noisy."

Write a suggestion or advice for each picture.

You could take the bus, or you could ask someone for a ride.

3 Communicate

A **Work** in a small group. Make suggestions or give advice.

- Helene spends too much money on food.
- Gregory spends too much money on clothes.
- Teresa spends too much money on rent.
- Youssef spends too much money on his cell phone plan.
- Melinda spends too much money on her car payments.

B **Share** your ideas with your classmates.

Lesson C Gerunds after prepositions

1 Grammar focus: questions and answers

In, *of*, *about*, and *for* are examples of prepositions. We often use prepositions in phrases with adjectives (excited about, interested in) and verbs (think about). Gerunds often follow these phrases. A gerund is the base form of a verb + *ing*.

Watch

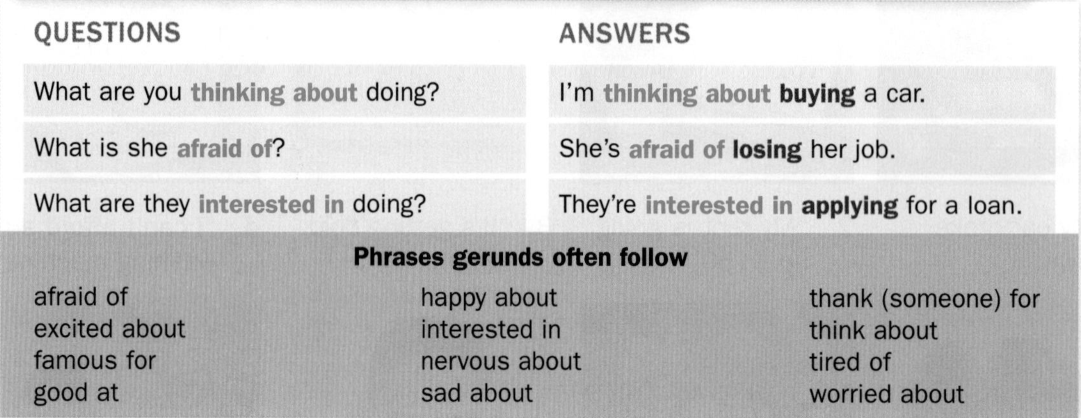

QUESTIONS	ANSWERS
What are you **thinking about** doing?	I'm **thinking about buying** a car.
What is she **afraid of**?	She's **afraid of losing** her job.
What are they **interested in** doing?	They're **interested in applying** for a loan.

Phrases gerunds often follow

afraid of	happy about	thank (someone) for
excited about	interested in	think about
famous for	nervous about	tired of
good at	sad about	worried about

2 Practice

A Write. Complete the sentences. Use the correct form of one of the words below.

apply find get lend make move open pay spend start

1. I'm worried about ___paying___ interest on my credit card balance.
2. Rob is afraid of ____________ into debt. He pays for everything with cash.
3. Have you thought about ____________ a checking account?
4. Elizabeth is happy about ____________ an apartment she can afford.
5. Elena is excited about ____________ classes at the community college.
6. I'm tired of ____________ payments on my car.
7. Franco isn't interested in ____________ for a loan.
8. Thank you for ____________ me money for school.
9. We're thinking about ____________ to a nicer neighborhood.
10. She's famous for ____________ a lot of money on clothes.

Listen and check your answers.

CD2, Track 13

B **Talk** with a partner. Ask and answer questions.

A What's she happy about?

B She's happy about opening a checking account.

1. happy about / open a checking account

2. thinking about / buy a computer

3. worried about / be in debt

4. interested in / study auto mechanics

5. tired of / wait in line

6. excited about / buy a new car

7. sad about / lose his phone

8. nervous about / drive in the snow

Write a sentence about each picture.

She's happy about opening a checking account.

3 Communicate

A **Work** in a small group. Ask and answer questions.

afraid of	excited about	happy about	responsible for
bad at	good at	interested in	tired of

A What are you afraid of?

B I'm afraid of spending too much money.

B **Share** information about your classmates.

Lesson D Reading

1 Before you read

Look at the reading tip. Skim the magazine article. Answer the questions.

1. What problem did the people have?
2. How did they solve it?

One way to organize information is to give problems and solutions.

2 Read

Read the magazine article. Listen and read again.

CD2, Track 14

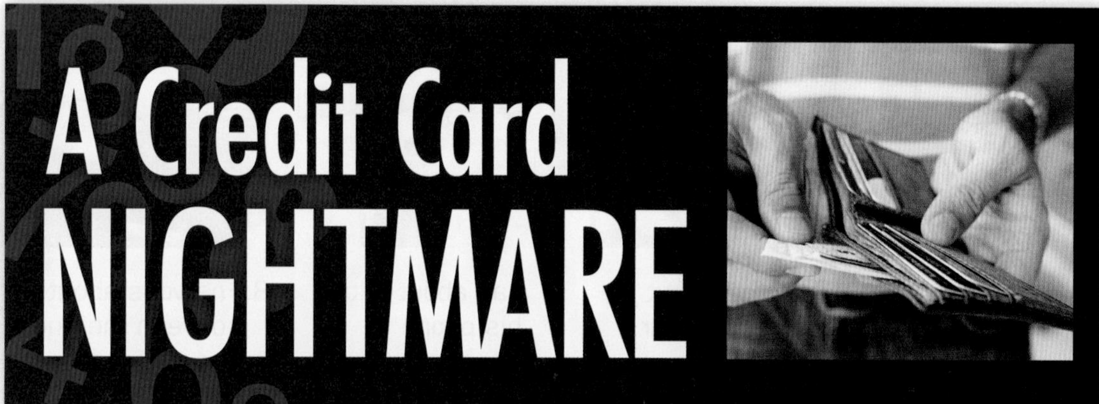

Sun Hi and Joseph Kim got their first credit card a week after they got married. At first, they paid off the balance every month.

The couple's problems began after they bought a new house. They bought new furniture, a big-screen television, and two new computers. To pay for everything, they applied for more and more credit. Soon they had six different credit cards, and they were more than $18,000 in debt.

"It was a nightmare!" says Mrs. Kim. "The interest rates were 19 percent to 24 percent. Our minimum payments were over $750 a month. We both got second jobs, but it wasn't enough. I was so worried about paying off the debt, I cried all the time."

Luckily, the Kims found a solution. They met Dolores Delgado, a debt counselor. With her help, they looked at all of their living expenses and made a family budget. They combined their six credit card payments into one monthly payment with a lower interest rate. Now, their monthly budget for all living expenses is $3,400. Together they earn $3,900 a month. That leaves $500 for paying off their debt.

"We've cut up our credit cards," says Mr. Kim. "No more expensive furniture! In five years, we can pay off our debt. Now we know. Credit cards are dangerous!"

3 After you read

A Check your understanding.

1. What word in the article means *terrible experience?*
2. What is the main idea of the article?
3. When did Mr. and Mrs. Kim get their first credit card?
4. When did their problems begin?
5. How did they pay for everything?
6. According to the article, what things did the Kims do to reduce their debt?
7. Do you think the Kims will have financial problems in the future? What evidence supports your answer?

B Build your vocabulary.

1. Find these words in the reading, and underline them.

credit card **debt counselor** **family budget** **interest rates** **minimum payments**

2. Work with a partner. Circle the correct answers.
   1. Look at the words in Exercise B1. They are compound nouns. In each of the two-word combinations, the first word is: a. a noun b. an adjective
   2. Look at the words again. The second word is: a. a noun b. an adjective
3. Match each compound noun with its meaning.

1. credit card ____	a. a spending plan that a family makes for itself
2. interest rate ____	b. a small plastic card that allows you to buy something now and pay for it later
3. minimum payment ____	c. the smallest payment you can make each month on a credit card
4. debt counselor ____	d. the rate – percentage – of interest that you must pay each month on a credit card balance
5. family budget ____	e. a person who helps you solve financial problems

4. Work with your classmates. Write other *noun* + *noun* combinations.

________________ ________________ ________________

C Talk with your classmates. Ask and answer the questions.

1. How many credit cards do you have? What interest rate do you pay?
2. What things do you usually use a credit card to pay for?
3. Are credit cards popular in your native country?
4. Do you think credit cards are helpful or harmful? Why?
5. Do you think a family budget is important? Why or why not?

For college and career readiness practice, please see pages 154–156.

Determine the main idea and supporting details in a news article about credit card debt; determine the meaning of compound nouns

Lesson E Writing

1 Before you write

A **Talk** with a partner. Look at the picture. What is the problem? What do you suggest?

B **Read** the letter from a newspaper advice column.

THE MONEY MAN

Dear Money Man,

I recently got a new job in a downtown office. I need to look nice every day. I've never worked in an office before, and I don't have the right clothes. Most of the women wear suits to work. How can I get a new wardrobe without spending my entire salary? Can you give me advice?

Not Clothes Crazy

Work with a partner. Answer the questions.

1. What is the woman's problem?
2. What do you suggest?

C **Read** the answer from the Money Man.

> **Dear Not Clothes Crazy,**
>
> It's important to look nice at your job, but you don't need to spend all your money on clothes. I have a few suggestions. First, why don't you buy a black suit with a skirt, jacket, and pants? Then wear a different blouse and jewelry every day for a different look. Second, you could shop at thrift stores. They often have excellent used clothes at very cheap prices. Third, how about talking to the other women in your office? They can tell you about good places to shop. Finally, you should make a monthly budget and follow it carefully. Following a budget is the best way to manage your money.
>
> **Money Man**

Use words like *first*, *second*, *third*, and *finally* to list your ideas.

Work with a partner. What does the Money Man suggest?

2 Write

Read the letter. Write an answer. Start with the problem and write two or more suggestions. Use Exercises 1A, 1B, and 1C to help you.

> **Dear Money Man,**
>
> My wife and I have three young children. We both work full-time. When we come home from work, we are very tired and don't want to cook. We eat in fast-food restaurants three or four times a week. It's very expensive. Last night, the bill was $44! How can we save money on dinner?
>
> **Fast-Food Dad**

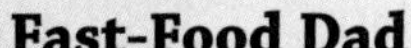

3 After you write

A **Check** your writing.

	Yes	No
1. I started with the problem.	☐	☐
2. I wrote two or more suggestions.	☐	☐
3. I used words like *first* and *second* to list my suggestions.	☐	☐

B **Share** your writing with a partner.

1. Take turns. Read your letter to a partner.
2. Comment on your partner's letter. Ask your partner a question about the letter. Tell your partner one thing you learned.

Lesson F Another view

1 Life-skills reading

TOWN **BANK** CHECKING ACCOUNTS

Choose the plan that's right for you!

	Regular Checking	*Premium Checking*
Monthly Service Fee	$8	$12
Minimum Daily Balance (to waive the monthly service fee)	$1,000	$5,000
Earn Interest	No	Yes
ATM and Bank Card	Free	Free
Free Checks	No	Yes
Free Internet Banking	Yes	Yes
Free Internet Bill Paying	Yes	Yes
Free Money Orders and Traveler's Checks	No	Yes

A **Read** the questions. Look at the bank brochure. Fill in the answer.

1. What does the Premium Checking plan offer?
   - (A) a free ATM card
   - (B) free internet bill paying
   - (C) free traveler's checks
   - (D) all of the above

2. With Premium Checking, how much do you need in your account to avoid a monthly service fee?
   - (A) $0
   - (B) $12
   - (C) $1,000
   - (D) $5,000

3. Which kind of checking account offers free Internet banking?
   - (A) Premium Checking
   - (B) Regular Checking
   - (C) both *a* and *b*
   - (D) neither *a* nor *b*

4. Which statement is true?
   - (A) Both plans offer free checks.
   - (B) Premium Checking pays interest.
   - (C) Only one plan offers a free ATM card.
   - (D) Regular Checking offers free money orders.

B **Solve** the problem. Give your opinion.

Larry has a checking account from Town Bank. When he writes a check, he often forgets to record the amount in his checkbook. Last month, he wrote two bad checks because his balance was too low. The bank charged him over $100. What should he do?

2 Grammar connections: collocations with *get* and *take*

Use *get* with adjectives and some nouns. Use *take* with other nouns.

get dressed	take a bus / a train / a taxi / a plane
get engaged / married / divorced	take notes / a test / a class
get lost / confused	take a break / a nap
get sick / better	take a bath / a shower
get upset / nervous / tired	take a vacation / a trip
get a job / laid off / fired	take pictures / photos

A **Talk** with a partner. Point to a circle. Your partner asks a question using *get* or *take*. Answer the question. Take turns.

A Do you get sick very often?
B No, I don't. I hardly ever get sick.

A Have you taken a vacation recently?
B Yes, I have. I took a vacation to Florida last year.

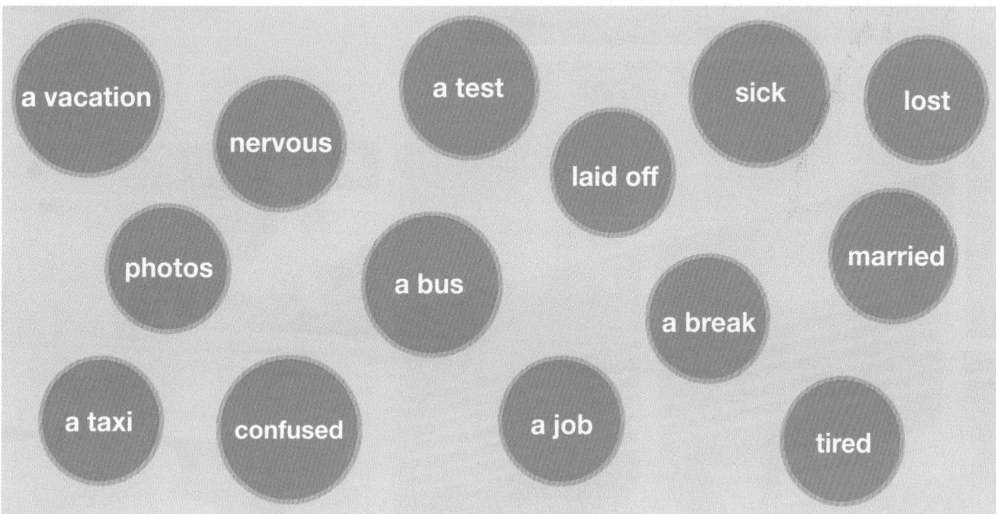

B **Share** information about your partner.

Manuel doesn't get sick very often.

Anton took a vacation last year. He went to Florida.

UNIT 8 WORK

Lesson A Listening

1 Before you listen

A What do you see?

B What is happening?

C What's the story?

2 Listen

CD2, Track 15

A **Listen** and answer the questions.

1. Who are the speakers?
2. What are they talking about?

CD2, Track 15

B **Listen again.** Complete the chart with information about Tony.

Topic	Tony's answers
1. job he is applying for	*shipping-and-receiving clerk*
2. native country	
3. current job	
4. strengths	
5. shift he prefers	

3 After you listen

A **Read.** Complete the story.

background	employed	interview	reliable
degree	gets along	personnel	strengths

Tony has been working as a teacher's assistant for about a year. He is also going to college part-time to get a ___*degree*___ (1) in accounting. Right now, Tony is at a job __________ (2) with Mr. Leong, the __________ (3) manager.

Mr. Leong asks about Tony's __________ (4). Tony says he is from Peru and has been living in the United States for two years. Next, Mr. Leong asks about Tony's work experience, and Tony says that now he is __________ (5) at a school. Finally, Mr. Leong asks about Tony's personal __________ (6). Tony says he is responsible and __________ (7), and he __________ (8) with everybody. Mr. Leong says he will contact Tony next week.

Listen and check your answers.

CD2, Track 16

B **Talk** with a partner. Ask and answer the questions.

Have you ever had a job interview? What happened?

Lesson B Present perfect continuous

1 Grammar focus: questions and statements with *for* and *since*

Use the present perfect continuous to talk about actions that started in the past, continue to now, and will probably continue in the future.

QUESTIONS	SHORT ANSWERS	
Have you **been living** here **for** a long time?	Yes, I **have**.	No, I **haven't**.
Has Tony **been working** here **for** a long time?	Yes, he **has**.	No, he **hasn't**.
Have they **been working** here **for** a long time?	Yes, they **have**.	No, they **haven't**.

How long **have** you **been looking** for a job?	**Since** October.
How long **has** Tony **been working** as a teacher's assistant?	**For** about a year.
How long **have** they **been working** at the school?	

STATEMENTS

I**'ve been waiting** **for** a long time.

Lida **has been waiting** **since** 2:00.

We**'ve been waiting** **all** morning.

USEFUL LANGUAGE
Use *since* with specific times.
Since 2011.
Use *for* with periods of time.
For two months.

2 Practice

A **Write.** Complete the sentences. Use the present perfect continuous with *for* or *since*.

1. **A** How long ___has___ Talia ___been practicing___ (practice) for her driving test?
   B ___For___ about three months.

2. **A** __________ you __________ (work) here for a long time?
   B No, I __________. I started six days ago.

3. **A** How long __________ Yin __________ (look) for a job?
   B __________ last year.

4. **A** __________ Mr. Rivera __________ (interview) people all day?
   B Yes, he __________.

5. **A** How long __________ you __________ (wait) to get an interview?
   B __________ March.

6. **A** How long __________ they __________ (go) to night school?
   B __________ one year.

Listen and check your answers. Then practice with a partner.

B **Talk** with a partner. Ask and answer questions. Use *for* or *since*.

A How long has Sandra been talking on the phone?
B For 20 minutes.

Sandra

Ron

Latifa

Jerry

1. talk / ________ 20 minutes
2. wait / ________ 8:00
3. study / ________ morning
4. practice keyboarding / ________ 10:30

Felix and Pablo

Sharon

Brad

Elena

5. paint the house / ________ two days
6. work in the restaurant / ________ 2011
7. look for a job / ________ several weeks
8. attend this school / ________ last semester

Write a sentence about each picture.

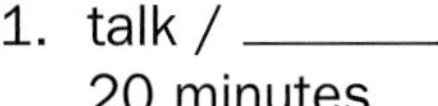

Sandra has been talking on the phone for 20 minutes.

3 Communicate

A **Talk** with your classmates. Find a person who does each activity. Ask how long the person has been doing it. Complete the chart.

A Do you drive?
B Yes, I do.

A How long have you been driving?
B For about six years. / Since 2012.

Activity	Name	How long?
drive	*Josefina*	*for six years / since 2012*
cook for yourself		
attend this school		
work in this country		
speak English		
use a computer		

B **Share** information about your classmates.

Lesson C Phrasal verbs

1 Grammar focus: separable phrasal verbs

A phrasal verb is a verb + preposition. The meaning of the phrasal verb is different from the meaning of the verb alone. These phrases are separable because you can put the second part of the phrase before or after the object.

Watch

STATEMENTS
Alfred **handed out** the papers.
He **handed** the papers **out**.
He **handed** them **out**.

Common separable phrasal verbs

call back	hand out	turn down
clean up	put away	turn off
fill out	throw out / away	turn up

USEFUL LANGUAGE
papers → them
application → it

2 Practice

A **Write.** Complete the sentences.

1. She's **handing out** papers.
   She's _handing_ the papers _out_.
   She's _handing_ them _out_.

2. He's ________ the cups.
   He's **throwing** the cups **away**.
   He's ________ them ________.

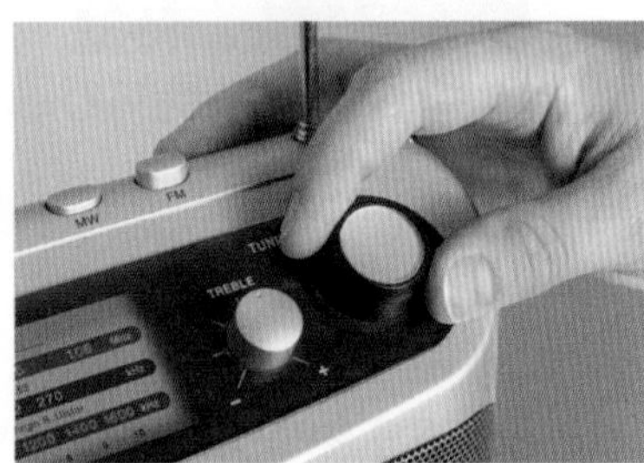

3. He's ________ the volume.
   He's ________ the volume ________.
   He's **turning** it **up**.

4. She's **filling out** a job application.
   She's ________ the application ________.
   She's ________ it ________.

5. She's ________ the lamp.
   She's **turning** the lamp **off**.
   She's ________ it ________.

6. He's **putting away** the clothes.
   He's ________ the clothes ________.
   He's ________ them ________.

Listen and check your answers.

CD2, Track 18

B **Talk** with a partner. Make requests. Use the verbs in the box.

A Please turn the lights off.

B OK. I'll turn them off.

call back clean up put away throw out turn down turn off

USEFUL LANGUAGE
To make a polite request, you can use:
Please . . .
Would you please . . . ?
Could you please . . . ?

1. lights

2. heat

3. lunchroom

TELEPHONE MESSAGE
TO DATE TIME
FROM
PHONE NO. EXT.
☐ PLEASE CALL ☐ RETURNED CALL ☐ WILL CALL AGAIN
MESSAGE

4. Mr. Jones

5. trash

6. books

Write sentences about each picture.

Please turn the lights off.

3 Communicate

A **Work** in a small group. Ask and answer the questions.

1. Have you ever filled out an application form? Where? When?
2. Did you put anything away last night? What was it?
3. Is there someone you need to call back? Who?
4. What things do you want to throw away?
5. What things do you turn on, off, or up?
6. Is there anything you need to clean up? What is it?

B **Share** information about your classmates.

Lesson D Reading

1 Before you read

Talk with your classmates. Answer the questions.

1. How many dates are in the reading? What are they?
2. What is the reading about?
3. What is a *blog*? Have you ever seen one?

Scan the text for specific information. Look quickly to find dates. When you find the information you need, stop reading.

2 Read

Read the blog. Listen and read again.

CD2, Track 19

www.edensblogaddress.com

EDEN'S BLOG

MONDAY 9/29

I had my interview today! I gave the interviewer a big smile and a firm handshake. I answered her questions with confidence. I'll let you know if I get the job.

THURSDAY 9/25

Great news! One of the companies from the job fair finally called me back! I've been preparing for the job interview all day. I'm really excited. I'm going to have a practice interview with some classmates today. That will prepare me for the real one.

WEDNESDAY 9/24

I've been feeling depressed about the job search lately, but my counselor at school told me I shouldn't give up. He said I need to be patient. Today, I organized my papers. I made lists of the places I have applied to and the people I have talked to. I also did some more research online.

TUESDAY 9/16

Today, I went to a job fair at my college. I filled out several applications and handed out some résumés. There were about 20 different companies there. Several of them said they were going to call me back. Wish me luck!

MONDAY 9/15

Hello fellow job searchers! I have been looking for a job for several weeks. Everyone tells me that it's critical to network, so I've been telling everyone I know. I've been calling friends, relatives, and teachers to tell them about my job search. If you have any good job-searching tips, please share them with me!

3 After you read

A **Scan** the blog for Eden's activities. Match them with the dates.

1. Monday 9/15 ____
2. Tuesday 9/16 ____
3. Wednesday 9/24 ____
4. Thursday 9/25 ____
5. Monday 9/29 ____

a. She had a practice interview with her classmates.
b. She had a job interview.
c. She organized her papers.
d. She's been telling everyone about her job search.
e. She went to a job fair.

B **Check** your understanding.

1. What is the main purpose of the blog?
2. Who did she network with?
3. How did she get a job interview?
4. According to the blog, what is a good way for Eden to prepare for the job interview?
5. In the Wednesday 9/24 entry, which word means *discouraged*?
6. Based on the most recent blog post, what can you assume about Eden's job interview?

C **Build** your vocabulary.

1. Read the dictionary entry for *critical*. How many definitions are there?

> **critical** /*adj*/ **1** saying that someone or something is bad or wrong **2** giving opinions on books, plays, films, etc. **3** very important; essential – **critically** /*adv*/

2. Find the vocabulary in the reading. Underline the words. Find each word in a dictionary. Copy the part of speech and the definition that best fits the reading.

Vocabulary	Part of speech	Definition
1. critical	*adjective*	*very important; essential*
2. network		
3. fair		
4. patient		
5. firm		
6. confidence		

D **Talk** with a partner. Ask and answer the questions.

1. What is your most critical goal right now?
2. If you are trying to find a job, who can you network with?
3. How can you show confidence in a job interview?

For college and career readiness practice, please see pages 157–159.

Determine the main idea and key details in a blog; use a dictionary to select the best definition for the context

Lesson E Writing

1 Before you write

A **Talk** with a partner. Who do you send thank-you emails to? Make a list. Share your list with the class.

B **Read** the thank-you email.

To: janice.hill@smartshop.com Reply Forward
Subject: Sept 29 interview

Dear Ms. Hill:

I would like to thank you for the job interview I had with you on Monday, September 29th. I appreciate the time you spent with me. Thank you for showing me around the store and introducing me to some of the employees. I felt very comfortable with them.

Thank you again for your time. I hope to hear from you soon.

Sincerely,

Eden Babayan

Work with a partner. Answer the questions.

1. Who wrote the email?
2. Who did she write it to?
3. What is the purpose of the email?
4. What information is in the first sentence?
5. How many times did the writer say thank you?
6. What does Eden want to happen next?
7. How does the writer end the email?

C **Plan** a formal thank-you email. Complete the information.

Name and address of the person or business you are thanking:

____

____

____

Reason for saying thank you:

____

____

____

Something specific you appreciate:

____

____

____

2 Write

Write a formal thank-you email to a person or a business. Say why you are thanking the person and mention something specific that you appreciated. Thank the person again at the end of the email. Use the email in Exercise 1B and the information in Exercise 1C to help you.

In a thank-you email, include:
- why you are thanking the person
- what you appreciate
- another thank you at the end

3 After you write

A **Check** your writing.

	Yes	No
1. My first sentence says why I am thanking the person.	☐	☐
2. I mentioned something specific that I appreciated.	☐	☐
3. I thanked the person again at the end of the email.	☐	☐

B **Share** your writing with a partner.

1. Take turns. Read your email to a partner.
2. Comment on your partner's email. Ask your partner a question about the email. Tell your partner one thing you learned.

Lesson F Another view

1 Life-skills reading

Occupational projections and worker characteristics			
Occupation	Job openings due to growth and replacements * 2014–2024	Percent Employment change, 2014–2024	Typical education needed for entry
Automotive service technicians and mechanics	237	5.3	Postsecondary technical nondegree award
Dental hygienists	70	18.6	Associate's degree
Food service managers	77	5.1	High school diploma or equivalent
Medical assistants	262	23.5	Post secondary technical nondegree
Retail salespersons	1,917	6.8	No formal educational credential
Veterinary technologists and technicians	274	18.7	Associate's degree

* Numbers in thousands
Source: https://www.bls.gov/emp/ep_table_107.htm

A **Read** the questions. Look at the chart. Fill in the answer.

1. Which statement is not true about the jobs in the chart?
   - (A) One requires an associate's degree.
   - (B) One requires a bachelor's degree.
   - (C) One requires technical training.
   - (D) There will be more jobs in 2024 than in 2014.

2. Which occupations will have the largest percent increase in growth from 2014-2024?
   - (A) automotive service technicians and retain salespersons
   - (B) veterinary technologists and technicians and medical assistants
   - (C) food service managers and dental hygienists
   - (D) retail salespersons and medical assistants

3. What is the growth in number of jobs from 2014–2024 for dental hygienists?
   - (A) 70
   - (B) 700
   - (C) 7,000
   - (D) 70,000

4. What is included in this chart?
   - (A) salary information for certain jobs
   - (B) information about the decline of certain occupations
   - (C) information about the amount of education necessary for certain jobs
   - (D) amount of work experience necessary for certain jobs

B **Solve** the problem. Give your opinion.

Alex has been working in a fast food restaurant for over a year. He works as a busser, cashier and cook. He would like to be a restaurant manager some day, but that requires a high school diploma or equivalent. He dropped out of high school after two years. What should he do?

2 Grammar connections: present continuous and present perfect continuous

Use the *present continuous* to talk about an activity that is happening at the moment of speaking.	Use the *present perfect continuous* to talk about an activity that started in the past and continues to the present.
My classmate **is writing** in her book right now.	I**'ve been writing** emails for two hours.

Watch

A **Work** in a small group. Play the game. Write your name on a small piece of paper. Flip a coin to move your paper. Then tell your group your answer to the question in the square. Use the present continuous or the present perfect continuous in your answer. Take turns.

"Choose someone in the classroom. What is he/she wearing?" OK. I'll describe Tonya. She's wearing . . .

Start here →	Choose someone in the classroom. What is he/she wearing? →	How long have you been studying English? →	What is your teacher doing right now?
How long have you been living in your current city and state?	← How have you been getting to school recently?	← What are you wearing right now?	← How long have you been living in your current home?
Choose someone in the classroom. What is he/she doing right now? →	How long has your teacher been teaching at your school? →	What do you think your best friend is doing right now? →	How long have you been playing this game?
Finish!	← Is anyone in your family working right now? Who? Where?	← What are you thinking about right now?	← What's one thing you've been doing for fun lately?

B **Share** information about your classmates.

Tonya is wearing a red and blue sweater.

REVIEW

1 Listening

Listen. Put a check (✓) under the correct name.

CD2, Track 20

	Clara	John
1. wants an SUV		✓
2. thinks a small car is better		
3. says an SUV is more comfortable		
4. wants to take friends for a ride		
5. wants to keep taking the bus		
6. wants to save money to buy a house		

Talk with a partner. Check your answers.

2 Grammar

A Write. Complete the story. Use the correct words.

Getting Work Experience

Hao *has been applying* (1. will apply / has been applying) for jobs as a computer technician since October. He ____________ (2. is having / has had) several interviews, but he hasn't gotten a job yet. He's afraid of ____________ (3. applying / apply) again until he gets some experience. His friend Terry gave him some good advice. He said Hao ____________ (4. could / should) think about ____________ (5. volunteer / volunteering) at Hao's son's school. Hao wants to call the school because the school ____________ (6. has been having / has) problems with the computer system for a few months. Hao is interested in ____________ (7. help / helping). It would be a win-win situation for both the school and Hao.

B Write. Look at the answers. Write the questions.

1. **A** Who ____?
   B Hao has been applying for a job.
2. **A** What ____?
   B He has been looking for a job as a computer technician.
3. **A** Where ____?
   B Hao wants to volunteer at his son's school.

Talk with a partner. Ask and answer the questions.

3 Pronunciation: linking sounds

A **Listen** to the phrasal verbs. Pay attention to the linking sounds.

1. clean up
2. think about
3. turn up
4. fill out
5. interested in
6. throw out
7. put on
8. tired of

CD2, Track 21

Listen again and repeat.

B **Listen and repeat.** Pay attention to the linking sounds in the phrasal verbs.

1. A What do you need to do?
   B I have to clean up the kitchen.
   A Can I help?
   B Sure. Could you throw out the trash?
   A I'd be happy to.

2. A Don't you think it's cold in here?
   B It's a little cold.
   A Why don't you turn up the heat?
   B That costs too much money. You can put on my jacket.

CD2, Track 22

C **Talk** with a partner. Practice the conversations. Pay attention to the linking sounds in the phrasal verbs.

1. A Do you need some help?
   B I'm interested in applying for a job here.
   A OK. Just fill out this application, and return it to me.
   B Thanks.
   A Don't forget to put your name on it.

2. A May I help you?
   B I may be interested in buying a big-screen TV.
   A We have some great deals. Let me show you.
   B Thanks, but I'd like to just look around some more.

3. A Do you want to go to a movie tonight?
   B What do you think about just staying home?
   A That's fine. There's a good game on TV.
   B OK. First help me clean up the kitchen. Then we can watch the game.

4. A I want to register for English classes.
   B Fill out this form, please.
   A Can you help me?
   B Sure. I just need to put away these papers.
   A Thank you.

D **Write** four questions. Use the words in Exercise 3A. Ask your partner. Remember to connect the sounds.

Did you clean up the kitchen last night?

1. ______________________________
2. ______________________________
3. ______________________________
4. ______________________________

UNIT 9 DAILY LIVING

Lesson A Listening

1 Before you listen

A What do you see?

B What is happening?

C What's the story?

1

3

2

4

5

NEIGHBORHOOD WATCH

PROGRAM IN FORCE

We report all Suspicious Persons & Activities to our Law Enforcement Agency

2 Listen

A **Listen** and answer the questions.

1. Who are the speakers?
2. What are they talking about?

CD2, Track 23

B **Listen again.** Take notes. Answer the questions.

CD2, Track 23

1. What happened at Monica and Todd's house?	*someone broke into it*
2. Where were Monica and Todd when the robbery happened?	
3. What did the robber steal?	
4. How has the neighborhood changed?	
5. What does Samantha think they should do?	

3 After you listen

A **Read.** Complete the story.

broke into   come over   crime   got in   mess   robbed   robber   stole   worried

Monica calls Samantha with bad news. While Monica and Todd were out, someone *broke into* (1) their home and ________ (2) their TV, DVD player, jewelry, and some cash. Monica is upset because the ________ (3) took her mother's ring. She says the person ________ (4) through a window in the back bedroom.

Samantha is ________ (5). She says they never used to have so much ________ (6) in their neighborhood. She tells Monica that last week someone ________ (7) their neighbor Mr. Purdy, too. Samantha thinks they should start a Neighborhood Watch program. Monica agrees, but first, she needs to clean up the ________ (8) in her house. Samantha offers to ________ (9) and help.

Listen and check your answers.

CD2, Track 24

B **Talk** with a partner.

Tell about a crime that happened to you or someone you know.

Lesson B Past continuous

1 Grammar focus: questions and answers

Use the past continuous to talk about actions that were happening at a specific time in the past. The actions were not completed at that time.

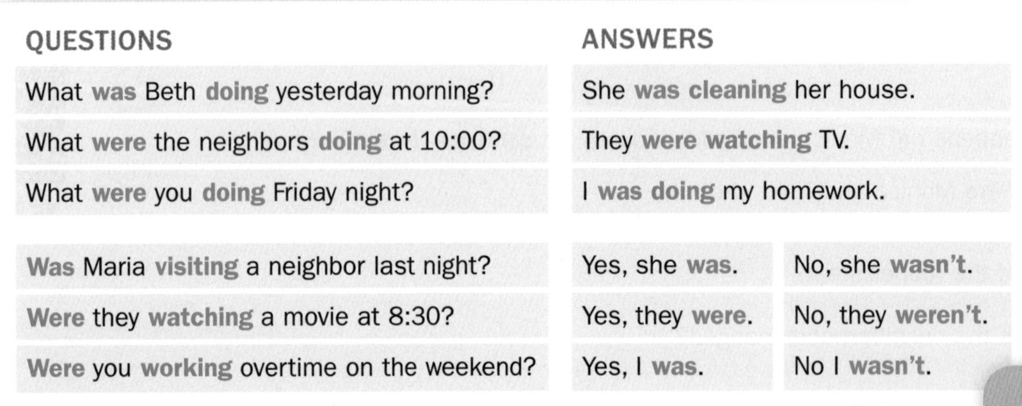

QUESTIONS	ANSWERS	
What **was** Beth **doing** yesterday morning?	She **was cleaning** her house.	
What **were** the neighbors **doing** at 10:00?	They **were watching** TV.	
What **were** you **doing** Friday night?	I **was doing** my homework.	
Was Maria **visiting** a neighbor last night?	Yes, she **was**.	No, she **wasn't**.
Were they **watching** a movie at 8:30?	Yes, they **were**.	No, they **weren't**.
Were you **working** overtime on the weekend?	Yes, I **was**.	No I **wasn't**.

wasn't = was not
weren't = were not

2 Practice

A Write. Complete the sentences. Use the verbs in the word box below. Use the past continuous.

attend babysit bake drive eat paint play study visit work ~~watch~~

What were you doing at 8:30 last night?

1. Roberto and Maya: We *were watching* a movie at the Rialto Theater.
2. Mi Young: I ______________ English at home last night.
3. Ciro: I ______________ to work.
4. Magda and Luis: We ______________ dinner at Kate's Kitchen Restaurant.
5. Ilian and Francine: We ______________ a Neighborhood Watch meeting.
6. Susana: I ______________ my grandchildren at my daughter's house.
7. Claudia: I ______________ a cake for my daughter's birthday party.
8. Leila and Mark: We ______________ the kitchen.
9. Daniel: I ______________ my friend and ______________ video games.
10. Mehri and Sari: We ______________ late at our hair salon.

Listen and check your answers.

B **Talk** with a partner. Look at the picture. Ask and answer questions. Use the past continuous and the verbs in the box.

A What was Bill doing at 7:00 p.m.?

B He was reading.

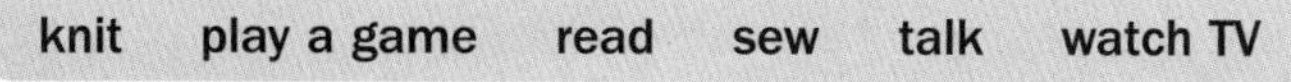

Write a sentence about each person.

Bill was reading.

3 Communicate

A Work in a small group. Ask and answer questions. Take notes in the chart.

A Sergio, were you at home at 9:00 a.m. yesterday?

B Yes, I was.

A What were you doing?

B I was sleeping.

Name	Hour	Time	Action
Sergio	*9:00 a.m.*	*yesterday*	*was sleeping*

B **Share** information about your classmates.

Lesson C Past continuous and simple past

1 Grammar focus: adverb clauses with *when* and *while*

Use *when* or *while* to begin an adverb clause to show that one past action interrupted another past action. Use *when* with the simple past for the action that interrupted. Use *while* with the past continuous to show the action that was happening before the interruption.

Watch

When the fire **started**, Maxine and Joel **were sleeping**.
While Maxine and Joel **were sleeping**, a fire **started** in the kitchen.
Maxine and Joel **were sleeping** **when** the fire **started**.
A fire **started** in the kitchen **while** Maxine and Joel **were sleeping**.

2 Practice

A **Write.** Complete the sentences. Use the past continuous or simple past.

First, look at the sentence and decide which past action was interrupted. Number the activity "1". Number the activity "2" that interrupted the past action.

1. While Dad (1) ___was working___ (work) in the garden, a thief (2) ___stole___ (steal) his car.
2. I ____________ (eat) lunch when the fire alarm suddenly ____________ (go off).
3. Ali ____________ (fall) off a ladder while he ____________ (paint) the ceiling.
4. When the earthquake ____________ (start), the students ____________ (take) a test.
5. I ____________ (make) a right turn when another car ____________ (hit) the back of my car.
6. While we ____________ (camp), it suddenly ____________ (begin) to rain.
7. Mr. and Mrs. Gomez ____________ (jog) in the park when a dog ____________ (begin) to chase them.
8. While Diana ____________ (work) outside, a stranger ____________ (drive) up to her house.
9. While we ____________ (drive) to the beach, someone ____________ (break) into our garage and ____________ (steal) our new lawn mower.

Listen and check your answers.

CD2, Track 26

B **Talk** with a partner. Look at the pictures. Ask and answer questions. Use *when* or *while*.

A What happened?

B While the woman was working, a tree fell on her house.

work | fall | drive | run out of gas

eat | get a parking ticket | cook dinner | the lights go out

Write sentences about what happened. Use *when* and *while*.

The woman was working when a tree fell on her house.

While the woman was working, a tree fell on her house.

3 Communicate

A **Work** with a partner. Describe a situation that happened to you. Answer the questions.

1. What happened?
2. When and where did it happen?
3. What were you doing when it happened?

B **Share** information about your partner.

Lesson D Reading

1 Before you read

Look at the picture. Answer the questions.

1. Who are the people in the picture?
2. What do you think is happening?
3. How do they probably feel?

2 Read

Read the newspaper article. Listen and read again.

Home Is More Than a Building

Claypool, AZ

A few months ago, Pedro Ramirez, 45, lost his job in a grocery store. To pay the bills, he got a part-time job at night. Several days later, Pedro's wife, Luisa, gave him a big surprise. She was pregnant with their third child. Pedro was happy but worried. "How am I going to support another child without a full-time job?" he wondered.

That evening, Pedro and Luisa got some more news. A fire was coming near their home. By the next morning, the fire was very close. The police ordered every family in the neighborhood to evacuate. The Ramirez family moved quickly. While Pedro was gathering their legal documents, Luisa grabbed the family photographs, and the children put their pets – a cat and a bird – in the family's van. Then, the family drove to the home of Luisa's sister, one hour away.

About 24 hours later, Pedro and Luisa got very bad news. The fire destroyed their home. They lost almost everything. With no home, only part-time work, and a baby coming, Pedro was even more worried about the future.

For the next 11 months, the Ramirez family stayed with Luisa's sister while workers were rebuilding their home. Many generous people helped them during that difficult time. Friends took them shopping for clothes. Strangers left gifts at their door. A group of children collected $500 to buy bicycles for the Ramirez children.

Because of all the help from friends and neighbors, the Ramirez family was able to rebuild their lives. Two months after the fire, Luisa mailed out holiday cards with this message: "Home is more than a building. Home is wherever there is love."

Time phrases show changes in time.
A few months ago, . . .
Several days later, . . .
That evening, . . .

3 After you read

A **Check** your understanding.

1. What is the main idea of this news article? Underline the details that support your answer.
2. Why did Pedro and Maria move to her sister's home?
3. Name three things that changed Pedro and Maria's life.
4. Who were the people that helped Pedro and Maria rebuild their lives?
5. In the second paragraph, what does the word *evacuate* mean?
6. How were Maria and Pedro able to overcome this difficult time?

B **Build** your vocabulary.

Find the words in the story and underline them. Circle the definitions that best match the reading.

1. support
   a. pay for necessary things
   b. find
   c. say that you agree with someone
2. evacuate
   a. clean
   b. go inside a house
   c. leave a dangerous place
3. gathering
   a. separating
   b. a group of things
   c. collecting
4. grabbed
   a. took quickly
   b. held someone with force
   c. stole
5. destroyed
   a. broke completely
   b. killed
   c. hurt
6. generous
   a. critical
   b. giving
   c. sad
7. strangers
   a. family
   b. friends
   c. people you don't know
8. message
   a. medical treatment
   b. communication
   c. a person who brings things

C **Talk** with a partner. Ask and answer the questions.

1. Tell your partner about an emergency situation that happened to you or your family. What happened?
2. Has someone been generous to you or your family? How?
3. How do you feel about accepting help from strangers?

For college and career readiness practice, please see pages 160–162.

Lesson E Writing

1 Before you write

A **Talk** with a partner. Think about an emergency. Answer the questions.

1. **Who** did it happen to?
2. **What** happened?
3. **When** did it happen?
4. **Where** did it happen?
5. **Why** or **how** did it happen?

B **Read** about an emergency.

Fire in Our Backyard

One evening last summer, my husband and I were preparing dinner together. My husband was cooking outside, and I was setting the table inside. Suddenly, my husband ran into the kitchen and shouted, "There's a fire in the backyard!" I ran outside and saw fire in the bushes next to our fence. I was really scared because my 70-year-old parents live next door. Luckily, my husband acted quickly. He called the fire department and then started putting water on the fire. The firefighters arrived quickly, and they easily put out the fire. They said a coal from the barbecue started it. My parents were very surprised when they saw the firefighters. They were watching the news in the living room, and they never knew there was a problem. My father said, "Let's go back and watch the news. Maybe we're on TV!"

Work with a partner. Answer the questions.

1. Who is the article about?
2. When did it happen?
3. Where did it happen?
4. What were the people doing when the emergency started?
5. What was the emergency?
6. Why was the writer scared?
7. How did the article end?

C **Write** a plan for a narrative paragraph about an emergency that happened to you or someone you know. Answer the questions.

1. Who is the paragraph about?	
2. Where did it happen?	
3. When did it happen?	
4. What were the people doing when the fire started?	
5. What was the emergency?	
6. How did the paragraph end?	

2 Write

Write a narrative paragraph about an emergency that happened to you or someone you know. Give the paragraph a title and write a concluding sentence. Use the information from Exercises 1B and 1C to help you.

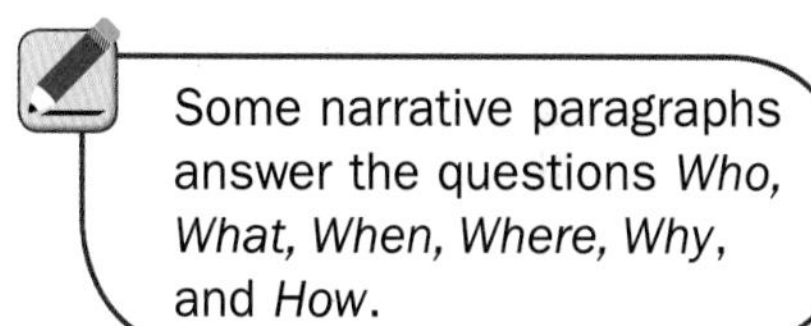

3 After you write

A **Check** your writing.

	Yes	No
1. I gave my paragraph a title.	☐	☐
2. I answered the questions *Who*, *What*, *When*, *Where*, *Why*, and *How*.	☐	☐
3. I wrote a concluding sentence.	☐	☐

B **Share** your writing with a partner.

1. Take turns. Read your paragraph to a partner.
2. Comment on your partner's paragraph. Ask your partner *Who, What, When, Where, Why*, and *How* questions about the story. Tell your partner one thing you learned.

Write a narrative paragraph about an emergency that answers the questions *Who, What, When, Where, Why*, and *How*

Lesson F Another view

1 Life-skills reading

Best States Rankings for Public Safety and Pre-K-12 Education (2015)

Best States for Public Safety (Low Property Crime Rate/Low Violent Crime Rate)	Best States for Pre-K-12 Education
1. Vermont	1. New Hampshire
2. Maine	2. New Jersey
3. New Hampshire	3. Massachusetts
4. Idaho	4. Connecticut
5. New Jersey	5. Vermont
6. Virginia	6. Iowa
7. Connecticut	7. Maryland
8. Wyoming	8. Minnesota
9. Rhode Island	9. Nebraska
10. Kentucky	10. Illinois
Source: https://www.usnews.com/news/best-states/rankings/crime-and-corrections/public-safety	Source: https://www.usnews.com/news/best-states/rankings/education/prek-12

A Read the questions. Look at the chart. Fill in the answer.

1. Which states on the chart have the highest public safety record?
   - (A) Vermont and Maine
   - (B) Vermont and New Hampshire
   - (C) New Hampshire and New Jersey
   - (D) Rhode Island and Kentucky

2. Which statement is true?
   - (A) New Hampshire has the best ranking for Pre-K-12 education.
   - (B) New Hampshire is in the top 5 in both public safety and Pre-K-12 education.
   - (C) Connecticut and Iowa are NOT in the top 5 for Public Safety.
   - (D) all of the above

3. How many states are listed only once in this chart?
   - (A) 8
   - (B) 12
   - (C) 4
   - (D) 6

4. Which statement is not true?
   - (A) Vermont and New Hampshire are listed in both public safety and pre-K-12 education.
   - (B) Wyoming is #8 in public safety.
   - (C) Kentucky is #10 in Public Safety.
   - (D) all of the above

B Solve the problem. Give your opinion.

Carlos has a wife and two young sons. He has been offered a great job in New Jersey. He currently lives in Florida, and all his family lives nearby. He wants to be able to provide his children with a good education, and he wants good public safety. However, the winters are very cold and Carlos has always lived close to his family. What should he do?

2 Grammar connections: three uses of the present continuous

There are three uses for the present continuous.

Events happening now	Farah **is wearing** new jeans right now.
Ongoing events	I'**m studying** in the library this week.
Events in the near future	Hiro **isn't working** next Saturday.

A **Work** in a small group. Complete the chart.

A What are you doing tonight, Farah?

B I'm studying English.

	Name: _______	Name: _______	Name: _______
1. What are you doing tonight?			
2. What are you looking at right now?			
3. What are you watching on TV this week?			
4. What are you doing next Saturday?			
5. What are you thinking about right now?			
6. What classes are you taking this term?			

B **Work** with a partner. Look at the questions in Exercise 2A. Answer the questions.

1. Which questions are about events happening now? ____________
2. Which questions are about ongoing events? ____________
3. Which questions are about events in the near future? ____________

Scan a chart for key details about public safety and pre-K-12 education; use the present continuous tense in three different ways

UNIT 10 FREE TIME

Lesson A Listening

1 Before you listen

Talk about the pictures.

A What do you see?

B What is happening?

C What's the story?

2 Listen

CD2, Track 28

A **Listen** and answer the questions.

1. Who are the speakers?
2. What are they talking about?

B **Listen again.** Complete the chart.

CD2, Track 28

	San Francisco		Camping
Transportation	Round-trip airfare per person: $ _____		Gas for the car: $ _____
Lodging	Hotel per night: $ _____	Tax: _____%	Campsite per night: $ _____

3 After you listen

CULTURE NOTE
Advertisements for hotels do not include the room tax. The tax adds 7% to 16% per night to the cost of the room.

A **Read.** Complete the story.

book a flight	**days off**	**exhausted**	**reserve**	**tax**
camping	**discounts**	**figure out**	**round-trip**	**tourist**

Felicia is *exhausted* (1). She needs a vacation. Her husband, Ricardo, says he can ask his boss for a few _____ (2). Felicia would like to go to San Francisco. They look for special travel _____ (3) on the Internet. If they _____ (4) at least seven days ahead, they can get a _____ (5) ticket for less than $200. On the other hand, hotel room rates will be high because summer is the most popular _____ (6) season. Also, there is a room _____ (7) on hotel rooms in San Francisco. They _____ (8) that a three-day trip to San Francisco will cost almost $1,200.

Felicia and her husband decide to change their plans. If they go _____ (9), they will save a lot of money and their daughter will have more fun. Felicia's husband will _____ (10) the campsite after he talks to his boss.

Listen and check your answers.

CD2, Track 29

B **Talk** with a partner. Answer the question.

Which would you prefer: a trip to San Francisco or camping in the mountains?

Lesson B Conditionals

1 Grammar focus: future real conditional

Use an *if* clause to talk about future possibility. Use the simple present in the *if* clause. Use the future in the main clause to talk about what could happen.

If the fare **is** cheap enough, we **will fly**.

We **will fly** **if** the fare **is** cheap enough.

If the weather **is** bad, she **won't go swimming**.

She **won't go swimming** **if** the weather **is** bad.

If they **get** time off from work, they **will visit** their relatives in California.

They **will visit** their relatives in California **if** they **get** time off from work.

USEFUL LANGUAGE
won't = will not

2 Practice

A **Write.** Complete the sentences. Use the simple present or future form of the verbs. Circle the future conditional clause.

1. Annette and William ___*will take*___ (take) their children to Sea Adventure next month (if William ___*gets*___ (get) a few days off.)
2. If they ________ (get) a discount, they ________ (reserve) a room at a hotel.
3. If prices ________ (be) too high, they ________ (not / take) an expensive vacation.
4. We ________ (have) a picnic on Saturday if it ________ (not / rain).
5. If you ________ (give) me the money, I ________ (buy) the concert tickets.
6. If you ________ (come) to Chicago, we ________ (meet) you at the airport.
7. They ________ (fly) to Miami next month if they ________ (find) a cheap flight.
8. We ________ (not / go) camping if the weather ________ (be) too hot.
9. If it ________ (rain), we ________ (have) the party inside.
10. If she ________ (need) a rental car, she ________ (look) for one online.

Listen and check your answers.

B **Talk** with a partner. Ask and answer questions about the pictures.

A What will John do if the weather is good?
B He'll play soccer.

A What will he do if the weather isn't good?
B He'll watch a movie.

USEFUL LANGUAGE
He'll = He will

1.

John

play soccer | watch a movie

2.

Melinda and Pedro

go hiking | go shopping

3.

Ken

go swimming | clean the house

4.

Andrea

work in the garden | read a book

5.

Kim and Tan

walk downtown | take the bus

Write a sentence about each picture.

If the weather is good, John will play soccer.

He'll watch a movie if the weather isn't good.

3 Communicate

A **Work** with a partner. Ask and answer questions. Take notes in the chart.

A What will you do if you have time off in the summer?
B I'll visit my family in Mexico.

1. have time off in the summer	*visit family in Mexico*
2. have a three-day weekend	
3. get some extra money	
4. the weather is beautiful next weekend	

B **Share** information about your partner.

Lesson C Future time clauses

1 Grammar focus: clauses with *after* and *before*

Use *after* and *before* to introduce adverb clauses to talk about the order of future plans. Use *after* + present tense verb to introduce the first event. Use the future tense in the main clause. Use *before* + present tense verb to introduce the second event. Use the future tense in the main clause.

After Kim **finishes** school, he **will take** a vacation.

Kim **will take** a vacation **after** he **finishes** school.

1st event–finish school.
2nd event–take a vacation

Before Kim **takes** a vacation, he **will finish** school.

Kim **will finish** school **before** he **takes** a vacation.

USEFUL LANGUAGE
Use a comma when *if*, *before*, and *after* clauses are at the beginning of a sentence.

2 Practice

A Write. Complete the sentences. Use the correct form of the verb. Write "1" above the first event. Write "2" above the second event.

1. Kara ___will talk___ (talk) [1] to a travel agent before she ___books___ (book) [2] a flight.
2. Before Cynthia ______ (leave) for Puerto Rico, she ______ (buy) some new clothes.
3. Donald ______ (take) a taxi to the hotel after he ______ (pick up) his baggage.
4. The campers ______ (make) a fire before they ______ (cook) their dinner.
5. After they ______ (finish) eating, they ______ (clean up) the campsite.
6. I ______ (call) you after I ______ (return) from my trip.
7. After I ______ (get) my passport, I ______ (make) the reservations.
8. Before we ______ (go) to Mexico, we ______ (learn) some words in Spanish.
9. Jack ______ (lock) the doors before he ______ (leave) for the airport.
10. Maria ______ (print) her boarding pass before she ______ (go) to the airport.

Listen and check your answers.

B **Talk** with a partner. Anita is going to the airport. Talk about her plans. Use *before* or *after*.

A After Anita checks in, she'll check her bag.

B Before Anita goes through security, she'll check her bag.

1. check in

2. check her bag

3. go through security

4. buy a cup of coffee

5. check her messages

6. read a magazine

7. get on the plane

8. turn off her cell phone

Write sentences about Anita. Use *before* and *after*.

Anita will go through security after she checks her bags.

3 Communicate

A **Imagine** you are going to take a weekend trip. Choose the location. Write three things you need to do before the trip.

B **Interview** a partner. Take notes in the chart.

A Where will you go on your trip?

B To the mountains.

A What will you do first?

B I'll reserve a campsite.

A What will you do after you reserve a campsite?

B I'll pack warm clothes.

A What will you do after that?

B I'll pack my camping supplies.

C **Share** information about your partner.

You
Location:
1. __________
2. __________
3. __________
Your partner
Location:
1. __________
2. __________
3. __________

Lesson D Reading

1 Before you read

Look at the picture. Answer the questions.

1. What do you see on the postcard?
2. Would you like to visit this place? Why or why not?

2 Read

Read the article from a tourist website. Listen and read again.

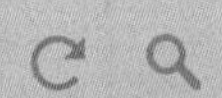

www.therock.com

The ROCK SAN FRANCISCO'S BIGGEST TOURIST ATTRACTION

Alcatraz, a small, rocky island in the middle of San Francisco Bay, was once the most famous prison in the United States. For a period of 29 years, from 1934 to 1963, over 1,500 dangerous criminals lived in the prison's 378 cells. People believed that it was impossible to escape from Alcatraz Island. However, in 1962, two brothers, John and Clarence Anglin, and another man named Frank Morris, escaped on a raft made of raincoats. A famous movie, *Escape from Alcatraz*, tells this amazing story. Other famous prisoners who lived on the island included Al Capone, the gangster, and Robert Stroud, the "Birdman of Alcatraz."

Alcatraz prison closed in 1963. The island became a national park, and since then it has been a major attraction for tourists from all over the world. These days, many people call Alcatraz by its popular name, "The Rock."

In the summer, it is wise to buy tickets to the island in advance because the ferries sell out. Evening tours are less crowded. The admission prices listed include the ferry, tickets, and an audio tour.

General admission	Day tours	Evening tours
Adult (18–61)	$45.25	$52.25
Child (5–17)	$31.00	$34.20
Senior (62+)	$43.25	$49.25

Words between commas sometimes explain the words before them.
For a period of 29 years, ***from 1934 to 1963, . . .***

3 After you read

A Check your understanding.

1. What is the main topic of this article?
2. What was Alcatraz in the past?
3. Why did dangerous criminals go to Alcatraz?
4. According to the article, why was the escape in 1962 surprising?
5. Underline the word "major" in the 2nd paragraph. What do you think this word means in this article? What words help you understand the meaning?
6. How long has Alcatraz been a tourist attraction?
7. Maria and her two sons, 11 and 13 years old, want to go to Alcatraz during the day. How much will this cost them?
8. Why do you think Alcatraz is a popular tourist attraction?

B Build your vocabulary.

1. Find the following words in the reading. Underline them.

admission attraction cells escape ferries in advance prison sell out

2. Work with a partner. Guess the meaning of the words. Note the clues that helped you. Then use a dictionary to check your guesses.

I guess that *attraction* means a place tourists want to visit. My clue was the phrase "biggest tourist attraction" in the title. The dictionary definition of *attraction [noun]* is "a thing or place that tourists like to see or visit."

3. Complete the sentences. Use the words from Exercise B1.

a. The Empire State Building in New York is a famous tourist ____________.
b. General ____________ for an evening tour for adults is $52.25.
c. Tickets to popular music concerts often ____________ very quickly.
d. We bought our tickets six months ____________.
e. To get to the Ellis Island Immigration Museum in New York, you have to take one of the ____________ from Manhattan.
f. Alcatraz used to be a ____________. Then it became a national park.
g. Each prisoner in Alcatraz lived in one of the 378 ____________.
h. Thirty-six men tried to ____________ from Alcatraz.

C Talk with a partner. Ask and answer the questions.

1. Tell about a popular tourist attraction in a city you have visited. What was the cost of admission?
2. What kinds of tickets do you usually buy in advance?
3. Have you ever taken a ferry ride? Where did you go?

For college and career readiness practice, please see pages 163–165.

Determine the main idea and key details in an article about a tourist attraction; use context clues and a dictionary to determine meaning

Lesson E Writing

1 Before you write

A **Work** with a partner. Write the name of a tourist attraction in your community. Make a list of things to do or see there.

Attraction: ______________________________

1. ____
2. ____
3. ____

B **Read** the paragraph.

One of the biggest tourist attractions in many cities in the United States is the county fair. A fair has something for everyone. It has a beautiful flower show and a photography exhibit. If you have children, they will love the Ferris wheel and the fast rides. If you like animals, you can watch many different animal competitions. The winner in each competition gets a blue ribbon. A fair also has displays of new products, such as cleaning products and cooking tools. When you get hungry, you can buy food from one of the many booths. After you have eaten dinner, you can listen to a concert of live music until late in the evening. Many fairs end with spectacular fireworks. There really is something for everyone at a fair.

C **Complete** the outline. Write five examples of things to do at the county fair.

Topic sentence: *A fair has something for everyone.*

Examples:

1. ______________________________
____

2. ______________________________
____

3. ______________________________
____

4. ______________________________
____

5. ______________________________
____

Conclusion: *There really is something for everyone at a fair.*

> Use complex sentences to make your writing more interesting. Complex sentences are sentences with a dependent clause.
> *If you have children, they will love the Ferris wheel and the fast rides.*
> *When you get hungry, you can buy food from at least 25 different booths.*

D **Work** with a partner. Look at the paragraph in Exercise 1B. Find four complex sentences. Underline them.

2 Write

Write a paragraph about a tourist attraction in your city. Include the topic sentence, at least three examples, and a conclusion. Use at least two complex sentences in your paragraph. Before you write, make an outline. Use Exercises 1B and 1C to help you.

3 After you write

A **Check** your writing.

	Yes	No
1. My paragraph has a topic sentence and a conclusion.	☐	☐
2. My paragraph has at least three examples.	☐	☐
3. My paragraph has complex sentences with *before*, *after*, *when*, or *if*.	☐	☐

B **Share** your writing with a partner.

1. Take turns. Read your paragraph to a partner.
2. Comment on your partner's paragraph. Ask your partner a question about the paragraph. Tell your partner one thing you learned.

Lesson F Another view

1 Life-skills reading

www.comparehotel.com

	GATEWAY INN 524 Memorial Highway Orlando, Florida 407-555-7000		WESTERN UNIVERSAL INN 4617 Southland Rd. Orlando, Florida 407-555-9100
Amenities	Restaurant in lobby (kids eat free), outdoor pool, fitness center, golf nearby, free transportation to local theme parks	Amenities	Breakfast buffet, outdoor pool, self-parking (free), in-room safe, iron, hair dryer, Internet access
Distance from destinations	Theme parks (3.5 miles)	Distance from destinations	Daytona Beach (47 miles), International Drive (1 mile), Winter Park (8 miles), Theme parks (12 miles)
Room rates	Budget: $100–$120 Standard: $130–$160 Deluxe: $200–$250	Room rates	Budget: $130–$165 Standard: $160–$175 Deluxe: $250–$300
Room tax	6%	Room tax	6%

A **Read** the questions. Look at the hotel information. Fill in the answer.

1. What is the rate for a standard room at the Gateway Inn?
   - (A) $100–$120
   - (B) $130–$160
   - (C) $160–$175
   - (D) $200–$250

2. Which statement is true?
   - (A) The Gateway Inn is less expensive than the Western Universal Inn.
   - (B) The Western Universal is farther away from theme parks than the Gateway Inn.
   - (C) Both hotels have pools.
   - (D) all of the above

3. Where can children eat for free?
   - (A) Gateway Inn
   - (B) Daytona Beach
   - (C) Western Universal Inn
   - (D) none of the above

4. Look at the examples of amenities in the two ads. Which of the following is the best definition for *amenities?*
   - (A) places to see near the hotels
   - (B) things that come with the hotel
   - (C) room taxes
   - (D) prices of different room types

B **Solve** the problem. Give your opinion.

Peter and Sophia went online and booked a room at the Gateway Inn three months before their vacation. When they arrived at the hotel and talked with other guests, they learned that the hotel was offering a special room rate that was cheaper than the one they booked online. What should they do?

2 Grammar connections: three uses of the present perfect

There are three uses of the present perfect.

Events that began in the past and continue to now	Keiko **has taken** English classes for six years.
Events that have happened before now (time unclear)	Jason **has been** to Canada.
Events that were repeated before now	I **have flown** on a plane six times.

A **Talk** with your classmates. Complete the chart.

A Have you been to another country on vacation, Elena?

B No, I haven't.

A Have you been to another country on vacation, Jason?

C Yes, I have. I've been to Canada.

Find someone who . . .	**Name**
has been to another country on vacation.	
has taken English classes for more than five years.	
hasn't missed a class since the beginning of the term.	
hasn't changed his/her hairstyle in the last five years.	
has flown on a plane more than once.	
has seen snow.	
has shopped online a lot recently.	
hasn't sent a text message in the last 24 hours.	
has lived in the same place for more than ten years.	
has lived in this country for less than a year.	
hasn't traveled by bus before.	

B **Share** information about your classmates.

Jason has been to Canada on vacation.

Keiko has taken English classes for six years.

Compare and contrast two hotel ads for key details; use the present perfect for three different purposes

REVIEW

1 Listening

CD2, Track 33

Listen. Put a check (✓) under *Yes* or *No*.

	Yes	No
1. Brad Spencer was missing for two nights.		✓
2. He disappeared Sunday.		
3. He was camping with his friends.		
4. He was wearing only a T-shirt and shorts.		
5. When the park police found him, he was playing his guitar.		
6. If Brad returns to the park, he's going to stay on the trails.		

Talk with a partner. Check your answers.

2 Grammar

A Write. Complete the story. Use the correct words.

A Problem in Chicago

Tina Foster is visiting Chicago for the first time. While she *was taking* (1. took / was taking) a walk in Lincoln Park early this morning, she ________ (2. lost / was losing) her wallet with all her cash, identification, and credit cards. When she got back to her hotel, she realized that her wallet ________ (3. missed / was missing). She is going to ________ (4. search / searching) the park. If she ________ (5. doesn't find / didn't find) her wallet, she ________ (6. calls / will call) the credit card companies. After she ________ (7. cancels / canceled) her credit cards, she ________ (8. will go / goes) to the nearest police station and file a police report.

B Write. Look at the answers. Write the questions.

1. **A** Who ________________________________?
   B Tina Foster is visiting Chicago for the first time.
2. **A** What ________________________________?
   B Tina was taking a walk when she lost her wallet.
3. **A** Where ________________________________?
   B She will file a police report at the nearest police station.

Talk with a partner. Ask and answer the questions.

3 Pronunciation: unstressed vowel

A **Listen** to the unstressed vowel sounds in these words. They are written in **green**. Many unstressed vowels sound like "uh."

CD2, Track 34

1. up-sét
2. a-bóut
3. fá-mi-ly
4. éx-tra
5. trá-vel
6. po-líce
7. va-cá-tion
8. dán-ge-rous
9. Sa-mán-tha
10. phó-to-graphs

Listen again and repeat.

B **Listen and repeat.** Then underline the unstressed vowels that sound like *uh* in these words.

CD2, Track 35

1. Samantha is upset.
2. Where's the travel agent?
3. The prison is dangerous.
4. It's about seven o'clock.
5. Did you take photographs?
6. Call the police!
7. She'll think about visiting her family.
8. I need a vacation.

Talk with a partner. Compare your answers.

C **Talk** with a partner. Practice the conversations. Pay attention to the unstressed vowel sounds in **green**.

1. **A** There was a lot of excitement at the Community Adult School yesterday!
   B What are you talking about?
   A There was a fire in the kitchen!
   B Did the fire department come?
   A Yes. A student heard the smoke alarm and called 911 right away.

2. **A** Betty is going to Washington next week!
   B Are you serious? Won't that cost a lot?
   A Well, she probably got a cheap ticket.
   B Is she traveling with her family?
   A No. Her husband's going to take care of the children.

D **Write** five questions. Use the words in Exercise 3A. Ask a partner your questions. Remember to pay attention to the unstressed vowel sound.

What makes you get upset?

1. ______________________
2. ______________________
3. ______________________
4. ______________________
5. ______________________

Reading Tip: Look at the title of the article. Make a guess. What are you going to read about?

Finding a Job that Fits Your Personality

"What's the best job for me?" This is a question that Betty Strickland hears again and again. Betty is an employment counselor at a community college in Ohio. She says, "People are often confused about their career choices. Many of them are working, but they are unhappy with their jobs."

To help her clients think about jobs, Betty asks each person to take a personality test – a test that gives a clear picture of one's personality. Sometimes these tests are online. They ask questions about a person's interests and habits. "When people understand their own personality, they can look at jobs that would be a good fit," she explains.

Betty tells the story of Jung Ho, a student who came to her for advice. While in school, he was earning a good salary as a part-time night watchman, but he was unhappy in his job. His personality test revealed that he is very outgoing – he is a natural leader, and he loves to socialize with others. Now Jung Ho is considering jobs such as a restaurant manager or a fitness trainer in a gym.

Betty also remembers Selena, a young woman who came to her for help. She was interested in a medical career, but she couldn't decide what job was best for her. Her test showed that she has an intellectual personality type. She is a thoughtful and analytical person. She prefers to work alone more than in a group. She has recently begun a training program to become a medical technician.

Finally, Ms. Strickland likes to tell about Samantha. Samantha's last job was as a file clerk in a small office, but she was bored. She quit after a few months. She's artistic and loves to sew and paint with bright colors. Her personality test demonstrated that she is extremely creative and imaginative. Samantha got very excited when Ms. Strickland told her that their school offers training programs in fashion design, graphic design, and floral design.

Ms. Strickland advises her clients, "If you want to be happy in your work, it's never too late to find the right job for your personality."

UNIT 1

1 Check your understanding

1. According to Betty Strickland, how are jobs and personalities related?
2. What is Ms. Strickland's job? Where does she work?
3. What are the personality types of Jung Ho, Selena, and Samantha?
4. What jobs are these three people considering now?
5. What advice does Ms. Strickland give about job happiness?

2 Build your vocabulary

A Find the two-word combinations in Column 1 in the paragraphs indicated and underline them. Make a sentence with both words that shows the meaning.

Two-word combinations	My sentence using both words
1. community college, **¶1**	*The college serves the community.*
2. personality test, **¶2**	
3. night watchman, **¶3**	
4. fitness trainer, **¶3**	
5. file clerk, **¶5**	
6. fashion design, **¶5**	

B Find each of the following academic words in the article and underline the sentence.

analytical creative medical revealed

Then, on another piece of paper, copy and complete the chart.

Academic word	Phrase or sentence from article	Part of speech	Dictionary definition	My sentence
analytical	*thoughtful and analytical person*	*adjective*	*logical and scientific*	*A scientist needs to be very analytical.*

3 Talk with a partner

Answer each question with evidence from the reading. Use one of the phrases in the Useful Language box.

1. What question do students always ask Ms. Strickland?
2. What is the purpose of personality tests?
3. Before choosing a job, why is it important to consider personality?

USEFUL LANGUAGE
Phrases to cite evidence:
According to this article, . . .
According to the author, . . .

Objective: CCR Anchor 9: Analyze how two or more texts address similar themes or topics in order to build knowledge or to compare the approaches the authors take.

4 Analyze the texts

Review the following texts to answer the questions below: (1) p. 12, *Your Personality and Your Job*; and (2) p. 136, *Finding a Job that Fits Your Personality*.

1. What is the main idea of both articles?
2. What three personality types do both articles discuss?
3. Which jobs do the two articles list for the three personality types?
4. Choose one of the people Ms. Strickland talks about. Explain how and why that person's goals changed as a result of the personality test.
5. Is the topic of these articles important for your life? Explain your answer.

5 Before you write

Copy and complete the graphic organizer on another piece of paper. Fill it in with (1) the main idea shared by the two articles, (2) the three personality types in the articles, (3) a list of the characteristics of each personality, and (4) an example of the impact of a personality test on a person for each personality type. Use information from Exercises 1–4 and evidence from the two articles. Finally, (5) fill in the conclusion with your answer to question five in Exercise 4.

Main Idea:		
1st Personality Type	**2nd Personality Type**	**3rd Personality Type**
Examples: Jobs for the Personality Types		
Examples: Impact of Personality Test		
Conclusion:		

6 Write

Write one paragraph to explain the connection between personality type and happiness in a job. Use the information from your graphic organizer.

7 After you write

A Check your writing. Did you include all the ideas in your graphic organizer?

B Share your writing with a partner.

a. Take turns. Read your writing to your partner.
b. Read your partner's writing to yourself. Compare it to your partner's graphic organizer.
c. Comment on your partner's writing: Ask one question; share one thing you learned.

Reading Tip: Dots, or bullet points, at the beginning of sentences introduce a list of ideas or examples. Look at the title and bullet points in the article. Make a guess. What are you going to learn about in this article? Read and see if you are right.

How to Be a Good Listener

Listening is an important skill, but for many students, it is the most difficult part of learning English. "People talk too fast!" says Marisol Ruiz, a student at Wilmont Community College. "When I don't understand a word, I feel discouraged and I stop listening."

There are actually two different kinds of listening. Each kind of listening has different strategies you can use to understand English.

Interactive listening is the first kind. In interactive listening, you speak to someone, and then you listen and respond to that person. Conversations and group discussions are examples of interactive listening.

Here are some strategies for improving your interactive listening skills.

- **Ask for help.** Say, "Please speak more slowly," or ask, "Excuse me. What did you say?"
- **Check the information.** If you think you haven't understood, repeat what you heard. Use your own words.
- **Make sure you're listening.** Don't think about what you're going to say next.

The second kind of listening is noninteractive. With noninteractive listening, you listen, but you don't speak. Watching movies and listening to music are examples of noninteractive listening. "I have lived in the United States for two years, and for me, watching movies or listening to the news on the radio is very difficult," Ahmed Omran says. "I can't ask questions about the things that I don't understand."

The following strategies can help improve your noninteractive listening skills.

- **Use what you know.** Think about the subject and try to think of the words you will hear in advance. For example, when you watch TV, a weather reporter might use the words rainy or sunny. Listen for those words.
- **Just listen.** Concentrate on listening. Be an active listener. Don't eat lunch or do other things while you're listening.
- **Don't stop listening.** Even if you don't understand something, keep on listening. You can make guesses and listen to other important information.

If you do all these things, not only will you become a better listener, your speaking skills will improve, too!

1 Check your understanding

1. What is the main idea of the article?
2. According to the article, what are the two kinds of listening?
3. What does the author say is the difference between the two kinds of listening?
4. What three strategies does the article identify for each kind of listening?
5. What is the author's opinion about listening as a skill in learning English?

2 Build your vocabulary

A Find the words in Column 1 in the paragraphs indicated and underline them. Next, use the context to decide the part of speech of each word (noun or verb) and write it in the chart. Then circle the best definition to match the part of speech.

Word	Part of speech	Definition
1. part, **¶1**	*noun*	a. to separate b. a piece of something, not all of it
2. use, **¶2**		a. to make useful b. purpose
3. check, **¶4**		a. to look at something to decide if it is correct b. a printed form you can use instead of money to make payments from your bank account
4. help, **¶4**		a. to make easier for someone to do something b. something that makes things easier
5. watch, **¶6**		a. to look at something for a period of time b. a small clock that you wear on your wrist
6. guesses, **¶6**		a. to give an answer that you think is right b. answers that you think are right, but you're not sure

B Find each of the following academic words in the article and underline the sentence.

concentrate interactive respond strategies

Then, on another piece of paper, copy and complete the chart.

Academic word	Phrase or sentence from article	Part of speech	Dictionary definition	My sentence
concentrate	*concentrate on listening*	*verb*	*to think hard about something*	*When I watch TV while studying I can't concentrate.*

3 Talk with a partner

Answer each question with evidence from the reading. Use one of the phrases in the Useful Language box.

USEFUL LANGUAGE
Phrases to cite evidence:
The author points out that . . .
The article points out that . . .

1. How can you ask for help when doing interactive listening?
2. What is an example of noninteractive listening?
3. If you practice these strategies for improving listening, what other skill will you improve?

Objective: CCR Anchor 9: Analyze how two or more texts address similar themes or topics in order to build knowledge or to compare the approaches the authors take.

4 Analyze the texts

Review the following texts to answer the questions below: (1) p. 24, *Strategies for Learning English*; and (2) p. 139, *How to Be a Good Listener*.

1. How are the topics of the two articles similar? Give examples from both articles to support your choice.
2. Strategy #3 in *Strategies for Learning English* is to guess. Which strategy is it most similar to in *How to Be a Good Listener?*
3. Identify a strategy that one article discusses and the other article does not discuss.
4. Read the last paragraph of both articles. How are the conclusions in each similar?
5. Choose one of the strategies that you have used in the past. How was it helpful or not helpful?

5 Before you write

Copy and complete the graphic organizer on another piece of paper. Fill it in with (1) the topic that the two articles share, (2) two examples of how the articles are the same, and (3) two examples of how they are different. Use information from Exercises 1–4 and evidence from the two articles. Finally, (4) use your answer to question five in Exercise 4 to fill in the conclusion.

Topic:	
Strategies for Learning English	***How to Be a Good Listener***
HOW THE SAME?	
HOW DIFFERENT?	
Conclusion:	

6 Write

Write one paragraph to explain the connection between personality type and happiness in a job. Use the information from your graphic organizer.

7 After you write

A Check your writing. Did you include all the ideas in your graphic organizer?

B Share your writing with a partner.

a. Take turns. Read your writing to your partner.
b. Read your partner's writing to yourself. Compare it to your partner's graphic organizer.
c. Comment on your partner's writing: Ask one question; share one thing you learned.

Reading Tip: Look at the first sentence of each paragraph. Make a guess. What are the main ideas? What is the article about? Read and find out.

Meet Your Neighbors at a Block Party!

by Cari Delacruz

Two years ago, I didn't know my neighbors at all. Today, my neighbors are my best friends. Everything changed because of our first block party.

A block party is a big outdoor party for people in the same neighborhood. Neighbors get together in front of their houses. They don't have to watch out for traffic because they ask the police to block off the street, and no cars can drive on it. People fill the street with tables and chairs instead. There are games for children and music and dancing for adults. There is also a potluck meal – each family brings some kind of food for everyone to share.

Two months before our first party, my neighbors came over because we wanted to set a date and identify volunteers for different jobs. One neighbor volunteered to find a band. Another neighbor agreed to get soda and ice cream. We planned games for the children. We also made invitations and distributed them to all of the families on our block.

We were worried about the weather, but the day of our party was warm and sunny. At 4:00, we closed the street. We started with a talent show, where people sang, did interesting tricks, played music, and told funny stories. One boy hit a soccer ball with his head 20 times! The show lasted two hours. The street was noisy, but no one complained because everyone had a lot of fun. We all wore name tags so we could learn everyone's name. We ate dinner together and enjoyed talking with our neighbors. After lots of dancing, the party ended at around 10:00.

Because of the block party, our street is friendlier and safer. We've created the Locust Avenue Neighborhood Association. My neighbors and I meet once a month and talk about how we can improve our neighborhood. And we've already started planning a bigger and better block party for next year!

1 Check your understanding

1. What is the main idea of the article?
2. According to the article, why don't people have to watch out for traffic at a block party?
3. What are two of the jobs the volunteers did to organize the block party?
4. What did neighbors do to learn each other's names?
5. According to the author, what were three positive results of the block party?

2 Build your vocabulary

A Find the two-word combinations in Column 1 in the paragraphs indicated and underline them. Make a sentence with both words that shows the meaning.

Two-word combinations	My sentence using both words
1. block party, **¶2**	*A block party is a party for people who live in the same block or neighborhood.*
2. block off, **¶2**	
3. potluck meal, **¶2**	
4. talent show, **¶4**	
5. name tags, **¶4**	
6. neighborhood association, **¶5**	

B Find each of the following academic words in the article and underline the sentence.

created distributed identify volunteered

Then, on another piece of paper, copy and complete the chart.

Academic word	Phrase or sentence from article	Part of speech	Dictionary definition	My sentence
created	*We've created the Locust Avenue Neighborhood Association . . .*	*verb*	*to originate or make*	*I created a presentation on the computer.*

3 Talk with a partner

Answer each question with evidence from the reading.
Use one of the phrases in the Useful Language box.

1. What is a block party?
2. What three things did the neighbors do to organize the block party?
3. What happened in the talent show?

USEFUL LANGUAGE
Phrases to cite evidence:
The article states that . . .
The author states that . . .

Objective: CCR Anchor 9: Analyze how two or more texts address similar themes or topics in order to build knowledge or to compare the approaches the authors take.

4 Analyze the texts

Review the following texts to answer the questions below: (1) p. 38, *Neighborhood Watch Success Story*; and (2) p. 142, *Meet Your Neighbors at a Block Party!*

1. In general, how are the topics of the two articles similar?
2. Describe how both neighborhood watch programs and block parties help neighbors to get to know each other.
3. Both articles describe volunteers. Compare the activities of volunteers in the neighborhood watch program and the block party.
4. How is the purpose of the activities in each article different?
5. To get to know your neighbors better, which of these activities would you like to try? Is there another activity not described that you would suggest? If so, describe it.

5 Before you write

Copy and complete the graphic organizer on another piece of paper. For each article, fill in (1) the topic that the two articles share, (2) the purpose of each article, and (3) examples of activities. Use information from Exercises 1–4 and evidence from the two articles. Finally, (4) use your answer to question five in Exercise 4 to fill in the conclusion.

Topic:		
	Neighborhood Watch Success Story	***Meet Your Neighbors at a Block Party!***
Purpose		
Example of activities		
Conclusion:		

6 Write

Write one paragraph that describes two or more solutions to help neighbors get to know each other. Use the information from your graphic organizer.

7 After you write

A Check your writing. Did you include all the ideas in your graphic organizer?

B Share your writing with a partner.

a. Take turns. Read your writing to your partner.
b. Read your partner's writing to yourself. Compare it to your partner's graphic organizer.
c. Comment on your partner's writing: Ask one question; share one thing you learned.

Reading Tip: Look at the first paragraph. Then look at the last paragraph. What is the main idea of this article? Think about the main idea as you read.

Medicine from Your Kitchen

A cold is probably the most common health problem in the world. Most people have one or two colds a year. When you have a cold, you often have a cough and a sore throat. You cannot breathe, your nose is congested, and you might have a fever. Although there is no cure for a cold, there are things you can do to feel better. Some people take medication. Other people use home remedies.

Home remedies are ways to treat an illness with foods and other items found at home. People may use them instead of going to the doctor or buying medication.

Here are some home remedies for colds that my grandmother always uses. My grandmother used to say, "Feed a cold. Starve a fever." This is an old idea. It means you should eat a lot if you have a cold, but you should not eat much if you have a fever. She thinks that chicken soup and toast are the best foods to eat when you have a cold. However, she says you should never have cheese or other milk products. They can aggravate a cold.

My grandmother also gives this advice: Drink a lot of liquids. She recommends that you consume up to eight glasses of water or juice a day and take vitamin C. She also says that hot water with lemon and honey can help you breathe more easily if you are congested and that a spoonful of red pepper in a glass of water will reduce a fever. If you have a cough, she thinks you should cook onions and put them on your chest while they are still warm.

Do these home remedies really help people recover? Some doctors say "yes," and other doctors say "no." But people have used them for hundreds of years to feel better when they have a cold, so it probably doesn't hurt to try.

1 Check your understanding

1. Look at the reading tip again. Restate the main idea of the article in your own words.
2. In your own words, explain the meaning of the expression *Feed a cold. Starve a fever.*
3. What home remedy does the author's grandmother suggest to reduce a fever?
4. In the fourth paragraph, what word does the author use that means the same as *drink*?
5. What does the author say doctors think of home remedies?

2 Build your vocabulary

A Find the words in Column 1 in the paragraphs indicated and underline them. For each, identify a clue to meaning. Then complete the chart.

Word	Clue to meaning	Guess	My sentence
1. common, ¶1	*Most people have . . .*	*shared by many people*	*Colds are common in the winter.*
2. congested, ¶1			
3. cure, ¶1			
4. starve, ¶3			
5. aggravate, ¶3			
6. reduce, ¶4			

B Find each of the following academic words in the article and underline the sentence.

consume found items recover

Then, on another piece of paper, copy and complete the chart.

Academic word	Phrase or sentence from article	Part of speech	Dictionary definition	My sentence
consume	*consume up to eight glasses*	*verb*	*to eat or drink*	*Don't consume milk products when you have a cold.*

3 Talk with a partner

Answer each question with evidence from the reading. Use one of the phrases in the Useful Language box.

1. Do home remedies help people get better?
2. Should people not eat when they have a fever?
3. Does drinking lots of water help people get better?

USEFUL LANGUAGE
Phrases to support an opinion:
I believe that . . . because . .
I think that . . . because . . .

Objective: CCR Anchor 9: Analyze how two or more texts address similar themes or topics in order to build knowledge or to compare the approaches the authors take.

4 Analyze the texts

Review the following texts to answer the questions below: (1) p. 50, *Two Beneficial Plants*; and (2) p. 145, *Medicine from Your Kitchen*.

1. What is the topic of the two articles?
2. Both articles describe remedies for colds. Describe one remedy from each article.
3. Both articles describe remedies for coughs. Describe one remedy from each article.
4. Both articles describe remedies for flu or fevers. Describe one remedy from each article.
5. Choose one of these remedies that you have tried or would like to try. Explain why you chose it.

5 Before you write

Copy and complete the graphic organizer on another piece of paper. Fill it in with (1) the topic that the two articles share, and (2) two examples for each key point. Use information from Exercises 1–4 and evidence from the two articles. Finally, (3) use your answer to question five in Exercise 4 to fill in the conclusion.

Topic:		
Remedies for Colds	**Remedies for Coughs**	**Remedies for Flu or Fever**
Examples	**Examples**	**Examples**
Conclusion:		

6 Write

Write one paragraph that explains how home remedies and plants may help some people feel better when they are sick. Use the information from your graphic organizer.

7 After you write

A Check your writing. Did you include all the ideas in your graphic organizer?

B Share your writing with a partner.

a. Take turns. Read your writing to your partner.
b. Read your partner's writing to yourself. Compare it to your partner's graphic organizer.
c. Comment on your partner's writing: Ask one question; share one thing you learned.

Reading Tip: Look at the bold words in the flyer. Make a guess. What do you think this flyer is about? Read and find out.

Summer Festival at Lakeshore Park

Thursday, July 1–Sunday, July 4
10:00 a.m.–10:00 p.m.

There's something for everyone each day of the Lakeshore Park Summer Festival, so come early and bring your whole family!

Fun Fair

Try all the exciting rides! Only $1.00 each.

Outdoor Food Court

Eat delicious dishes from local ethnic restaurants for $4.00 to $6.00. Hot dogs for only $1.00!

Art Exhibit

See unique paintings, photos, and pottery from local artists.

International Film Festival

Enjoy five films from a different country each day. For the price of one daily movie pass, watch one movie – or all five! Movies start at 2:00 p.m. and end by 10:00 p.m. Check our Web site for the movie list. **Admission: $8.00.**

See the daily schedule below.

Thursday, July 1	**Mexico**
Friday, July 2	**China**
Saturday, July 3	**India**
Sunday, July 4	**U.S.A.**

Sounds of the City

Hear superb musicians on three outdoor stages every evening from 7:00 p.m. to 10:30 p.m. The Rock Stage has the best young bands from all over the city. The International Stage has new sounds from around the world. The Golden Songs Stage has the great music you remember from the 1960s and 1970s. **Admission: $3.00.**

Crafts Tent

Bring your kids here for fun with art every day at 4:30 p.m. Draw, paint, and make fun paper toys. For ages 4 to 10. Parents must stay with their children. **Admission: free.**

Special Events

Friday, 7:30 p.m.
Salsa Dance Contest
Show us your best dance steps and win great prizes – cash, gift certificates for local restaurants, and salsa CDs.

Saturday, 8:00 p.m.
Outdoor Concert by the City Youth Choir
More than 100 remarkable young voices sing together in a performance you'll never forget.

Sunday, 9:00 p.m.
Independence Day Fireworks Show
Bring a blanket or a chair to sit on.

1 Check your understanding

1. What is the flyer for? When is it?
2. Your friend likes movies. Which activity do you recommend?
3. How many stages are there and which kind of music can you hear at each one?
4. In your opinion, which activities would children probably like to attend?
5. According to the author, who is the festival for?

2 Build your vocabulary

A For each activity listed, find a positive word that describes it. Then complete the chart with that word and the word it describes.

Activity	Positive adjective	Word it describes
Art Exhibit	*Unique*	*paintings, photos, pottery*
Crafts Tent		
Fun Fair		
Outdoor Concert by the City Youth Choir		
Outdoor Food Court		
Salsa Dance Concert		
Sounds of the City		

B Find each of the following academic words in the article and underline the sentence.

ethnic exhibit schedule site

Then, on another piece of paper, copy and complete the chart.

Academic word	Phrase or sentence from article	Part of speech	Dictionary definition	My sentence
ethnic	*dishes from local ethnic restaurants*	*adjective*	*related to group characteristics, such as race or culture*	*My favorite ethnic food is Chinese.*

3 Talk with a partner

Answer each question with evidence from the reading. Use one of the phrases in the Useful Language box.

USEFUL LANGUAGE
Phrases to support an opinion:
I believe that . . . because . . .
I think that . . . because . . .

1. Would children like the crafts tent?
2. Which event would a competitive person like? What are some of the prizes for the winner?
3. Which outdoor stage would people in their 50s probably enjoy?

Objective: CCR Anchor 9: Analyze how two or more texts address similar themes or topics in order to build knowledge or to compare the approaches the authors take.

4 Analyze the texts

Review the following texts to answer the questions below: (1) p. 64, *Salsa Starz*; and (2) p. 148, *Summer Festival at Lakeshore Park*.

1. How are the topics of the two articles similar?
2. In which season do the activities occur? Why do you think they are held then?
3. Who probably goes to the concerts at Century Park? Who probably goes to the Summer Festival at Lakeshore Park? Why do you think that?
4. What unexpected thing happened in Salsa Starz that caused the concert to end early? If that happens at Summer Festival at Lakeshore Park, which activities would have to be canceled?
5. Which of the two events – the Salsa Starz concert or the Summer Festival – would you rather attend? Provide examples from both articles to support your choices.

5 Before you write

Copy and complete the graphic organizer on another piece of paper. Fill it in with (1) the topic, (2) the event names, (3) three reasons for choosing one event, and (4) three reasons for not choosing the other event. Use information from Exercises 1–4 and evidence from the two articles. Finally, (5) use your answer from question five in Exercise 4 to fill in the conclusion.

Topic:	
Where I want to go	**Where I don't want to go**
Reasons	
What I like	**What I don't like**
Conclusion:	

6 Write

Write one paragraph that explains which of two events – the Salsa Starz concert or the Summer Festival at Lakeshore Park – you would prefer to go to. Give three examples of why you chose this event rather than the other one. Use information from your graphic organizer.

7 After you write

A Check your writing. Did you include all the ideas in your graphic organizer?

B Share your writing with a partner.

a. Take turns. Read your writing to your partner.
b. Read your partner's writing to yourself. Compare it to your partner's graphic organizer.
c. Comment on your partner's writing: Ask one question; share one thing you learned.

Reading Tip: Read the first and last paragraphs of the article. Who is the article about? What is the main idea?

Time Rules Can Be Confusing

Worldwide, just as there are many different cultures, there are many different expectations about time rules. When people come from different countries to study in the United States, they often feel confused – or lack understanding – because of differences in time rules in their countries and the United States. Each paragraph below highlights an experience that a student from another country had while studying in the United States.

Rafael Silva, from Brazil. Rafael came to the the US for a summer English program. In the beginning, he was lonely because he didn't have any friends.When David, his English tutor, invited him to a party, he was very excited because he hoped to make new friends. David told him the party started at 6 p.m. and there would be food. When Rafael arrived at around 8 p.m., he was shocked. There were only a few people and there was no food. David told Rafael he was late. He explained that the party started at 6 p.m., everyone ate, and then went to another party.

Lailani Ocampo, from the Philippines. A very good student in her native country, Lailani decided to continue her medical studies in the United States. Because she was an excellent and diligent student, her instructor was very surprised that Lailani wasn't in class for the final exam. The instructor thought she must be very sick. Her instructor was even more surprised to learn why Lailani had missed the end-of-semester test – her grandmother recently arrived from the Philippines, so she spent the day with her grandmother. Then it was Lailani's turn to be surprised – she needed to retake the class because the instructor failed her.

Bao Wong, from China. Interested in engineering, Bao applied for a part-time job at an engineering firm. His interview was scheduled for 8:15 a.m. Bao arrived at 7:45 a.m.. He was stunned that the office didn't even open until 8:00. In his country, people not only arrive early for appointments, they also try to finish any business before the appointment "so as not to waste anyone's time." There was no conversation before the interview and the interview began promptly at 8:15, so he did not expect to get the job. Bao was astonished when the company offered it to him.

Rafael, Lailani and Bao come from different countries, but each believes that differences in expectations in time issues between the United States and their own country can result in confusion.

UNIT 6

1 Check your understanding

1. What is the main idea of the article?
2. Did Rafael meet a lot of new people at the party? How do you know?
3. Did the instructor say that it was all right for Lailani to miss the final exam? What sentence in the article answers this question?
4. Why did Bao think he wouldn't get the part-time job? Restate the reason in your own words.
5. Read the last paragraph. Why do you think the author wrote this article?

2 Build your vocabulary

A Find and underline in the article each word listed on the chart. Which words are positive? Which words are negative? What clues helped you guess?

Word	Positive	Negative	Clue
1. confused, ¶1		✓	*Lack understanding because of differences*
2. excited, ¶2			
3. shocked, ¶2			
4. diligent, ¶3			
5. stunned, ¶4			
6. astonished, ¶4			

B Find each of the following academic words in the article and underline the sentence.

highlight medical scheduled issues

Then, on another piece of paper, copy and complete the chart.

Academic word	Phrase or sentence from article	Part of speech	Dictionary definition	My sentence
highlight	*Each paragraph below highlights an experience that a student from another country had while studying in the United States.*	*verb*	*emphasize something*	*I want to highlight the differences between my country and the United states.*

3 Talk with a partner

Answer each question with evidence from the reading. Use one of the phrases in the Useful Language box.

1. Describe a misunderstanding in a social situation.
2. Describe a misunderstanding in a class situation.
3. Describe a misunderstanding in a business situation.

USEFUL LANGUAGE
Phrases to cite an example:
An example from the article is . . .
An example the author gave is . . .

Objective: CCR Anchor 9: Analyze how two or more texts address similar themes or topics in order to build knowledge or to compare the approaches the authors take.

4 Analyze the texts

Review the following articles to answer the questions below: (1) p. 76, *Rules about Time*; and (2) p. 151, *Time Rules Can Be Confusing*.

1. What is the main idea of both articles?
2. What is the United States time rule about business meetings and personal appointments? Why was Bao confused?
3. What is the United States time rule about social events? Why was Rafael confused?
4. What is the United States time rule about scheduled classes or appointments? Why was Lailani confused?
5. Do you think time rules in the United States are confusing? Why or why not? Use evidence from both articles to support your answer.

5 Before you write

Copy and complete the graphic organizer on another piece of paper. Fill it in with (1) the main idea shared by the articles, (2) the three time rules from the article *Rules about Time,* and (3) for each rule, an example from the article *Time Rules Can Be Confusing* of how that rule caused confusion. Use information from Exercises 1–4 and evidence from the two articles. Finally, (4) use your answer to question five in Exercise 4 to fill in the conclusion.

Main Idea:		
Time Rule 1	**Time Rule 2**	**Time Rule 3**
Example	**Example**	**Example**
Conclusion:		

6 Write

Write one paragraph to explain how some time rules in the United States may cause problems for students from different countries. Use the information from your graphic organizer.

7 After you write

A Check your writing. Did you include all the ideas in your graphic organizer?

B Share your writing with a partner.

a. Take turns. Read your writing to your partner.
b. Read your partner's writing to yourself. Compare it to your partner's graphic organizer.
c. Comment on your partner's writing: Ask one question; share one thing you learned.

Reading Tip: Words like *first, second,* and *finally* often introduce the order in which you should do something. Look for those words in the article. Think about them as you read.

A Penny Saved Is a Penny Earned

Susan has a great job as a nursing assistant, but she has a problem. She is thinking about buying a used car; however, she doesn't have any money in a savings account, and she is afraid of getting into a lot of debt. She doesn't spend much on expensive clothes or entertainment, but she never seems to have enough money.

"I worry about paying my bills," Susan says. "I use my credit card a lot, and I usually make only the minimum payment. Unfortunately, my credit card has a high interest rate. What can I do?"

Many people have the same problem. The solution is simple. Susan needs a personal budget – a plan for spending her money. Making a budget is not difficult. All it takes is three easy steps. Here is financial advice for people like Susan.

First, you should make a list of all your daily expenses for one month. Keep a piece of paper in your wallet, and write down everything you buy. Don't forget incidental expenses, like a cup of coffee or a magazine.

Second, at the end of the month, you should look at your expenses. Combine them into categories, or groups, such as clothing and entertainment. Then, write down your other expenses – monthly bills like rent and electricity. Add up the numbers. What's the total amount you spent last month? It may surprise you.

Finally, think about adjusting your spending habits, especially if you want to save for something special. You should look at your major expenses first. For example, maybe one of your largest expenses is $200 a month for food. Try changing your shopping habits so that you save $10 a month on grocery bills. You should also look at the small things that you buy every day. "Every afternoon at work, I buy a $3 snack, such as a cupcake or muffin," says Susan. "If I bring a snack from home, I can save $60 every month and use that money to buy a car sooner."

When you make a budget and follow it carefully, you will have more money for the important things in your life. After all, a penny saved is a penny earned.

1 Check your understanding

1. What is the main idea of the article?
2. What is Susan worried about? Why?
3. What are two problems Susan has with her credit card?
4. The author gives threes steps for making a budget. What are they?
5. What is the author's opinion about making a budget?

2 Build your vocabulary

A Find the words in Column 1 in the paragraphs indicated and underline them. For each, identify a clue to its meaning. Then complete the chart.

Word	Clue to meaning	Dictionary definition
1. budget, **¶3**	*a plan for spending her money*	*a financial plan*
2. list, **¶4**		
3. incidental, **¶4**		
4. categories, **¶5**		
5. add up, **¶5**		
6. snack, **¶6**		

B Find each of the following academic words in the article and underline the sentence.

adjust credit major minimum

Then, on another piece of paper, copy and complete the chart.

Academic word	Phrase or sentence from article	Part of speech	Dictionary definition	My sentence
adjust	*think about adjusting your spending habits*	*verb*	*Change*	*Maybe you can adjust your work schedule.*

3 Talk with a partner

Answer each question with evidence from the reading. Use one of the phrases in the Useful Language box.

1. What is Susan afraid of?
2. How can people adjust their spending habits?
3. What happens when you make a budget and follow it carefully?

USEFUL LANGUAGE
Phrases to cite evidence:
The author points out that . . .
The article points out that . . .

Objective: CCR Anchor 9: Analyze how two or more texts address similar themes or topics in order to build knowledge or to compare the approaches the authors take.

4 Analyze the texts

Review the following texts to answer the questions below: (1) p. 90, *A Credit Card Nightmare*; and (2) p. 154, *A Penny Saved Is a Penny Earned*.

1. What is the topic that the two articles share?
2. How are the financial problems discussed in the two articles similar?
3. How are the financial problems discussed in the two articles different?
4. Both articles give several solutions to financial problems. Name two from each article.
5. Select the solution you think is most important and explain why or suggest another solution and explain why it is important, too.

5 Before you write

Copy and complete the graphic organizer on another piece of paper. Fill it in with (1) the topic that the two articles share, (2) three financial problems from each article, and (3) three financial solutions from each article. Use information from Exercises 1–4 and evidence from the two articles. Finally, (4) use your answer to question five in Exercise 4 to fill in the conclusion.

Topic:		
	A Credit Card Nightmare	***A Penny Saved is a Penny Earned***
Financial Problems		
Financial Solutions		
Conclusion:		

6 Write

Write one paragraph that identifies problems and solutions for people with financial problems. Use the information from your graphic organizer.

7 After you write

A Check your writing. Did you include all the ideas in your graphic organizer?

B Share your writing with a partner.

a. Take turns. Read your writing to your partner.
b. Read your partner's writing to yourself. Compare it to your partner's graphic organizer.
c. Comment on your partner's writing: Ask one question; share one thing you learned.

Reading Tip: Look at the title. Then read the first sentence in each paragraph. What are the three key points? Read to find out more about each.

How I Got My Job

The interview is the most critical step in getting a job – and the most difficult. Here are some interview tips from people who have succeeded in their job search.

Grace Huang, sales assistant

"I think it's really important to make a good first impression. Remember, interviewers talk to a lot of people; you want them to remember you in a positive way! You should always be on time for your appointment. Arrive early, and greet the interviewer with a firm handshake and a smile. At the end of the interview, shake hands again and thank your interviewer. I always send a thank-you letter after each interview. On my first day at work, my new boss said that I was the only applicant who sent a letter!"

Tomas Martinez, computer technician

"You need to prepare before you go to an interview. I always try to research something about each company and prepare questions to ask the interviewer. When you ask questions about the company and the job, it indicates that you're really interested. Before I started my interviews, I practiced with a friend. He asked me questions and helped me prepare to talk about my work experience and my background. I also filled out job applications for practice."

Sita Pillai, office manager

"I think the most important factor is the way you speak. I try to be enthusiastic and positive about the job and to speak with confidence. You should never answer a question with just 'yes' or 'no.' Explain all of your answers! This will help the interviewer to know about your strengths. And here's one more tip. English isn't my native language, and I sometimes talk too fast when I'm nervous. If the interviewer has problems understanding you, speak more slowly."

1 Check your understanding

1. What is the main idea of the article?
2. What did Grace Huang do that made her stand out as an applicant?
3. According to Sita Pillai, why is it important to explain your answers at an interview rather than answer with just *yes* or *no*?
4 What does Tomas Martinez do before an interview to show the interviewer that he's interested in the job?
5. In the fourth paragraph, what word does the author use that means the same as *positive qualities*?

2 Build your vocabulary

A Find the words in Column 1 in the paragraphs indicated, underline them, and identify the part of speech. Many words have more than one definition. Look up the words in a dictionary and complete the chart with the definition that best fits the article.

Word	Part of speech	Definition
1. interview, **¶1**	*noun*	*A formal meeting in which a person who is interested in getting a job is asked questions.*
2. impression, **¶2**		
3. positive, **¶2**		
4. experience, **¶3**		
5. enthusiastic, **¶4**		
6. native, **¶4**		

B Find each of the following academic words in the article and underline the sentence.

assistant factor indicates research

Then, on another piece of paper, copy and complete the chart.

Academic word	Phrase or sentence from article	Part of speech	Dictionary definition	My sentence
assistant	*Grace Huang, sales assistant*	*noun*	*a person who helps another at work*	*The assistant manager works directly under the manager.*

3 Talk with a partner

Answer each question with evidence from the reading.
Use one of the phrases in the Useful Language box.

USEFUL LANGUAGE
Phrases to cite evidence:
Some examples from the article are …
A few examples from the article are …

1. What are two ways to make a good impression at an interview?
2. What are two ways to prepare before an interview?
3. What are three things you can you do about the way you speak during an interview?

Objective: CCR Anchor 9: Analyze how two or more texts address similar themes or topics in order to build knowledge or to compare the approaches the authors take.

4 Analyze the texts

Review the following texts to answer the questions below: (1) p.102, *Eden's Blog*; and (2) p. 157, *How I Got My Job*.

1. What is the topic shared by the two articles?
2. Both articles say it is important to practice before an interview. Describe one way to practice from each article.
3. Both articles describe how to make a good first impression. What's one strategy from each article?
4. Both articles discuss how to prepare for the interview. What did each article say about that?
5. In your opinion, which of the three interview tips is the most important? Explain your reason for choosing it.

5 Before you write

Copy and complete the graphic organizer on another piece of paper. Fill it in with (1) the topic shared by the articles, and (2) two examples for each key point. Use information from Exercises 1–4 and evidence from the two articles. Finally, (3) use your answer to question five in Exercise 4 to fill in a conclusion.

Topic:		
Make a Good First Impression	**Preparing**	**Speaking**
Examples 1:	**Examples 1:**	**Examples 1:**
Examples 2:	**Examples 2:**	**Examples 2:**
Conclusion:		

6 Write

Write one paragraph that explains three keys to a successful job interview. Use the information from your graphic organizer.

7 After you write

A Check your writing. Did you include all the ideas in your graphic organizer?

B Share your writing with a partner.

a. Take turns. Read your writing to your partner.
b. Read your partner's writing to yourself. Compare it to your partner's graphic organizer.
c. Comment on your partner's writing: Ask one question; share one thing you learned.

Reading Tip: Read the title. Skim the first paragraph. Skim the last paragraph. Why is the title *Meals and Smiles*?

Meals and Smiles

Barbara Watson is 73 years old and lives alone. Barbara had an operation a few months ago. When she came home from the hospital, she couldn't walk or drive a car. Buying food and cooking meals were very challenging for her. Then a friend told Barbara about Meals on Wheels. Now Barbara has a hot lunch delivered to her house every day. She has a sandwich and salad delivered for dinner, too.

Meals on Wheels is an organization of volunteers. Every day, they provide meals to people over the age of 60 who cannot cook or shop for themselves. Gordon Chen has been delivering meals to senior citizens for more than four years. Every Tuesday at 11:00 a.m., he picks up the food at the kitchen of a local school and delivers it to 10 different men and women around town.

"I love visiting with these people," says Gordon. "Sometimes they don't have any other visitors all day."

"I'm always happy to see Gordon and the other volunteers," says Barbara. "They help me more than any medicine!"

Meals on Wheels started in England in the 1940s and then moved to other countries. The program ensures that senior citizens eat more nutritious food by using fresh ingredients. Seniors pay a small amount for each meal, or meals are free for those with low incomes.

Many different kinds of people volunteer for Meals on Wheels. Teenagers, college students, neighborhood groups, and even some retired people help to prepare the meals. Once the meals are ready, nearly half a million people deliver more than a million meals to seniors in the United States every day.

And these volunteers do much more than transport meals. "While I was volunteering, I also checked the safety and health of these senior citizens," says a former volunteer. When volunteers notice a problem, they call for help. And most importantly, with every meal, they deliver a smile.

1 Check your understanding

1. Read the reading tip again. How did the first and last paragraphs explain the title?
2. What are three ways that volunteers for Meals on Wheels help senior citizens?
3. How much do seniors pay for Meals on Wheels?
4. Is there a big need for Meals on Wheels? How do you know?
5. Aside from bringing meals, what does the author see as the most important service that volunteers provide?

2 Build your vocabulary

A Find the words in Column 1 in the paragraphs indicated and underline them. Then complete the chart by selecting one meaning for each word and identifying the clue in the article that guided your choice.

Word	Meaning		Clue
1. organization, ¶2	(a.) people	b. things	volunteers
2. provide, ¶2	a. give	b. take	
3. nutritious, ¶5	a. unhealthy	b. healthy	
4. prepare, ¶6	a. make	b. eat	
5. former, ¶7	a. still	b. no longer	
6. notice, ¶7	a. see	b. write about	

B Find each of the following academic words in the article and underline the sentence.

challenging ensure incomes transport

Then, on another piece of paper, copy and complete the chart.

Academic word	Phrase or sentence from article	Part of speech	Dictionary definition	My sentence
incomes	*Seniors pay a small amount for each meal, or meals are free for those with low incomes.*	*noun*	*the amount of money received over a period of time*	*Many people have low incomes*

3 Talk with a partner

Answer each question with evidence from the reading. Use one of the phrases in the Useful Language box.

1. Who does Meals on Wheels provide meals to?
2. In the United States, how many meals does Meals on Wheels provide to seniors daily?
3. In addition to delivering meals, what is another thing volunteers may do?

USEFUL LANGUAGE
Phrases to cite evidence:
According to this article, . . .
According to the author, . . .

Objective: CCR Anchor 9: Analyze how two or more texts address similar themes or topics in order to build knowledge or to compare the approaches the authors take.

4 Analyze the texts

Review the following texts to answer the questions below: (1) p. 116. *Home is More Than a Building*; and (2) p. 160, *Meals and Smiles*.

1. What is the main idea of both articles?
2. Both articles describe problems that people have. Describe one problem from each article.
3. Both articles describe how friends, families or volunteers help people with problems. Describe two examples from each article.
4. Both articles describe the types of people that volunteered or helped out. How are they similar or different?
5. In your opinion, what is the most important thing that friends, families or volunteers can do to help people who have problems? Use examples from the article to support your answer.

5 Before you write

Copy and complete the graphic organizer on another piece of paper. Fill it in with: (1) the main idea shared by the two articles, (2) the problem that each article identifies, and (3) for each problem, who helped and what they did. Use information from Exercises 1–4 and evidence from the articles. Finally, (4) use your answer to question five in Exercise 4 to fill in the conclusion.

Main Idea:	
Home is More Than a Building	***Meals and Smiles***
Problem	
Who helped	
What they did	
Conclusion:	

6 Write

Write a one-paragraph summary of the two articles. Use the information from your graphic organizer.

7 After you write

A Check your writing. Did you include all the ideas in your graphic organizer?

B Share your writing with a partner.

a. Take turns. Read your writing to your partner.
b. Read your partner's writing to yourself. Compare it to your partner's graphic organizer.
c. Comment on your partner's writing: Ask one question; share one thing you learned.

Reading Tip: Look at the title and the bold face headings. Make a guess. Who is the article about? What will you learn about him? Read and find out.

The Flower Man of Houston, Texas

A folk artist is an artist with little or no formal art education. A folk artist has a story to tell, which he tells in his art. He shows through his art the culture of the people – the folk – he knows best.

Who is the Flower Man?

Cleveland Turner is a well-known folk artist in Houston, Texas. His nickname is the "Flower Man" because he lives in a very unusual house. Cleveland's house is bright yellow, but if you decide to visit this popular tourist attraction, you might not notice the color at all. That's because Cleveland has decorated his entire house with artificial and real flowers. There are also dolls, paintings, tools, household appliances, and more covering his house. There's a red ceramic cow on the roof and art on the gate and on the fence around the yard. The yard itself is filled with unusual objects: old street signs, plastic plants, musical instruments, another red cow, and every kind of junk you can think of.

How did this happen?

In 1983, Cleveland was sick, homeless, living on the streets, and sleeping under bridges. A woman found him and took him to a hospital for help. While he was in the hospital, he had a dream. He saw beautiful, colorful flowers and junk flying around him. When he woke up, he decided to build a "dream" house with colorful things, like the flowers and objects in his dream.

The Flower Man's house is an ongoing project. It's always changing. Sometimes visitors, especially children, will take something away from the house. Sometimes visitors bring things for the house. But Cleveland says he prefers finding things himself. So, every day he rides his Flowercycle – his bicycle and his only form of transportation – around Houston, looking for more items to decorate his house. And yes, the Flowercycle is covered in flowers – from front to back!

Admission to the Flower Man's house is free. If you decide to go, be prepared to meet the famous artist himself. When Cleveland is home, he often welcomes visitors personally, with a smile, and asks his visitors to sign his guest book.

1 Check your understanding

1. What is the article about? Did you guess correctly before you read?
2. According to the article, what is a folk artist?
3. What does Cleveland Turner's yard look like?
4. Why did Cleveland Turner decide to decorate his house the way he did?
5. If you visit Cleveland Turner's house, why might you not notice the color of the house?

2 Build your vocabulary

A Find the words in Column 1 in the paragraphs indicated and underline them. Then, look the words up in the dictionary. Complete the chart with the clue that helped you know its meaning and the dictionary definition that matches the meaning in the article.

Word	Clue	Dictionary definition
1. nickname, ¶2	*His nickname is the "Flower Man."*	*an informal name for someone*
2. artificial, ¶2		
3. junk, ¶2		
4. homeless, ¶3		
5. covere, ¶4		
6. guest book, ¶6		

B Find each of the following academic words in the article and underline the sentence.

culture items ongoing project

Then, on another piece of paper, copy and complete the chart.

Academic word	Phrase or sentence from article	Part of speech	Dictionary definition	My sentence
culture	*He shows through his art the culture of the people*	*noun*	*The way of life of a particular people in a given period*	*Each country has a different culture.*

3 Talk with a partner

Answer each question with evidence from the reading. Use one of the phrases in the Useful Language box.

1. Why is Cleveland Turner called the "Flower man?"
2. How was the Flower Man's life before he went to the hospital?
3. How is the Flower Man's house an ongoing project?

USEFUL LANGUAGE
Phrases to cite evidence:
The article states that . . .
The author states that . . .

Objective: CCR Anchor 9: Analyze how two or more texts address similar themes or topics in order to build knowledge or to compare the approaches the authors take.

4 Analyze the texts

Review the following texts to answer the questions below: (1) p. 128, *The Rock – San Francisco's Biggest Tourist Attraction*; and (2) p. 163, *The Flower Man of Houston, Texas*.

1. How are the topics of the two articles similar?
2. How did the two tourist attractions originate?
3. What are two differences between the tourist attractions?
4. What evidence in the articles suggests that the attraction in Houston will change more in the future than the attraction in San Francisco?
5. Which tourist attraction would you prefer to visit? Provide information from both articles to explain your choice.

5 Before you write

Copy and complete the graphic organizer on another piece of paper. Fill it in with (1) the topic shared by the two articles, and (2) the differences between the two attractions. Use information from Exercises 1–4 and the two articles. Finally, (3) use your answer to question five in Exercise 4 to fill in the conclusion.

Topic:		
Differences	***The Rock***	***The Flower Man***
What		
Where		
Nickname		
How originated		
What it was previously		
Cost		
Conclusion:		

6 Write

Write one paragraph that contrasts the two tourist attractions described in the two articles. Use the information from your graphic organizer.

7 After you write

A Check your writing. Did you include all the ideas in your graphic organizer?

B Share your writing with a partner.

a. Take turns. Read your writing to your partner.
b. Read your partner's writing to yourself. Compare it to your partner's graphic organizer.
c. Comment on your partner's writing: Ask one question; share one thing you learned.

AUDIO SCRIPT

Welcome

Page 3, Exercise 2A – CD1, Track 2

A Hi, Silvia. What do you want to do in the future?
B I want to open my own beauty salon someday.
A What steps do you need to take?
B First, I need to go to beauty school for two years.
A What's the next step after that?
B Second, I need to take an exam to get my license.
A And after that?
B Third, I need to work in a salon to get experience.
A That sounds great. Do you have any other goals?
B I hope to become a business owner in five years. I don't want to work for anyone else.

Page 4, Exercises 3A and 3B – CD1, Track 3

1. Javier Molina works at a grocery store.
2. He puts groceries in bags for customers.
3. Javier is working at the store right now.
4. He is helping a woman with her bags of groceries.
5. He is talking to the woman.
6. He works every day from 9 a.m. to 5 p.m.
7. He likes his job, but he wants to do something different in the future.
8. Javier is going to cooking school at night.
9. He wants to be a chef at a restaurant.
10. He is planning to graduate from cooking school in six months.

Page 4, Exercise 3C – CD1, Track 4

Oksana Petrova is from Russia. She is living in Philadelphia right now. She works at an elementary school. She has a job as a teacher's assistant. She is working at the school right now. She is helping the students with math at the moment.
Oksana wants to become a teacher in the U.S. She studies English every evening. She plans to take elementary education classes at the community college next year. She is saving her money right now, because college classes are very expensive.

Page 5, Exercises 4A and 4B – CD1, Track 5

1. Diego Mata moved to the United States in 2005.
2. He got a job at a gas station.
3. He also took classes in English and auto mechanics.
4. Diego will finish his classes in auto mechanics next month.
5. He will look for a job when he is finished.
6. Diego liked his job at the gas station.
7. He will also like working as a mechanic.
8. He lived in an apartment last year.
9. He will move to a house next year.
10. He will also get married next summer.

Page 5, Exercise 4C – CD1, Track 6

1. **A** When did you move to this city?
   B I moved here in 2011.
2. **A** How long will you stay here?
   B Maybe I will stay here for one more year.
3. **A** Where did you live before you moved here?
   B I lived in Taiwan.
4. **A** How long will you study English in the future?
   B I will study English for two more years.

Unit 1: Personal information

Page 7, Exercises 2A and 2B – CD1, Track 7

A Hey, Danny, I am so tired this morning. I need a break. Let's get a cup of coffee.
B You're always tired on Mondays, Fernando. So, how was your weekend? Wild, as usual?
A Yeah, I guess. You know I like dancing, right? Well, last night, my girlfriend and I went to that new Cuban dance club – Club Havana.
B Oh, the one on, uh, Fourteenth Street?
A Yeah. Fourteenth Street. The place was full of people, and the music was incredible. We danced until, oh, it was about 1:30 in the morning. . . . Hey, you know what? You should come with us next time.
B Me? No. Oh, no. I don't like dancing.
A You're kidding. You don't like dancing? You really don't like dancing?
B Yeah, well, you know, Fernando, you're really outgoing and friendly, but I'm not outgoing. I'm not a party animal like you. I'm kind of shy. When I was a kid, I disliked going to parties, and I never learned how to dance.
A Really? That's too bad. But then, what do you enjoy doing?
B OK. This weekend, for example, I had a really nice, quiet weekend. I worked on my car, I watched some TV, I studied for my business class, and . . .
A Wow, Danny! You mean you were home the whole time? You didn't go anywhere?
B Nope. I was home alone the whole weekend. Well, I went to the autoparts store. See, I like staying home more than going out. But I'd like to find a girlfriend who likes staying home, too.
A A girlfriend? How are you going to find a girlfriend if you stay home all the time?
B Good question. Come on. Let's get back to work.

Page 7, Exercise 3A – CD1, Track 8

Fernando and Danny are talking about their weekend. Fernando is a very friendly and outgoing person. He enjoys dancing. Last night, he went to a dance club and stayed until late. Danny thinks Fernando is a party animal.
Danny is different from Fernando. He is shy and quiet. He dislikes dancing. Danny was home alone the whole weekend. He likes staying at home more than going out. He wants a girlfriend who likes staying home, too.

Page 8, Exercise 2A – CD1, Track 9

1. Does Katrina like shopping for clothes online?
2. My brother enjoys playing soccer.
3. Mrs. Tanaka doesn't mind cleaning the house
4. Do you prefer eating at home or in restaurants?
5. I love listening to the birds in the morning.
6. Do you enjoy using social media?
7. Most people don't enjoy paying bills every month.
8. Winston dislikes doing English homework.
9. I hate waiting for the bus.
10. Do you prefer going to bed early or late?
11. Danny avoids taking dance lessons.
12. Would you mind closing that window?

Page 10, Exercise 2A – CD1, Track 10

1. Sally enjoys cooking more than washing dishes.
2. Sally likes washing dishes less than cooking.
3. Alfredo loves listening to music as much as playing an instrument.
4. Alfredo enjoys playing an instrument as much as listening to music.
5. Pam likes working less than going to school.
6. Pam enjoys going to school more than working.
7. Marta enjoys painting more than jogging.
8. Marta likes jogging less than painting.

Page 12, Exercise 2 – CD1, Track 11

Your Personality and Your Job
What is the perfect job for you? It depends a lot on your personality. People think, act, and feel in different ways, and there are interesting jobs for every kind of person. Three common personality types are outgoing, intellectual, and creative.
Outgoing people enjoy meeting others and helping them. They are good talkers. They are friendly, and they get along well with other people. They often become nurses, counselors, teachers, or social workers.
Intellectual people like thinking about problems and finding answers to hard questions. They often enjoy reading and playing games like chess. Many intellectual people like working alone more than working in a group. They may become scientists, computer programmers, or writers.
Creative people enjoy making things. They like to imagine things that are new and different. Many of them become artists such as painters, dancers, or musicians. Architects, designers, and photographers are other examples of creative jobs.
Before you choose a career, think about your personality type. If you want to be happy in your work, choose the right job for your personality.

Unit 2: At school

Page 19, Exercises 2A and 2B – CD1, Track 12

A Hi, Alex.
B Hi, Bella.
A How long have you been in the library?
B For about two hours.
A How's it going?
B Um, not great.
A Why? What's the matter?

B I'm so discouraged. Look at this mess! I have to finish reading this book. Then I have to write a paper and study for a test. Where do I start!
A Well, Alex, have you ever tried making a to-do list?
B A to-do list?
A Yeah. You make a list of all the things you have to do. Then you do the most important things first.
B A to-do list. No, I've never tried that. I usually try to do six things at the same time. Let's see. Right now, the most important thing is to finish reading this book. But it's so boring. I can't concentrate.
A You need to be more active, Alex. Don't just read the book. You know, underline important ideas, write notes, repeat the main ideas to yourself. Those things will help you concentrate.
B Hmm. I think I can do that. But there's another problem.
A What's that?
B Too many new words! I can't remember all of them.
A Hmm. Well, here's an idea. Write important words on index cards. Take the cards with you, and study them everywhere – on the bus, during your break at work, and before you go to bed . . .
B OK, OK! I get it: study smarter – not harder. Thanks, Bella.

Page 19, Exercise 3A – CD1, Track 13

Alex has been at the library for a long time, and he is discouraged. He has many things to do. He needs to study for a test and write a paper. He needs to finish reading a book, but he can't concentrate. He says the book is boring.
Alex's friend Bella gives him some study advice. First, she tells Alex to make a list of all the things he needs to do. Next, she says he has to be a more active reader. Finally, she tells him to write vocabulary words on index cards
and study them when he has free time. With Bella's help, Alex plans to study smarter, not harder.

Page 20, Exercise 2A – CD1, Track 14

1. **A** How long has Manya been in the computer lab?
   B Since six o'clock.
2. **A** How long has Avi known Bella
   B For four months.
3. **A** How long has Kayla worked at the library?
   B Since September.
4. **A** How long has Mrs. Bateson taught at the adult school?
   B For 20 years.
5. **A** How long have you lived in Canada?
   B For one year.
6. **A** How long has Omar had two jobs?
   B Since last year.
7. **A** How long has Pete waited for the bus?
   B For one hour.

Page 22, Exercise 2A – CD1, Track 15

1. **A** Has Laura ever talked to her school counselor?
   B No, she hasn't.
2. **A** Have you ever forgotten your teacher's name?
   B Yes, I have.
3. **A** Has Joseph ever read a book in English?
   B No, he hasn't. But he wants to.
4. **A** Have Mary and Paula ever been late to school?
   B No, they haven't.
5. **A** Have you ever tried to speak English with your neighbors?
   B Yes, I have.
6. **A** Has Tomas ever taken the wrong bus to school?
   B No, he hasn't.

Page 24, Exercise 2 – CD1, Track 16

Strategies for Learning English
Have you ever felt discouraged because it's hard to speak and understand English? Don't give up! Here are three strategies to help you learn faster and remember more.

Strategy # 1 – Set goals.
Have you ever set goals for learning English? When you set goals, you decide what you want to learn. After you determine your purpose for learning, you can make a plan to help you reach your goals. Maybe your goal is to learn more vocabulary. There are many ways to do this. For example, you can read in English for 15 minutes every day. You can also learn one new word every day.

Strategy # 2 – Look for opportunities to practice English.
Talk to everyone. Speak with people in the store, at work, and in the park. Don't worry about making mistakes. And don't forget to ask questions. For example, if your teacher uses a word you don't understand, ask a question like "What does that word mean?"

Strategy # 3 – Guess.
Don't try to translate every word. When you read, concentrate on clues such as pictures or other words in the sentence to help you understand. You can also make guesses when you are talking to people. For example, look at their faces and hand gestures – the way they move their hands – to help you guess the meaning.
Set goals, look for opportunities to practice, and guess. Do these things every day, and you will learn more English!

Review: Units 1 and 2

Page 30, Exercise 1 – CD1, Track 17

A How long have you been here, Marisol?
B Umm . . . about two months.
A Really? You're a good student, Marisol. How did you learn English so quickly?
B Well, Vladimir, I ask a lot of questions in class. When I don't understand the teacher, I raise my hand and ask him to explain. I enjoy learning that way.
A I'm too shy to raise my hand in class.
B Well, why don't you ask the teacher your questions after class?
A Yeah. That's a good idea. Sometimes I just ask the person next to me.
B Oh, so then you're not so shy.
A Actually, I'm not really very outgoing, you know. . . . Hey, Marisol, do you write vocabulary on index cards so you can study on the bus? That's what I do.
B Well, I don't have much time to study like that. But I talk to my co-workers a lot. I listen to their conversations and learn new words that way. I like talking to them.
A And you know, I like talking to you. You give me great ideas, Marisol. Thanks a lot. See you next time.

Page 31, Exercise 3A – CD1, Track 18

1. She loves playing cards with friends.
2. He hates working in the garden.
3. Do you like being alone?
4. She enjoys cooking less than eating.
5. I like living in the city.
6. How long has Shen studied English?
7. He's been here for six months.
8. Have you ever studied Korean?
9. I've never studied Chinese.
10. He graduated from college in 2013.

Page 31, Exercise 3B – CD1, Track 19

1. What is the perfect job for you?
2. The perfect job depends on your personality.
3. Have you ever felt discouraged?
4. Have you ever set goals for learning English?
5. What does that word mean?
6. Intellectual people often enjoy working alone.
7. She has volunteered at a hospital for two years.
8. He got married in 2010.
9. How long have you lived in your present house?
10. She spends a lot of time studying at the library.

Unit 3: Friends and family

Page 33, Exercises 2A and 2B – CD1, Track 20

A Hello?
B Maria? Hi, It's Ana.
A Hey. Hi, Ana. How are you?
B Good, thanks. But I've been super busy. . . . Listen, Maria, do you have a minute to talk? Are you eating dinner?
A No, we've eaten. What's up?
B Well, I need a favor.
A Sure, Ana, what is it?
B The smoke alarm in my kitchen is beeping. Beep, beep, beep. I need to change the battery, but the ceiling's too high. Can I borrow your ladder?
A Sure, but I have a better idea. Um, Daniel can come over and change the battery for -you.
B Really? Are you sure he has enough time?
A Oh, Ana, you know Daniel. He is never too busy to help a neighbor. He'll come over in five minutes.
B Thanks. I really appreciate it. I owe you one. See you . . .
A Wait, Ana, I want to ask you something. Did you hear our noisy neighbors last Saturday night? They had a party until three in the morning. Because of the noise, we couldn't sleep at all.
B Gosh, that's too bad, Maria. I didn't hear anything. But you should complain to the manager.
A Yeah, I know. I'll do it tomorrow.

Page 33, Exercise 3A – CD1, Track 21

Ana and Maria are neighbors. Ana calls Maria because she needs a favor. The smoke alarm in Ana's kitchen is beeping. She needs to change the battery, but the ceiling in her kitchen is too high. Ana asks to borrow Maria's ladder.
Maria says her husband, Daniel, will come over with a ladder and help Ana. Ana says, "I owe you one." This means she appreciates Maria and Daniel's help, and she will do a favor for them in the future.
Next, Maria tells Ana about their noisy neighbors. The neighbors had a party on Saturday night. Because of the noise, Maria and Daniel couldn't sleep. Ana tells Maria that she should complain to the apartment manager.

Page 34, Exercise 2A – CD1, Track 22

A Nice Surprise
Lei wanted to bake a cake because it was her neighbor Margy's birthday. Lei needed to go to the store because she didn't have any flour. However, her car had a flat tire. She probably got the flat tire because her tires were very old. Because of this problem, she couldn't drive to the store. She couldn't walk to the store because of the distance. It was more than a mile away. Lei had a clever idea. She went to Margy and asked to borrow a cup of flour. Margy was happy to help because she had a lot of flour and because she was a good neighbor. Two hours later, Lei returned to Margy's house with a beautiful cake. When Margy opened the door, Lei shouted, "Happy birthday!" Margy was very surprised and happy. Because of the nice surprise, Margy had a wonderful birthday!

Page 36, Exercise 2A – CD1, Track 23

Too Far to Visit
My neighbors – the Mansours – have four children. Their house isn't big enough. Mr. and Mrs. Mansour think it's too expensive to live in the city. Their rent is too high. Last weekend, the Mansours bought a house outside the city. It has four bedrooms. It's big enough for the whole family. However, the new house is too far from Mr. Mansour's job, so he's going to look for a new job. Mr. Mansour is an experienced engineer. He's experienced enough to find a new job. I will miss the Mansours. I probably can't visit them. Their new house isn't close enough for me to visit. It's too expensive to take a taxi there. When I'm rich enough to buy a car, I will visit them.

Page 38, Exercise 2 – CD1, Track 24

Neighborhood Watch Success Story
by Latisha Holmes, President, Rolling Hills Neighborhood Watch
People often ask me about the role of Neighborhood Watch. My answer is *Because of Neighborhood Watch, our neighborhood is safer and nicer*. Members of Neighborhood Watch help each other and look after the neighborhood. For example, we look after our neighbors' houses when they aren't home. We help elderly neighbors with yard work. Once a month, we get together to paint over graffiti. Last Wednesday, the Neighborhood Watch team had another success story. Around 8:30 p.m., members of our Neighborhood Watch were out on a walk. Near the Corner Café, they noticed two men next to George Garcia's car. George lives on Rolling Hills Drive. The men were trying to break into the car. Suddenly, the car alarm went off. The men ran away and got into a car down the street. But they weren't quick enough. Our Neighborhood Watch members wrote down the car's license plate number and called the police. Later that night, the police arrested the two men.
I would like to congratulate our Neighborhood Watch team on their good work. Because so many people participate in Neighborhood Watch, Rolling Hills is a safer neighborhood Today.
For information about Neighborhood Watch, please call 773-555-1234.

Unit 4: Health

Page 45, Exercises 2A and 2B – CD1, Track 25

A Hello, Stanley. I haven't seen you for some time. How've you been?
B Busy. I've been working really hard.
A I see. So what brings you here today?
B Well, you know, I've always been healthy, but, uh, I've been really tired lately.
A Uh-huh. Well, let's take a look at your chart. . . . Ah, I see you've gained 20 pounds since last year.
B Yeah. I used to exercise a lot, but now I just work. Work, eat, and sleep.
A Well, you know, gaining weight can make you feel tired, Stanley. You need to start exercising again. Can you try walking for 30 minutes each day?
B I don't have time. I'm working a lot these days – sometimes 10, even 12, hours a day.
A Hmm. Well, then, can you walk or ride a bicycle to work? And at work, don't use the elevator. Take the stairs.
B Well, I guess, I can try.
A Good. Now, let's see. You also have high blood pressure. Tell me about your diet. What have you eaten since yesterday?
B Well, last night I had a hamburger with fries and a soft drink.
A Fat, salt, and sugar! They're all bad for your blood pressure, Stanley. What about today?
B I haven't eaten anything today.
A No breakfast? Well, of course you feel tired! You need to change your diet, Stanley. Eat more fish and more vegetables. Give up fast food. No hamburgers! No fries! They're really bad for your health.
B That's really hard. I'm so busy right now. I don't have time to –
A Listen, Stanley. You're 40 years old. Do you want to have a heart attack? This is my advice. You need to make real changes, or you'll need to start taking pills and all kinds of medication.
B OK. I'll try.

Page 45, Exercise 3A – CD1, Track 26

Stanley is at the doctor's office. His health has always been good, but he has been really tired lately. The doctor looks at Stanley's chart. He sees a couple of problems. One problem is Stanley's weight. He has gained 20 pounds. Another problem is his blood pressure. The doctor tells him he needs regular exercise – for example, walking or riding a bike. He also tells Stanley to change his diet – to eat more fish and vegetables. If Stanley doesn't do these things, he will need to take pills and other medication. Stanley wants to be healthy, so he is going to try to follow the doctor's advice.

Page 46, Exercise 2A – CD1, Track 27

Lola has been unhappy recently. She hasn't gone to the gym lately. And she hasn't watched her weight. She hasn't eaten healthy food, either. She has eaten a lot of french fries and has drunk lots of soft drinks. She has gained a lot of weight, and her blood pressure has gone up, too.
William has started to get in shape lately. He has lost weight recently. His blood pressure has gone down, too. He's eaten a lot of vegetables, and he has stopped eating red meat. He has given up hamburgers, french fries, and soft drinks. But he hasn't given up ice cream!

Page 48, Exercise 2A – CD1, Track 28

1. **A** Did he use to stay up all night?
   B Yes, he did, but he goes to bed early now.
2. **A** How often do you eat meat?
   B I used to eat meat every night, but now I usually have fish.
3. **A** Did she used to drive to work?
   B No, she didn't. She used to ride her bike, but now she drives.
4. **A** What do they usually do after work?
   B They used to go straight home, but now they take dance classes twice a week.
5. **A** Do you exercise every day?
   B I used to exercise every day, but now I exercise only on weekends.
6. **A** Did you used to eat red meat?
   B Yes, I did, but now I'm a vegetarian.
7. **A** Do you take the stairs?
   B No I don't. I used to, but now I take the elevator.
8. **A** Does he usually eat dessert?
   B Not now, but he used to.

Page 50, Exercise 2 – CD1, Track 29

Two Beneficial Plants
Since the beginning of history, people in every culture have used plants to stay healthy and to prevent sickness. Garlic and chamomile are two beneficial plants.
Garlic is a plant in the onion family.
The green stem and the leaves of the garlic plant grow above the ground. The root – the part under the ground – is a bulb with sections called cloves. They look like the pieces of an orange. The bulb is the part that people have traditionally used for medicine. They have used it for insect bites, cuts, earaches, and coughs. Today, some people also use it to treat high blood pressure and high cholesterol.
Chamomile is a small, pretty plant with flowers that bloom from late summer to early fall. The flowers have white petals and a yellow center. Many people use dried chamomile flowers to make tea. Some people give the tea to babies with upset stomachs. They also drink chamomile tea to feel better when they have a cold or the flu, poor digestion, or trouble falling asleep.
For thousands of years, people everywhere have grown garlic, chamomile, and other

herbal medicines in their gardens. Today, you can buy them in health-food stores. You can get them in dried, powdered, or pill form.

Review: Units 3 and 4

Page 56, Exercise 1 – CD1, Track 30

A Hello?
B Hi, Sara. This is Jenny. Remember me?
A Hey, Jenny! How have you been lately? We haven't talked in ages!
B Sorry about that, Sara. I used to have time to call friends after work. I just don't have enough time now.
A That's too bad. I have lots of time now that I work part-time! I used to work 50 hours a week; now I only work 20. But I've gotten lazy! I used to exercise a lot more.
B You're lucky you have free time, Sara. Because of my schedule, I eat fast food and don't exercise regularly. I used to cook healthy food for myself. Not anymore!
A It sounds like we both need to start taking care of ourselves, the way we used to do.
B I have an idea, Sara. Let's meet a few evenings a week and take a walk. I sit all day. I used to take the stairs at work, but I don't even do that anymore!
A I really like your idea. We can motivate each other. And we can catch up on each other's lives, too!

Page 57, Exercise 3A – CD1, Track 31

1. this morning
2. sore throat
3. That's too bad!
4. health problems
5. the neighbors
6. on South Street
7. they are
8. this month
9. asked them
10. three times
11. How are things?
12. thanks

Page 57, Exercise 3B – CD1, Track 32

1. **A** Where's Tommy this morning?
   B He's sick. He has a sore throat.
   A That's too bad!
   B He often has health problems.
   A I'm sorry to hear that.
2. **A** The neighbors on South Street are really noisy.
   B Yes, they are.
   A This month, I've asked them three times to be quiet.
   B Let's write them a letter.
   A That's a good idea.

Unit 5: Around town

Page 59, Exercises 2A and 2B – CD1, Track 33

A Mei, I'm so glad tomorrow is Friday. It's been a long week.
B That's for sure. Hmm. What would you like to do this weekend, Wen?
A Well, there are a few movies we haven't seen yet, or we could go to a concert downtown.
B Oh, we can't afford to go to concerts, Wen. They're too expensive. And I'm sort of tired of going to the movies.
A OK, so let's do something different on Sunday, something we haven't done yet this summer.
B Like what? Got any ideas?
A Let's check the newspaper for community events. Maybe we'll find something free right here in the neighborhood. Let's take a look. . . . Hmm. We have a lot of options. Here's something interesting. There's a concert in the park on Sunday at noon, admission is free.
B And here, look, there's a free walking tour of the gardens on Sunday at eleven o'clock.
A Here's another option, Mei. The Museum of Art is free the first Sunday of every month. There's an exhibit of modern art showing now. The museum opens at 10:00 a.m.
B Oh. And here's something at the library: free storytelling for children on Sunday at 10:30. Everything is happening on the same day at the same time! What do you want to do, Wen?
A Why don't we go to the library first?
B OK.
A Then, let's plan to go to the concert if the weather is nice. And then maybe later, we can go to the art museum.
B Yeah. That sounds good. I'll check the weather forecast for the weekend. Then we can decide.

Page 59, Exercise 3A – CD1, Track 34

It is Thursday. Wen and Mei are talking about their plans for the weekend. They can't afford to spend a lot of money on entertainment. They decide to check the newspaper for free community events on Sunday. They have many options. There's an outdoor concert in the park, a walking tour of the gardens, a modern art exhibit at the art museum, and storytelling for children at the library. All these events have free admission.
The problem is that all these things are happening on Sunday at the same time.
Mei and Wen decide to take their son to the storytelling first. Then, if the weather is nice, they will go to the concert. Later, they might go to the art museum.

Page 60, Exercise 2A – CD1, Track 35

1. **A** How much do you expect to pay for the concert?
   B No more than $25.00.
2. **A** What have you decided to do for your birthday?
   B I'm going to an exhibit at the art museum.
3. **A** Can you afford to buy a ticket for the show?
   B Not really. I need to start saving money.
4. **A** What did you agree to do next weekend?
   B We agreed to go to the park.
5. **A** How is Tom going to go to the park?
   B He intends to ride his bike.
6. **A** Have you ever refused to go on a trip with your family?
   B No, I haven't.
7. **A** What did they promise their relatives?
   B They promised to visit this weekend.
8. **A** What is Chen going to eat at the picnic?
   B He wants to eat ice-cream and cake.

Page 62, Exercise 2A – CD1, Track 36

1. It's 11:00 p.m. The salsa concert has already ended.
2. It's 8:00 a.m. The science museum opens at nine. It hasn't opened yet.
3. It's July 5th. The Independence Day parade has already finished.
4. It's the beginning of August. School begins in September. School activities haven't begun yet.
5. It's 2:00 a.m. The dance club stays open until 3:00. It hasn't closed yet.
6. It's Friday evening. The weekend has already started.
7. It's 7:45 p.m. The movie starts at 8:00. We haven't missed the movie yet.
8. It's Monday. I've already bought tickets for next Sunday's soccer game.
9. It's Sunday night. Have you done the homework yet?
10. There's a new Japanese restaurant down the street. Have you eaten there yet?
11. It's 8:30 a.m. The children have already left for school.
12. There's a new art exhibit at the museum. Have you seen it yet?

Page 64, Exercise 2 – CD1, Track 37

Salsa Starz at Century Park
If you missed the outdoor concert at Century Park last Saturday evening, you missed a great night of salsa music and dancing – and the admission was free!
The performers were the popular band Salsa Starz. Bandleader Ernesto Sanchez led the five-piece group and two dancers. Sanchez is a versatile musician. He sang and played maracas and guitar. The other musicians were also superb. The group's excellent playing and great energy galvanized the crowd. No one sat down during the entire show!
However, the evening had some problems. At first, the sound level of the music was excessive. I had to wear earplugs. Then, the level was too low. The change in sound was irritating. In addition, the stage was plain and unremarkable. I expected to see lights and lots of color at the performance. The weather was another problem. The night started out clear. By 10:00 p.m., some ominous black clouds moved in, and soon it started to rain. The band intended to play until eleven, but the show ended early because of the rain.
Century Park has free concerts every Saturday evening in July and August. If you haven't attended one of these concerts yet, plan to go next weekend. But take an umbrella!

Unit 6: Time

Page 71, Exercises 2A and 2B – CD2, Track 2

A Winston, what are you doing?
B I'm thinking.
A No, you're not. You're procrastinating. You always procrastinate. I'm getting very impatient with you! I asked you to take out the trash two hours ago, and you haven't done it yet.
B Aw, Mom.
A Do you have homework?
B Yeah, but . . . I can't decide what to do first.
A Hmm. Would you like some help?
B Well, uh, yeah, I guess.
A OK. So, why don't you make a to-do list. You know, write down all the tasks you have to do.
B OK. I've got . . . math, an English essay, and a history project.
A Uh-huh. What else?

B I have to practice guitar. I have a lesson tomorrow.
A And don't forget the trash. Write that down, too.
B OK. Now what?
A Prioritize. What are you going to do first, second, third, and so on?
B Well, guitar is first. It's the most fun.
A Nuh-uh. I don't think so. Homework and chores are first. Guitar is last.
B OK. Should I start with math, English, or history?
A Hmm. When are they due?
B Math and English are due tomorrow.
A And the history project?
B The deadline is next week. On Tuesday.
A OK. So do math and English tonight. You can do the history project over the weekend.
B OK, math and English tonight. Which one should I do first?
A Well, I always do the hardest thing first.
B English is a lot harder than math.
A OK. So English, then math, then guitar. But before you do anything . . .
B Yeah, I know. Take out the trash.
A Right.

Page 71, Exercise 3A – CD2, Track 3

Winston is listening to music in his room. His mother comes in and tells him to stop procrastinating. She is very impatient because he hasn't taken out the trash and he hasn't done his homework.
Winston has too many things to do. His mother suggests making a to-do list. First, she tells him to list all the tasks he needs to do. Next, she tells him to prioritize – to put his tasks in order of importance. His mother says he needs to do his homework and chores first. He decides to do his English and math homework first because they are due the next day. He also has a history project, but the deadline is next Tuesday. After he finishes his homework, he will practice guitar. But before he does anything else, he has to take out the trash.

Page 72, Exercise 2A – CD2, Track 4

1. When you have many things to do, make a to-do list.
2. When you have a deadline, write it on your calendar.
3. Don't let people interrupt you when you need to concentrate.
4. When you want to focus on a task, turn off the television.
5. When you feel tired, take a break.
6. Give yourself a reward when you finish something difficult.
7. Don't procrastinate when you have a deadline.
8. When you are tired, don't do difficult tasks.
9. Prioritize tasks when you have many things to do.

Page 74, Exercise 2A – CD2, Track 5

1. After Bonnie takes a shower, she gets dressed.
2. Bonnie takes a shower before she gets dressed.
3. Before Bonnie makes coffee, she gets dressed.
4. Bonnie makes coffee after she gets dressed.
5. Bonnie brings in the newspaper before she eats breakfast.
6. Bonnie eats breakfast after she brings in the newspaper.
7. After Bonnie eats breakfast, she leaves for work.
8. Before Bonnie leaves for work, she eats breakfast.
9. After Bonne makes coffee, she brings in the newspaper.
10. Before Bonnie brings in the newspaper, she makes coffee.

Page 76, Exercise 2 – CD2, Track 6

Rules About Time
Every culture has rules about time. These rules are usually unspoken, but everybody knows them.
In some countries such as the United States, England, and Canada, punctuality is an unspoken rule. It is important to be on time, especially in business. People usually arrive a little early for business appointments. Business meetings and personal appointments often have strict beginning and ending times. When you are late, other people might think you are rude, disorganized, or irresponsible. These countries also have cultural rules about time in social situations. For example, when an invitation for dinner says 6:00 p.m., it is impolite to arrive more than five or ten minutes late. On the other hand, when the invitation is for a party from 6:00 to 8:00 or a reception from 3:30 to 5:30, you can arrive anytime between those hours. For public events with specific starting times – movies, concerts, sports events – you should arrive a few minutes before the event begins. In fact, some theaters do not allow people to enter if they arrive after the event has started.
Other cultures have different rules about time. In Brazil, it is not unusual for guests to arrive an hour or two after a social event begins. In the Philippines, it is not uncommon for people to miss scheduled events – a class or an appointment – to meet a friend at the airport. Many Filipinos believe that relationships with people are more important than keeping a schedule.
When you are living or working with people from different cultures, it is important to know that culture's unspoken rules about time. Without this knowledge, there can be misunderstandings.

Review: Units 5 and 6

Page 82, Exercise 1 – CD2, Track 7

A Hey, Minh. So where do you plan to go on vacation?
B I've decided to visit my family in Vietnam.
A Fantastic. Have you bought your tickets yet?
B Not yet, Trina. I plan to buy them this week. What about you? What do you plan to do during your vacation?
A Well, I want to go to Las Vegas.
B Las Vegas?
A Yeah. I've already made my reservations. My husband and I won three free nights at a big hotel.
B You're kidding! How did you win that?
A We just filled out a form at a shopping mall.
B Wow! Is it really free?
A I think so. But when we get there, we have to listen to a lecture about vacation timeshares.
B Do you intend to buy a place in a hotel for vacations?
A No, but we intend to have fun in a free one.

Page 83, Exercise 3A – CD2, Track 8

1. Study English.
2. Start the computer.
3. Tell the story.
4. What state do you live in?
5. Go to the store.
6. Students need to study.
7. Let's see the Salsa Starz.
8. Stop procrastinating.

Page 83, Exercise 3B – CD2, Track 9

1. **A** Hi, Stuart. I'm going to the store. What do you need?
   B Can you get me some stamps? It's the first of the month, and I have to pay bills.
   A Sure.
   B Thanks. I'll start writing the checks now and stop procrastinating.
2. **A** Hello, Stephanie.
   B Hi, Steve. Are you still a student here?
   A Yes. I'm studying appliance repair.
   B Really? Maybe you can fix my stove when you're finished.
   A I hope so.

Unit 7: Shopping

Page 85, Exercises 2A and 2B – CD2, Track 10

A Julie, look at this car! "Automatic transmission, airconditioning, leather seats, sunroof, power windows . . ." It's got everything, and it's only $27,500.
B Ken, are you crazy? With tax and fees, that's about $30,000! We can't afford $30,000 for a car! Where . . . where are we going to get the money? The balance in our savings account is less than $8,000!
A No problem. Look here. It says, "Special financing available. Only 4 percent interest with 60 months to pay off the loan!"
B Sixty months to pay! That's five years! We're going to pay for that car every month for five years. Ken, you know I'm afraid of getting into debt. We have bills to pay every month, and we need to save money for college for the kids.
A Well, Julie, tell me: Do we need a car, or don't we need a car? Our old one always needs repair, and it's . . .
B OK, OK. We do need a car. But we don't need a new car. We could look for a used car. Let's go across the street and look. I'm sure we can find a good used car for $10,000 or even less than that.
A Yeah, but, Julie, look at this car. It's a beauty! We should get it. We can buy the car on credit. Everybody does it!
B No, not everybody! My father always paid cash for everything. He didn't even have a credit card!
A Well, your father never had any fun. And, I'm not your father!

Page 85, Exercise 3A – CD2, Track 11

Ken and his wife, Julie, are looking at cars. Ken wants to buy a new car that costs over $27,000. Julie thinks that they can't afford to spend that much money. The balance in their savings account is less than $8,000. She's

afraid of getting into debt. But Ken says they can get financing to help pay for the new car. The interest rate is low, and they can take five years to pay off the loan. Ken isn't worried about buying things on credit.
Julie disagrees. She suggests that they could buy a used car. She says her father never had a credit card. He always paid cash for everything.

Page 86, Exercise 2A – CD2, Track 12

1. **A** My rent is going up again. What should I do?
   B Here's my advice. You're a good tenant. I think you should talk to your landlord.
2. **A** I have to fix my credit. What should I do?
   B You should talk to a debt counselor. He can help you.
3. **A** Can you suggest a nice restaurant? It's my wife's birthday.
   B You could try Chao's. Or how about Anita's?
4. **A** It's my niece's sixteenth birthday next week. What could I get her?
   B Why don't you get tickets to a concert? Or you could buy her a CD.
5. **A** That vocational school is very expensive. I can't afford it. Can you give me any advice?
   B Well, you're a good student. I think you should apply for a scholarship.
6. **A** I need a new car. Where do you suggest I look for one?
   B How about looking in the newspaper? Or you could look online.
7. **A** I just got another parking ticket. It's getting harder and harder to park in this neighborhood.
   B. I think you should sell that car. You don't really need it.
8. **A** I'm going to be in New York City in July. Any ideas for things to do?
   B Well, you could see a show on Broadway, or you could walk in Central Park, or you could go to an art museum. There are so many things to do.

Page 88, Exercise 2A – CD2, Track 13

1. I'm worried about paying interest on my credit card balance.
2. Rob is afraid of getting into debt. He pays for everything with cash.
3. Have you thought about opening a checking account?
4. Elizabeth is happy about finding an apartment she can afford.
5. Elena is excited about starting classes at the community college.
6. I'm tired of making payments on my car.
7. Franco isn't interested in applying for a loan.
8. Thank you for lending me money for school.
9. We're thinking about moving to a nicer neighborhood.
10. She's famous for spending a lot of money on clothes.

Page 90, Exercise 2 – CD2, Track 14

A Credit Card Nightmare
Sun Hi and Joseph Kim got their first credit card a week after they got married. At first, they paid off the balance every month.
The couple's problems began after they bought a new house. They bought new furniture, a big-screen television, and two new computers. To pay for everything, they applied for more and more credit. Soon they had six different credit cards, and they were more than $18,000 in debt.
"It was a nightmare!" says Mrs. Kim. "The interest rates were 19 percent to 24 percent. Our minimum payments were over $750 a month. We both got second jobs, but it wasn't enough. I was so worried about paying off the debt, I cried all the time."
Luckily, the Kims found a solution. They met Dolores Delgado, a debt
counselor. With her help, they looked at all of their living expenses and made a family budget. They combined their six credit card payments into one monthly payment with a lower interest rate. Now, their monthly budget for all living expenses is $3,400. Together they earn $3,900 a month. That leaves $500 for paying off their debt.
"We've cut up our credit cards," says Mr. Kim. "No more expensive furniture! In five years, we can pay off our debt. Now we know. Credit cards are dangerous!

Unit 8: Work

Page 97, Exercises 2A and 2B – CD2, Track 15

A Good morning, Tony. Thanks for coming in. I'm Ken Leong, personnel manager for the company.
B Nice to meet you, Mr. Leong.
A So, I have your résumé right here, and I understand you're interested in the job of shipping-and-receiving clerk.
B Yes, that's right. I'm applying for the shipping-and-receiving clerk position.
A OK. I'd like to ask you a few questions.
B Sure, go ahead.
A Uh. First of all, could you tell me a little about your background? Where are you from? What kind of work have you done?
B Well, I was born in Peru and lived there for 18 years. I finished high school there, and then I came here with my family. I've been living here for two years.
A OK. And are you currently employed?
B Uh. Sorry?
A Are you working now?
B Yes, I've been working part-time as a teacher's assistant at an elementary school for about a year. And I'm also going to community college at night. I want to get a degree in accounting.
A Oh. That's good. What office machines can you use?
B Uh. I can use a computer, a fax machine, a scanner, and a copying machine.
A Excellent. Those skills will be useful in this job. You'll need to take inventory and order supplies. Now, Tony, can you tell me about some of your strengths?
B Um. Excuse me?
A Your strengths – you know, your personal qualities. What makes you a good person for this job?
B Well, I'm very responsible and reliable. If I have a deadline, I come in early or stay late to finish the job. Also, I get along with everyone. I never have problems working with people. I like everyone, and they like me.
A That's great. Can you work any shift?
B Well, I prefer the day shift because I have classes at night.
A OK, Tony. There's going to be an opening in the day shift soon. I'll get back to you next week sometime.
B Thank you, Mr. Leong. I appreciate that. It was nice to meet you.
A You, too. I'll give you a call.

Page 97, Exercise 3A – CD2, Track 16

Tony has been working as a teacher's assistant for about a year. He is also going to college part-time to get a degree in accounting. Right now, Tony is at a job interview with Mr. Leong, the personnel manager.
Mr. Leong asks about Tony's background. Tony says he is from Peru and has been living in the United States for two years. Next, Mr. Leong asks about Tony's work experience, and Tony says that now he is employed at a school. Finally, Mr. Leong asks about Tony's personal strengths. Tony says he is responsible and reliable, and he gets along with everybody. Mr. Leong says he will contact Tony next week.

Page 98, Exercise 2A – CD2, Track 17

1. **A** How long has Talia been practicing for her driving test?
   B For about three months.
2. **A** Have you been working here for a long time?
   B No, I haven't. I started six days ago.
3. **A** How long has Yin been looking for a job?
   B Since last year.
4. **A** Has Mr. Rivera been interviewing people all day?
   B Yes, he has.
5. **A** How long have you been waiting to get an interview?
   B Since March.
6. **A** How long have they been going to night school?
   B For one year.

Page 100, Exercise 2A – CD2, Track 18

1. She's handing out papers.
   She's handing the papers out.
   She's handing them out.
2. He's throwing away the cups.
   He's throwing the cups away.
   He's throwing them away.
3. He's turning up the volume.
   He's turning the volume up.
   He's turning it up.
4. She's filling out a job application.
   She's filling the application out.
   She's filling it out.
5. She's turning off the lamp.
   She's turning the lamp off.
   She's turning it off.
6. He's putting away the clothes.
   He's putting the clothes away.
   He's putting them away.

Page 102, Exercise 2 – CD2, Track 19

Eden's Blog

Monday 9/29
I had my interview today! I gave the interviewer a big smile and a firm handshake. I answered her questions with confidence. I'll let you know if I get the job

Thursday 9/25
Great news! One of the companies from the job fair finally called me back! I've been preparing for the job interview all day. I'm really excited. I'm going to have a practice interview with some classmates today. That will prepare me for the real one.

Wednesday 9/24
I've been feeling depressed about the job search lately, but my counselor at school told me I shouldn't give up. He said I need to be patient. Today, I organized my papers. I made lists of the places I have applied to and the people I have talked to. I also did some more research online.

Tuesday 9/16
Today, I went to a job fair at my college. I filled out several applications and handed out some résumés. There were about 20 different companies there. Several of them said they were going to call me back. Wish me luck!

Monday 9/15
Hello fellow job searchers! I have been looking for a job for several weeks. Everyone tells me that it's critical to network, so I've been telling everyone I know. I've been calling friends, relatives, and teachers to tell them about my job search. If you have any good job-searching tips, please share them with me!

Review: Units 7 and 8

Page 108, Exercise 1 – CD2, Track 20

A Hey, hi, John!
B Oh, hi, Clara.
A What a long week. I'm glad it's Friday.
B Me, too, Clara. And look! The bus is on time today!
A And you don't have to drive in all that rush-hour traffic.
B I know. But I've been taking this bus a long time, and I'm thinking about buying a car. I'm interested in finding a used SUV.
A An SUV? You should think about buying a smaller car. You can save a lot more money. And you can save on gas, too.
B Hey, I'm a big guy. I can't fit in a small car. I'm worried about getting a car that's too small for me. . . . But, hey, you could get a smaller car. I'll come to work with you and save my gas money. Then I can buy my SUV and take my friends for a ride after work.
A Sorry, John. I'm not interested in buying a car. I like the bus just fine. I'm saving my money to buy a house someday. Oh, here's my stop! See you Monday!

Page 109, Exercise 3A – CD2, Track 21

1. clean up
2. think about
3. turn up
4. fill out
5. interested in
6. throw out
7. put on
8. tired of

Page 109, Exercise 3B – CD2, Track 22

1. **A** What do you need to do?
   B I have to clean up the kitchen.
   A Can I help?
   B Sure. Could you throw out the trash?
   A I'd be happy to.
2. **A** Don't you think it's cold in here?
   B It's a little cold.
   A Why don't you turn up the heat?
   B That costs too much money. You can put on my jacket.

Unit 9: Daily living

Page 111, Exercises 2A and 2B – CD2, Track 23

A Hello?
B Samantha, this is Monica.
A Monica! I've been waiting for you to call. But, um, you sound really strange. Are you OK?
B Well, actually, no! I'm not. . . . Not at all. Somebody broke into our house tonight.
A Broke into your house? That's terrible! When? How?
B Well, around 7:30, we went over to the Morenos' next door to watch a movie. And while we were there, someone broke into our house and robbed us. They stole our TV, DVD player, jewelry, and some cash. I still can't believe it.
A Ugh. That's awful. How did the robber get in?
B He broke a window in the back bedroom. You should see the mess – there's glass all over the floor, and there are books and CDs and clothes all over the place. And, Samantha, they took my mother's ring. I'm so upset.
A Oh, did you call the police?
B Of course. They've already been here.
A What's happening to our neighborhood? We never used to have so much crime. When the kids were little, we didn't even lock the front door!
B Well, I'm just glad we weren't home when it happened.
A Oh, Monica, I feel so bad for you. And I'm worried. Did you hear someone robbed Mr. Purdy last week, too, while he was out taking a walk? I think we should start a Neighborhood Watch program, don't you?
B Yeah, we've been talking about that for months. I agree, it's time we finally did it. But right now, I have to clean up this mess.
A Do you want me to come over, Monica? I could help you clean up.
B You're the best, Samantha. Yeah, come as quickly as you can. Thanks.

Page 111, Exercise 3A – CD2, Track 24

Monica calls Samantha with bad news. While Monica and Todd were out, someone broke into their home and stole their TV, DVD player, jewelry, and some cash. Monica is upset because the robber took her mother's ring. She says the person got in through a window in the back bedroom.
Samantha is worried. She says they never used to have so much crime in their neighborhood. She tells Monica that last week someone robbed their neighbor Mr. Purdy, too. Samantha thinks they should start a Neighborhood Watch program. Monica agrees, but first she needs to clean up the mess in her house. Samantha offers to come over and help.

Page 112, Exercise 2A – CD2, Track 25

What were you doing at 8:30 last night?

1. We were watching a movie at the Rialto Theater.
2. I was studying English at home last night.
3. I was driving to work.
4. We were eating dinner at Kate's Kitchen Restaurant.
5. We were attending a Neighborhood Watch meeting.
6. I was babysitting my grandchildren at my daughter's house.
7. I was baking a cake for my daughter's birthday party.
8. We were painting the kitchen.
9. I was visiting my friend and playing video games
10. We were working late at our hair salon.

Page 114, Exercise 2A – CD2, Track 26

1. While Dad was working in the garden, a thief stole his car.
2. I was eating lunch when the fire alarm suddenly went off.
3. Ali fell off a ladder while he was painting the ceiling.
4. When the earthquake started, the students were taking a test.
5. I was making a right turn when another car hit the back of my car.
6. While we were camping, it suddenly began to rain.
7. Mr. and Mrs. Gomez were jogging in the park when a dog began to chase them.
8. While Diana was working outside, a stranger drove up to her house.
9. While we were driving to the beach, someone broke into our garage and stole our new lawn mower.

Page 116, Exercise 2 – CD2, Track 27

Home Is More Than a Building
A few months ago, Pedro Ramirez, 45, lost his job in a grocery store. To pay the bills, he got a part-time job at night. Several days later, Pedro's wife, Luisa, gave him a big surprise. She was pregnant with their third child. Pedro was happy but worried. "How am I going to support another child without a full-time job?" he wondered.
That evening, Pedro and Luisa got some more news. A fire was coming near their home. By the next morning, the fire was very close. The police ordered every family in the neighborhood to evacuate. The Ramirez family moved quickly. While Pedro was gathering their legal documents, Luisa grabbed the family photographs, and the children put their pets – a cat and a bird – in the family's van. Then, the family drove to the home of Luisa's sister, one hour away.
About 24 hours later, Pedro and Luisa got very bad news. The fire destroyed their home. They lost almost everything. With no home, only part-time work, and a baby coming, Pedro was even more worried about the future.
For the next eleven months, the Ramirez family stayed with Luisa's sister while workers were rebuilding their home. Many generous people helped them during that difficult time. Friends took them shopping for clothes. Strangers left gifts at their door. A group of children collected $500 to buy bicycles for the Ramirez Children.
Because of all the help from friends and neighbors, the Ramirez family was able to rebuild their lives. Two months after the fire, Luisa mailed out holiday cards with this message: "Home is more than a building. Home is wherever there is love."

Unit 10: Free time

Page 123, Exercises 2A and 2B – CD2, Track 28

A I'm so exhausted! I really need a vacation.
B You know, my work is pretty slow right now. I can talk to my boss. Maybe he'll give me a few days off.
A Oh, Ricardo, what a great idea. We haven't had a family vacation in two years.
B Where would you like to go, Felicia?
A We could go to San Francisco. Michelle's six – she's old enough to enjoy it, don't you think?
B Well, let's see if there are any deals on any of the Internet travel sites. . . . Look, if we book a flight seven days ahead, we can get a round-trip ticket for $200.
A That's not too expensive. Are there any discounts for children?
B Hmm. Let's see . . . I don't think so.
A Oh, that's too bad. What about hotel rates?
B Not cheap. Summer is the height of the tourist season. If we stay in a nice hotel, it's going to cost at least $250 a night.
A Plus the room tax, don't forget. You have to add on an extra 14 percent or something like that.
B Right. I forgot about that. So if the three of us take this trip, and if we stay in San Francisco just three days, it's going to cost almost $1,200.
A That's a lot to spend for just a three-day vacation, Ricardo. Maybe we should just go camping instead.
B Yeah, you're probably right. We could go to Big Bear Lake. If we do that, how much will it cost?
A Well, gas will probably cost about $100, the campsite will cost about $35 a night, and then there's food – but that won't be too much if we grill hamburgers.
B Michelle will probably have more fun camping, too.
A I agree. So what do you think? Should we make a reservation?
B I'll reserve the campsite after I talk to my boss tomorrow.
A I hope he says yes. We really need a vacation.

Page 123, Exercise 3A – CD2, Track 29

Felicia is exhausted. She needs a vacation. Her husband, Ricardo, says he can ask his boss for a few days off. Felicia would like to go to San Francisco. They look for special travel discounts on the Internet. If they book a flight at least seven days ahead, they can get a round-trip ticket for less than $200. On the other hand, hotel room rates will be high because summer is the most popular tourist season. Also, there is a room tax on hotel rooms in San Francisco. They figure out that a three-day trip to San Francisco will cost almost $1,200.
Felicia and her husband decide to change their plans. If they go camping, they will save a lot of money and their daughter will have more fun. Felicia's husband will reserve the campsite after he talks to his boss.

Page 124, Exercise 2A – CD2, Track 30

1. Annette and William will take their children to Sea Adventure next month if William gets a few days off.
2. If they get a discount, they will reserve a room at a hotel.
3. If prices are too high, they won't take an expensive vacation.
4. We will have a picnic on Saturday if it doesn't rain.
5. If you give me the money, I will buy the concert tickets.
6. If you come to Chicago, we will meet you at the airport.
7. They will fly to Miami next month if they find a cheap flight.
8. We won't go camping if the weather is too hot.
9. If it rains, we will have the party inside.
10. If she needs a rental car, she will look for one online.

Page 126, Exercise 2A – CD2, Track 31

1. Kara will talk to a travel agent before she books a flight.
2. Before Cynthia leaves for Puerto Rico, she will buy some new clothes.
3. Donald will take a taxi to the hotel after he picks up his baggage.
4. The campers will make a fire before they cook their dinner.
5. After they finish eating, they will clean up the campsite.
6. I will call you after I return from my trip.
7. After I get my passport, I will make the reservations.
8. Before we go to Mexico, we will learn some words in Spanish.
9. Jack will lock the doors before he leaves for the airport.
10. Maria will print her boarding pass before she goes to the airport.

Page 128, Exercise 2 – CD2, Track 32

The Rock: San Francisco's Biggest Tourist Attraction
Alcatraz, a small, rocky island in the middle of San Francisco Bay, was once the most famous prison in the United States. For a period of 29 years, from 1934 to 1963, over 1,500 dangerous criminals lived in the prison's 378 cells. People believed that it was impossible to escape from Alcatraz Island. However, in 1962, two brothers, John and Clarence Anglin, and another man named Frank Morris escaped on a raft made of raincoats. A famous movie, Escape from Alcatraz, tells this amazing story. Other famous prisoners who lived on the island included Al Capone, the gangster, and Robert Stroud, the "Birdman of Alcatraz." Alcatraz prison closed in 1963. The island became a national park, and since then, it has been a major attraction for tourists from all over the world. These days, many people call Alcatraz by its popular name, "The Rock."
In the summer, it is wise to buy tickets to the island in advance because the ferries sell out. Evening tours are less crowded. The admission prices listed include the ferry, tickets, and an audio tour.
General admission:
Adults (18–61), $45.25 for a day tour and $52.25 for an evening tour
Children (5–11), $31.00 for a day tour and $34.20 for an evening tour
Seniors (62 or older), $43.25 for a day tour and 49.25 for an evening tour

Review: Units 9 and 10

Page 134, Exercise 1 – CD2, Track 33

A This is a KPST Radio special report.
B Park police have found a Denver man who was missing overnight in Rocky River National Park. Brad Spencer disappeared sometime on Sunday after camping Saturday night at Timber Creek. His wife, Paula Spencer, became worried when he didn't return to their campsite Sunday evening.
Mrs. Spencer told KPST News . . .
C When I talked to Brad early Sunday, he was planning a short hike. It was a beautiful day, and he was wearing only a T-shirt and shorts. I got really worried when he wasn't back by eight o'clock in the evening. It was getting cold and dark. That's when I decided to call the park police.
B Paula's husband, Brad, got lost while he was bird-watching. Fortunately, he was carrying matches, and he was able to start a fire to keep warm. When park rangers found him around six o'clock Monday morning, he was sleeping next to the fire, over a mile from the closest trail. A happy and hungry Mr. Spencer told KPST . . .
D I learned a good lesson. If I ever go hiking here again, I'm going to carry food and stay on the trails!
A This is Roberta Chang with KPST Radio.

Page 135, Exercise 3A – CD2, Track 34

1. upset
2. about
3. family
4. extra
5. travel
6. police
7. vacation
8. dangerous
9. Samantha
10. photographs

Page 135, Exercise 3B – CD2, Track 35

1. Samantha is upset.
2. Where's the travel agent?
3. The prison is dangerous.
4. It's about seven o'clock.
5. Did you take photographs?
6. Call the police!
7. She'll think about visiting her family.
8. I need a vacation.

ACKNOWLEDGMENTS

The authors and publishers acknowledge the following sources of copyright material and are grateful for the permissions granted. While every effort has been made, it has not always been possible to identify the sources of all the material used, or to trace all copyright holders. If any omissions are brought to our notice, we will be happy to include the appropriate acknowledgments on reprinting and in the next update to the digital edition, as applicable.

Key: B = Below, BL = Below Left, BR = Below Right, C = Centre, L = Left, R = Right, T = Top, TL = Top Left, TR = Top Right.

Photos
All below images are sourced from Getty Images.

p. 2 (T): Hero Images; p. 2 (BL): Enis Aksoy/DigitalVision Vectors; p. 2 (BR): Ivcandy/DigitalVision Vectors; p. 6 (TL): shironosov/iStock/Getty Images Plus; p. 6 (BL): Newton Daly/DigitalVision; p. 6 (TR): Hill Street Studios/Blend Images; p. 6 (BR): PeopleImages/E+; p. 12 (T): andresr/E+; p. 12 (C): simonkr/E+; p. 12 (B): Daria Botieva/Eyeem; p. 14 (a): ONOKY - Eric Audras/Brand X Pictures; p. 14 (b, d): Hill Street Studios/Blend Images; p. 14 (c): Tetra Images; p. 14 (e): XiXinXing/iStock/Getty Images Plus; p. 14 (f): Joos Mind/Iconica; p. 16 (T): Hero Images; p. 16 (C): Yagi Studio/DigitalVision; p. 16 (B): isitsharp/E+; p. 18 (1): Wavebreakmedia Ltd/Wavebreak Media/Getty Images Plus; p. 18 (2): alejandrophotography/iStock/Getty Images Plus; p. 18 (3): TommL/E+; p. 18 (to do list): NuarZakaria/iStock/Getty Images Plus; p. 18 (index card): NorthStar203/iStock/Getty Images Plus; p. 18 (5): BernardaSv/iStock/Getty Images Plus; p. 29 (L): Jetta Productions/Blend Images; p. 29 (R): EastFenceImage/iStock/Getty Images Plus; p. 32 (1): aanton/iStock/Getty Images Plus; p. 32 (2): Hill Street Studios/Blend Images/Getty Images Plus; p. 32 (3): Wavebreakmedia Ltd/Lightwavemedia/Getty Images Plus; p. 32 (4): lisafx/iStock/Getty Images Plus; p. 32 (5): powerofforever/iStock/Getty Images Plus; p. 44 (1, 2): DigitalVision; p. 42 (3): Dan Dalton/Caiaimage; p. 42 (4): Nico De Pasquale Photography/Moment; p. 42 (5): Jedrzej Kaminski/EyeEm; p. 46 (T): skynesher/E+; p. 46 (B): RobertoDavid/iStock/Getty Images Plus; p. 50 (L): Joseph Clark/DigitalVision; p. 50 (R): emotionk/iStock/Getty Images Plus; p. 58 (1): Lane Oatey/Blue Jean Images; p. 58 (2): smontgom65/iStock Editorial/Getty Images Plus; p. 58 (3): George Munday/Perspectives; p. 58 (4): Les Stocker/Photolibrary; p. 58 (5): Shalom Ormsby/Blend Images; p. 63 (T): Buero Monaco/Corbis; p. 63 (B): Frank P. Wartenberg/Picture Press; p. 64: David Silverman/Getty Images News; p. 69 (L): Michael Interisano/Design Pics; p. 69 (R): Image Source; p. 70 (1): Sontaya Numpha/EyeEm; p. 70 (2): MachineHeadz/iStock/Getty Images Plus; p. 70 (3): JGI/Jamie Grill/Blend Images; p. 70 (guitar): DonNichols/iStock/Getty Images Plus; p. 70 (trash): maurusone/iStock/Getty Images Plus; p. 84 (1): WendellandCarolyn/iStock Editorial/Getty Images Plus; p. 84 (2): Westend61; p. 84 (3): APL; p. 84 (4): Stratol/E+; p. 84 (5): tillsonburg/E+; p. 90 (T): Simon Potter/Cultura; p. 90 (B): Rick Gomez/Blend Images; p. 92: Chabruken/Taxi; p. 96 (1): XiXinXing/iStock/Getty Images Plus; p. 96 (2): PeopleImages/iStock/Getty Images Plus; p. 96 (3): Emma Innocenti/DigitalVision; p. 96 (4): crisserbug/E+; p. 96 (5): wakila/E+; p. 99 (1): Hero Images; p. 99 (2): Westend61; p. 99 (3): John Fedele/Blend Images; p. 99 (4): Sam Edwards/OJO Images; p. 99 (5): Hill Street Studios/Blend Images; p. 99 (6): Andersen Ross/The Image Bank; p. 99 (7): Rawpixel/iStock/Getty Images Plus; p. 99 (8): WANDER WOMEN COLLECTIVE/DigitalVision; p. 100 (1): Ababsolutum/E+; p. 100 (2): TheTraumaTeam/iStock/Getty Images Plus; p. 100 (3): dorioconnell/E+; p. 100 (4): milindri/iStock/Getty Images Plus; p. 100 (5): Tetra Images; p. 100 (6): Daniel Allan/Photographer's Choice RF; p. 101 (1): FernandoAH/E+; p. 101 (2): Thomas Northcut/Photodisc; p. 101 (3): harmpeti/iStock/Getty Images Plus; p. 101 (4): AnthonyRosenberg/iStock/Getty Images Plus; p. 101 (5): ito akihiro/amana images; p. 101 (6): Wavebreakmedia/iStock/Getty Images Plus; p. 102: Klaus Tiedge/Blend Images; p. 110 (1): strickke/E+; p. 110 (2): kimberrywood/iStock/Getty Images Plus; p. 110 (3): Image Source/DigitalVision; p. 110 (4): MachineHeadz/iStock/Getty Images Plus; p. 110 (5): SweetBabeeJay/iStock Editorial/Getty Images Plus; p. 112: avid_creative/E+; p. 121: Gallo Images; p. 122 (1): Westend61; p. 122 (2): svetikd/E+; p. 122 (3): Coyright Roy Prasad/Moment; p. 122 (4): MoiseevVladislav/iStock/Getty Images Plus; p. 122 (5): John Warburton-Lee/AWL Images; p. 122 (6): Thomas Barwick/Taxi; p. 128: Danita Delimont/Gallo Images; p. 130 (L): Stephen Beifuss/EyeEm; p. 130 (C): 2ndLookGraphics/E+; p. 130 (R): Danita Delimont/Gallo Images; p. 132 (plane): dell640/iStock/Getty Images Plus; p. 132 (book): Arudolf/iStock/Getty Images Plus; p. 132 (house): Gina Sabatella/Moment Mobile; p. 132 (snowman): Jose Luis Pelaez/Iconica; p. 132 (mobile): Thinkstock/iStock; p. 132 (online shopping): Devrimb/iStock/Getty Images Plus; p. 132 (bus):Grafissimo/E+; p. 148: amtitus/DigitalVision Vectors.

The following images are from other image libraries:

p. 43, p. 81, p. 107: United States coin images from the United States Mint.

Illustrations
p. 9, p. 36, p. 47 (1, 2, 3, 4): Travis Foster; p. 9 (Joe, the students), p. 10, p. 17, p. 47 (5, 6), p. 73, p. 75, p. 87 (5, 6), p. 89, p. 92, p. 113, p. 115, p. 116, p. 118, p. 125 (5), p. 127 (2, 5, 6): QBS Learning; p. 34, p. 127 (1, 3, 4, 7, 8): Nina Edwards; p. 35, p. 125 (1, 2, 3, 4): Cyrille Berger; p. 37, p. 38, p. 49: Brad Hamann; p. 87 (1, 2, 3, 4, 5, 6): Kenneth Batelman; p. 93: Monika Roe.

Front cover photography by Peathegee Inc/Blend Images/GettyImages.

Back cover photography by pressureUA/iStock/Getty Images Plus/GettyImages; Adidet Chaiwattanakul/EyeEm; pixelfit/E+/GettyImages.

Audio produced by CityVox.